"Excellent adventure. I feel like I've lived another's life."
RUSSELL CROWE

"A wonderful, interesting, crazy, desperately beautiful journey."
JANN ARDEN

"Doyle is exuberant, irreverent, hilariously funny
and a heart-on-the-sleeve Newfoundler.
As a writer he's all that and a bag of chips."
MICHAEL CRUMMEY

"Funny, wise and self-deprecating, this book is hard to put down."
JIM CUDDY

Praise for WHERE I BELONG

"[A] rough-hewn saga growing up poor but happy on the Rock. . . . You'll love the skillful way Doyle teases his involvement with the band into the narrative. . . . Even better is the way you see Doyle slowly but inevitably following the invisible flight path that would take him to the career he was always meant to have."

Toronto Star

"Alternately laugh-out-loud funny, tearfully nostalgic, and stunningly beautiful, the stories in *Where I Belong* have nothing to do with the famous and everything to do with the legendary. . . . Alan has crafted a coming-of-age story that reads almost like a male version of *A Tree Grows in Brooklyn* in its Irish sensibility, episodic narrative, and rapturously detailed universe small in physical scale but infinite in colour and character. . . . The beating heart of life itself runs through this book."

Huffington Post

"A poignant and often comical memoir of growing up in Petty Harbour."

The Telegram (St. John's)

"If you're lucky enough to have spent any time with Alan, then you may have heard one or two of these stories before. If you haven't, this book is the next best thing."

Ed Robertson, of Barenaked Ladies

"There are great big smiles to be found on nearly every page. A beautiful memoir of heart and place."

Linwood Barclay, author of *A Tap on the Window*

"To many people, Petty Harbour's geographic isolation, bleak surroundings, and limited economic opportunities would have placed limits on their lives, limits from which they would have never recovered. To my friend Alan Doyle, they were just a challenge to overcome, and this strange and eccentric village would offer a well of experience, enough to fuel a lifetime of creativity. "

Bob Hallett, of Great Big Sea

"Stratocasters, goalie pads, skin mags and cutting tongues, Alan's charming and sometimes uproarious tale of growing up in Newfoundland has it all."

Edward Riche, author of *Rare Birds*

"Doyle [is] a master storyteller in a land rich in that resource. *Where I Belong* brought back some amazing memories of growing up in a small fishing community and what was to be life outside our hometown. From the first time I laid eyes on him, Alan's been *that* guy, the funny, charming dude cursed with charisma, with the talent to back it up. This book gives great insight into that super-talented, creative and insightful mind of a true entertainer."

Perry Chafe, co-creator/writer of *Republic of Doyle*

"Alan Doyle the writer, like Alan Doyle the person, is charming, funny, a natural storyteller who can be sweet without sliding into sentimentality, who can be honest without tumbling into darkness. The book breezes along the path that leads to Great Big Sea, and couldn't feel more authentic. If you know the place, you know these fantastic characters are real."

Stephen Brunt, author of *Gretzky's Tears: Hockey, Canada and the Day Everything Changed*

"In *Where I Belong*, Alan uses his natural 'master storyteller superpower' to draw you in as a reader in much the same way he does while holding court in the pub or in his own kitchen. This book shines a light on a very particular place and time in Newfoundland's history, as seen through the eyes of one of the province's greatest talents."

Allan Hawco, co-creator/star of *Republic of Doyle*

ALAN DOYLE

WHERE I BELONG

Anchor Canada

Library and Archives of Canada Cataloguing in Publication data is available upon request.

ISBN 978-0-385-68038-7

Photographs on the cover, tip-in and pages 9, 30, 54–56, 63, 68–69, 73, 74, 90 (right), 98–99, 116–117, 121, 122, 188, 214–215, 228 and 245 Copyright © Brian Ricks Photography, www.brianricks.com

Photo on page 88 Copyright © Robert O'Brien

Cartoon on page 281 Copyright © Kevin Tobin

Photo frames, celtic knot and paint texture from Shutterstock.com

Cover and interior design: Kelly Hill

Printed and bound in the USA

Published in Canada by Anchor Canada, a division of Random House of Canada Limited, a Penguin Random House Company

www.penguinrandomhouse.ca

10 9 8 7 6 5 4 3 2 1

Penguin
Random House
ANCHOR CANADA

For Mom and Dad

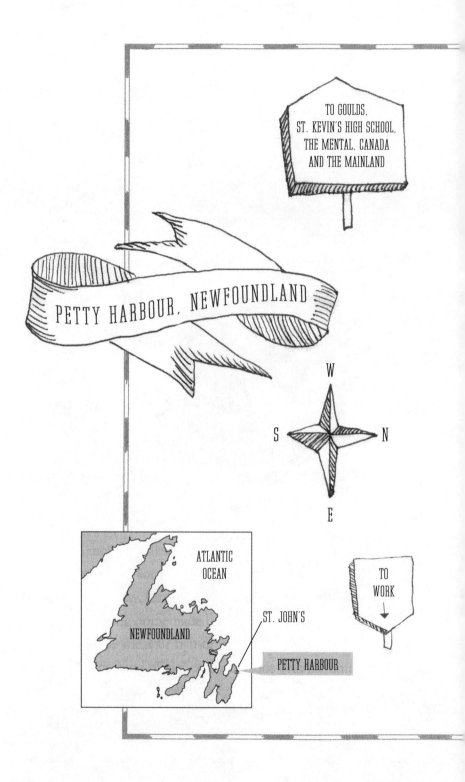

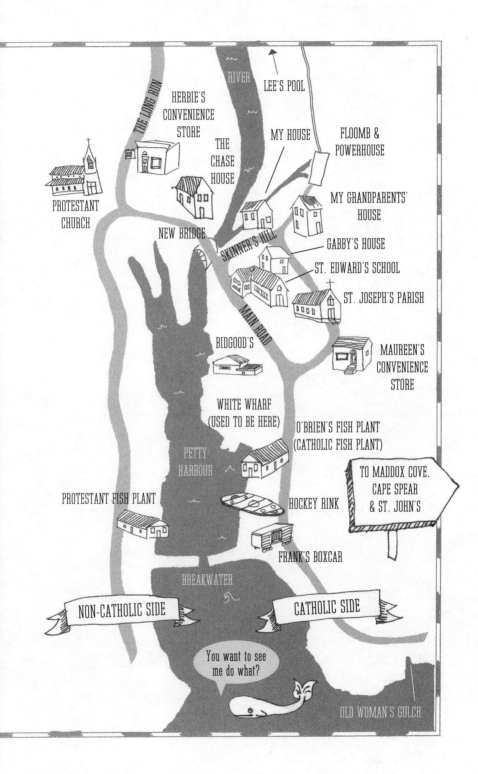

Contents

Foreword

by Jann Arden

What I want to do right now is tell you everything that happened in this book. I want to load each and every person I meet into a bus and drive them to a lovely little place called Petty Harbour in Newfoundland. I want to go to the Protestant grocery store and order a giant roast from the owner, Herbie, and take it to Alan Doyle's mother's house and have her cook it for us, with a mound of mashed potatoes and gravy made from rocks and sea water and a whole lot of love. (Maybe we should fly? That would be quicker.)

Where I Belong is such a wonderful, interesting, crazy, desperately beautiful journey back through time. Every single page holds so many treasures. I have been a long-time fan of Alan Doyle. I have always loved his music and his heart and his passion for everything he does. This book is no different. I had to keep reminding myself that this was a memoir and that each and every unbelievable event was indeed true. I often felt like I was in some sort of strange and whimsical movie complete with heroes and damsels and wicked nuns who cast dreadful spells over their innocent young flocks.

Alan writes words that are soaked in sea air and salt and, sometimes, a lovely, quiet solitude. You can taste them on the tip of your tongue. You can see and feel and hear everything he so meticulously describes.

This book really does feel like a song. Alan's musicality seeps through his prose, giving every tale a touch of his poetic soul. *Where I Belong* is a rolling, jaunty, whiskey-laced ballad, an ode, if you will, that will have you thirsting for more. When I turned the last page, I honestly felt sad. I didn't want it to end.

I want to track down Mr. Doyle and buy him a glass of whatever in the world he fancies and dance a jig. I want to celebrate his life and his accomplishments. It's not often that you want to meet every single character you've read about in a book. But that's what I would do if I could. I'd sit at a giant, long table with everyone Alan has introduced me to over these hundreds of pages, and I'd smile and eat and drink with them for hours on end.

—*Jann Arden*

Author's Note

I am from Newfoundland. Therefore, I am a bit of a story-teller. The stories of Newfoundlanders are often confused with fairy tales and the stuff of fiction, as the people, places and events in them seem exaggerated or outright invented. But in Newfoundland, truth really is stranger than fiction.

One of the greatest rewards I have had in publishing *Where I Belong* is the number of people who have told me that the book brought them back to a time and place they remembered from their own young lives. People from farming, logging and mining towns who told me they were reminded of their own childhoods by reading tales from a little fishing town in Newfoundland. Folks from my own province and the rest of Atlantic Canada who remarked that the description of my early days in Petty Harbour echoed their memories of growing up by the sea. I suppose I am always most grateful, and somewhat surprised (and relieved), when a person from home says, "You got it right."

This is a memoir, and I have gone through considerable effort to confirm dates, timelines, and all the stories I have shared here are true to my memories of them. The folks in my stories—the kids, fishermen, shopkeepers, priests, and members of my own extended family—appear in the book in the moments that their lives intersected with mine. In many cases, I have changed the names of characters, as I would not want any folks to think I was writing in a whole or complete way about anyone they recognize.

But all the people are real. All the places did or still exist, and all of the events actually occurred. Events of several days may be condensed into one, and events from several places may be presented here as having occurred at a single location. But no people, places, or events have been imagined.

This is a true story. I could not have made this stuff up if I tried.

Thanks for reading.

Cheers,

Alan Doyle

Boy on Bridge

Spin the planet like a globe. Stop it with your finger when you see blue. There's a good chance you stopped in the Atlantic Ocean. Look up to where the ocean narrows a bit and find the Old Country of Ireland. Follow west through the deep blue until you come to the New Country of Canada. If you are clever enough, you'll spot an odd-shaped island. If you're lucky enough, you'll visit it one day.

Look closer. On the eastern edge of that island, you'll find a little piece of land that sticks out closer to Ireland than any other piece in all of North America. Just below that you'll come to a bay with one wide-open cove and one very protected harbour.

Look closer again at the little harbour, that safe haven sheltered from the winds and isolated from everywhere else by its steep hills to the north, south and west. To the seaward east, the hills open ever so slightly to the cold Atlantic and all Her gifts and gales. Tiny fishing boats and fishermen journey onto her waters, and for the most part, She brings them back home again.

Look closer still and you will see a little town. You'll see how it's fed by a river, a perfect little river that splits the town in half. You'll see houses on either side, and two tiny schools, one on each side. You'll also see two small fish processing plants and two convenience stores. Also, two churches.

You'll notice the only thing that joins one side of the river to the other: a simple, single-lane bridge. In a bit more now and you'll likely see a boy on that bridge. He's got his hands in his pockets to keep them safe from the chilling winds off the water. His foot is tapping to a song in his head. Some might think this young fella seems happy enough to stand right where he is, but if you look just close enough, you'll see his eyes tell a different story.

He looks up and down; his gaze travels to the river below him and way up to the top of the hills beyond the town. He appears to be wondering which way to go. His eyes follow the valley to the road that leads out of town, past the harbour and into the great big sea.

There was once a boy who lived in a tiny fishing village on an island in the middle of the ocean.

That boy is me. This is my story.

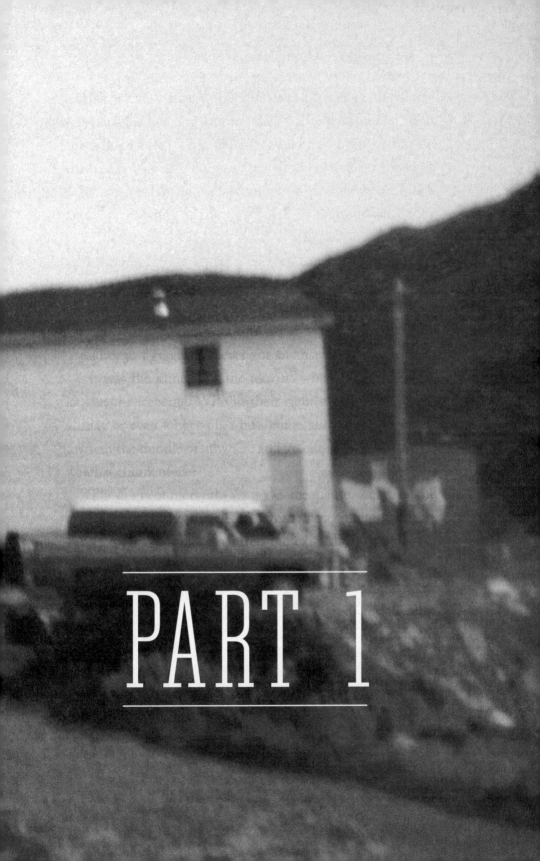

PART 1

CHAPTER I

Rough Side Out

When I was a boy, I had no idea. About many things. I knew a few facts here and there, but I was absolutely sure about very little. I had more questions than answers. I was more curious than certain. Here is a list of the few things I knew.

I knew I lived in Petty Harbour, a postcard-perfect, traditional fishing community, just twenty kilometres or so away from St. John's, the capital city of Newfoundland. I knew I was Catholic and not Protestant like that dubious crowd from the other side of the river. I knew I loved music and the Montreal Canadiens. That's about it. I was certain about very little else. Come to think of it, even these facts were cause for confusion.

I knew what town I lived in but was not totally sure what country. I thought I lived in a country called Canada, but my grandfather insisted I lived in a country called Newfoundland. I thought Newfoundland was my province, and Mom said that was the truth of it. But then she also said we should never say that out loud when Granda was on the whiskey.

I knew we were Petty Harbour folk. We lived around the Bay, and as such, we were Baymen. I did not live in town, so I was not a Townie, which is what most Newfoundlanders call St. John's people. Townies agreed that I was indeed a Bayman. But as far as my Baymen cousins from more rural Newfoundland were concerned, I may as well have been a Townie because I lived so close to the city. Also, most of the Petty Harbour Doyles worked in town and none of the Doyles were fishermen, as Baymen typically are. So this made me wonder if we were actually Baymen or Townies after all. Confused? So was I.

I did know I was Catholic and not Protestant. But I also knew that no matter how closely I looked at those strangers across the river, I couldn't see much difference between us and them. They went to a different school than we did, but they wore the same clothes and did the same jobs and liked the same sports. On rare occasions when I attended the Protestant church for weddings or funerals, their church services didn't seem to be that different from ours. Why, I wondered, didn't we just make one big church? Or why didn't we go to their church or they come to ours? I was told in no uncertain terms that I was most definitely a Catholic, but I honestly could not figure out why I had to be part of one religion or the other.

I knew I belonged to a musical family and I loved music more than anything, but not just the kind my friends at school liked. My parents and extended family were well versed in Newfoundland and Irish music, especially the Clancy Brothers, and beloved singer-songwriters like Johnny Cash, Cat Stevens and Kris Kristofferson. My uncles, who I idolized, played in a rock 'n' roll band. They played live covers of artists like Buddy Holly and Elvis and Creedence Clearwater Revival and the Beatles. They had records of heavier bands I loved like Led Zeppelin and Cream. From a young age, I was surrounded by music of all kinds, but I really had no idea what kind of music I was supposed to like.

I knew that hockey was a big deal in Petty Harbour, and just about everybody around me cheered for the Detroit Red Wings. Gordie Howe had made such an impression on his generation that children born into a Red Wings household had no choice but to follow suit. My father was a Wings fan, but in a gesture of true open-mindedness, he did not insist that I follow him down the Gordie path. When I was around ten years old, the Montreal Canadiens won four Stanley Cups in a row and I fell in love with the Habs. I was the only Canadiens fan in the extended Doyle family, and folks insisted I must be cracked. So I knew in my hockey heart I loved the Habs, but I was made to feel like that was a terrible mistake.

Somehow, through all this, I knew I belonged to Petty Harbour. There was never a doubt about it. I was a Petty Harbour Dog, born and bred. Now don't get me wrong. When I was young, I didn't spend a lot of time dwelling on who I was or what I was, whether I was a Canadian Newfoundlander or a Newfoundland Canadian. But there were times when I did feel that even though I knew where I was from, I didn't quite know how I fit in. Here was wee Alan Doyle, son of Tom and Jean, neither Townie nor Bayman, not quite a true Catholic but certainly not a Protestant, a music lover who wasn't sure what music to love most. And all I really wanted to be when I grew up was a rock star or the goalie for the Montreal Canadiens, but I was pretty sure neither of those careers was achievable.

So what was I was supposed to do? How was I supposed to act? I really had no idea.

And that was the best thing that could have ever happened to me.

I was born on May 17, 1969, in St. Clare's Hospital in St. John's, North America's oldest city, in Newfoundland, Canada. My parents and I were born on the same island, but while I was born a Canadian, they were born Newfoundlanders. In 1949, Newfoundland joined Canada, or Canada joined Newfoundland, as so many of our citizens say to this day. Many still believe that vote was rigged, but the statistics say that 51 percent of Newfoundlanders were for the union and only 49 against it. I can still hear my grandfather, long after the fact, explaining his opinion on the matter.

"They picked the right day to sign that declaration, April first. 'Cause they were all a bunch of fools to join up with the Canadian Wolf. Well, I did not suck the Wolf's tit and I'm not going to start today or any day. I am a Newfoundlander like my father and his father before that."

Once he got started on this subject, he'd usually stay on it awhile, and if he was really riled, he'd start invoking the Devil himself.

"I swear to ye all that the Daemon Canada will one day take away everything that is ours, including the very fish in the bay that brought us all to life. I just hope I'm not alive to see it, b'y."

My paternal grandparents, Bernard and Frances Doyle. But to me, they were Granda and Nan.

Granda was a staunch Newfoundlander (and not at all a Canadian) to the day he died. I remember him asking one of my older cousins about a recent trip to Toronto.

"So you were up to Canada, were ye?"

"Uh . . . yes," my cousin answered, trying not to stir the dragon.

"What are they like up there?" Granda asked with honest curiosity.

"They are quite nice, actually."

"Yeah, I heard they were." Granda grinned and went back to watching the news.

Canada puzzled me as a kid. It seemed like a faraway land we saw on TV or read about in the newspaper, but it had very little to do with us directly. It may as well have been Sweden or Malta for all the connection I had with it. Yet somehow, I knew I did not agree with Granda's assessment. I would never say it out loud, but I kind of liked Canada. What I knew about it, anyway.

I loved hockey and watching *The Tommy Hunter Show* on the CBC. I fantasized about big cities like Toronto, and especially about Montreal. I longed to speak French like those people from Quebec. I knew I was officially born in Canada, but where did I really belong?

I can still hear my grandmother's voice in my head as I ask that question: "Now, honey," she says, "Tom Best may be *from* Petty Harbour, but he is not *belong* to Petty Harbour." *Is not* belong. That's the way we say it. And that was always the distinction. If you came to our town from anywhere else in the world, you'd be part of the community, but you could never expect to belong to it. So did Newfoundlanders come to Canada? Did we belong there? I was not sure.

The day after my birth, I was brought home to the town where I belong—the fishing town of Petty Harbour, on the Southern Shore of the Avalon Peninsula. Petty Harbour itself had a population of around five hundred people. It still does. Originally, it was called Petit Havre, but that was when the French occupied the Southern Shore. They had named it well.

This tiny town sheltered on three sides by tall hills was a perfect launching point for a small-boat inshore fishery. To the east is a narrow opening in the hills to Motion Bay and to both the bounty and the terrors of the North Atlantic. Two artificial breakwaters jut out on either side of the harbour, leaving an opening only a few metres across for small and medium-sized boats to pass through. The result is a protected port, a safe haven where in older times small boats holding one, two or three fishermen could row

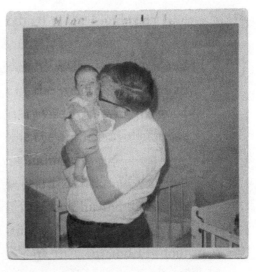

Me and my dad, Tom Doyle, 1969. I was one month old. You'll notice two cribs in the photo. My sister, Kim, slept in one while Bernie and I slept in the other. Mom tells of how I was so eager to get out of there that I jammed my head between the rails and my dad had to use a hacksaw to set me free.

or steam out to fertile fishing grounds in a matter of minutes.

My father, Tom Doyle, is belong to Petty Harbour. He was born on Skinner's Hill. When I was a kid, there was only one way to get there. As you enter the town from the higher hills to the west, from the farming town of the Goulds, you'll drive along a long run of straight road called the Long Run. Then, as you make your way around the turn on the south side of the river and harbour, you'll drive onto a road that winds all the way down to the ocean on the south side. This is called Southside Road. The main road (conveniently called Main Road) turns north of Southside Road

7

and then crosses New Bridge over the river that splits Petty Harbour in two. New Bridge replaced the Old Bridge long before I was born. Even though it was older than me and most of my friends when I was growing up, we still called it New Bridge. (There is now a new New Bridge, built in 1986, but it is still just called New Bridge.) It serves as the only connection between one side of the town and the other.

This bridge served an even bigger function for me. It's where I stood, hundreds if not thousands of times in my young life, wondering what the Protestant crowd on the other side were up to, waiting for a school bus, hitchhiking to the neighbouring town, watching boats come and go as they had for centuries and, most of all, daydreaming—daydreaming about what else was out there beyond the hills and harbour. When searching for a title for my first-ever solo CD in 2012, I discovered I'd had an acting credit from the late seventies, when I stood on that very bridge as an extra in a made-for-TV film, *Whale for the Killing*. "Boy on Bridge, Alan Doyle," the Internet Movie Database read. I could hardly believe I'd been officially called "Boy on Bridge," as that's how I've always pictured myself in my most formative years in the town I call home.

On the other side of the bridge you can take a detour up Skinner's Hill (named after Bishop Skinner; finally, a landmark named after a person, a rarity in Petty Harbour), which, as I said before, is where my dad was born, the second of ten children.

He and his siblings inherited a love of singing from my grandparents and great-uncles. If you grew up in Petty

It is a long run into Petty Harbour.

Skinner's Hill is named for Bishop Skinner.
To this day, there are many Doyles up that hill.

The road on the south side of town. We really were not great at nomenclature.

9

Harbour, chances are you could sing. That's just the way it was. And the Doyles were known all over town as particularly good singers. Just ask anyone in Petty Harbour and they'll tell you, "Oh, the Doyle family? All the Doyles in Petty Harbour sing. The Doyles are the best singers in the world. No better singers than them anywhere."

When my father was young, like all the boys of his age, he was bused to St. John's to attend high school at a Catholic boy's college, under the close eye of the Christian Brothers. And soon after finishing high school and a trades course, he faced the daunting task of finding work in a province that had very little of it. After a few stints on delivery trucks, he eventually found steady employment, not in the fishery like almost everyone else, but as an orderly and nursing assistant at the only psychiatric hospital in St. John's. Whenever I was asked as a kid what my father did, I would say, "Fadder works in The Mental," and naturally, everyone knew exactly what this meant.

My mother, Regina "Jean" Pittman, is belong to Marystown on the Southern Burin Peninsula of Newfoundland, about three hundred kilometres from Petty Harbour, the youngest of seven children. She was schooled and learned to play piano and piano-accordion under the careful watch of Catholic nuns. Like many girls her age, she finished high school when she was sixteen. Then, like almost all girls from rural Newfoundland, she got on a bus in June and was shipped off to St. John's to the Sisters of Mercy Convent to train as a nun, a nurse or, Mom's vocation of choice, a schoolteacher.

Yes, Mom is belong to Marystown, and you can't belong

to more than one place so she never quite belonged to Petty Harbour. She once told me how lonely and isolated she felt in the town when she was posted there to teach at the tender age of only eighteen, far away from her home in Marystown. My maternal grandmother, Charlotte, was a very strong and sensible woman. She believed in duty and honour, and when my mother began a contract to teach in the one-room schoolhouse in Petty Harbour, she made my mother stay right to the end of the school year instead of quitting at Christmas like Mom wanted.

And so, my grandmother Charlotte made her youngest daughter go back to Petty Harbour and without knowing it led my mother to my father. She and Dad became acquainted in town. I asked my mom and dad about how they fell in love. "What was it you saw in each other?" Dad looked at Mom. Mom looked at Dad. "Alan, dear," Mom said, "now that's a really good question." Then Dad shrugged his shoulders and replied, "It was simple, I s'pose. She could play and I could sing." And that was that.

Mom's main instrument is the piano. I remember being in

Mom and Dad cutting their wedding cake while the photographer cut off their heads. Most Newfoundland wedding pics from pre-1970 must have had the same photographer because there is an overabundance of such half-headed shots from this era.

my crib at home and hearing her play. I remember her teaching some local kid to play "Mary Had a Little Lamb" as she reached her long arms around to lay her hands over theirs on the keyboard.

Mom became the town's choirmaster and the go-to musician for weddings, funerals, christenings and community concerts. Dad and his brothers were the singers in town, and I guess that meant Mom and Dad were a good match. To hear them talk about it, their entire social life when they were young revolved around music. Weeknights: choir and concert practice. Weekends: singing and masses, and then kitchen-party singalongs with the neighbours. They were married in November 1965, and in perfect Catholic form, Mom was pregnant by January. They quickly started building a small two-storey house on a dirty, rocky, inhospitable precipice on Skinner's Hill, right across from my grandparents' place.

It was impossible ground. It still is. Any sensible person from a farming community would have taken one look at that hill and walked the other way. But not my folks. They started by pouring a concrete wall on the lowest side of the property to create a level surface, and against all laws of physics and gravity, they somehow managed to build a solid structure and keep a house standing on a ninety-degree bend in the road. My father and a few of his friends spent weekends and evenings shelling up and roofing the modest little house, about three hundred square feet per floor. That's the way it was in rural Newfoundland. You didn't call professionals to build you a house or put a roof on it. You called the boys, and you got a few cases of beer and you did it yourselves.

The houses back then in Petty Harbour, and most every house in Newfoundland, actually, were made of wood—clapboard on the outside. The way most North American lumberyards manufactured clapboard was with one smooth, sanded side and the other rough—full of cracks and splinters and grooves. The rough side was meant to face inward, while the smooth, finished side was supposed to face out. But us Newfoundlanders, being unique in our ways and far more practical than most, would often nail the clapboard rough side out because paint would stick to it better. Come to think of it, that's the way most Newfoundland houses and Newfoundlanders themselves are built: rough side out.

The Doyle family home, circa 1975, where I grew up on Skinner's Hill. None of the cars pictured belonged to us. If you look closely, you can see some blurry kids scampering across the rocks on the top left. I'm most likely one of those kids.

Our house was painted white. That's how you knew it was ours. White place. Green trim. On Skinner's Hill. There was no front stoop, or "bridge" as it is often called in Newfoundland, just a front door and a back one, and you never came in the front one, except if you were special . . . like my Granda. I can't remember a time when I went into the house through that front door.

My older sister, Kim, was born in September 1966, and the day before Christmas Eve, as soon as the first floor of my folks' house was complete, they moved in. "Complete" in this case meant the house had a kitchen with an electric stove and a fridge, and interior panelling covering all the studs. The living room at that time was not yet "complete"—just a rough board floor and no wall coverings to speak of. That was it. The second floor remained undeveloped, without even so much as stairs leading up to it.

Perhaps you're thinking that I've missed something. Maybe you're wondering, "Wouldn't them Doyles require a bathroom? After all, there were three of them, and they had a new baby to mind." Well, it's true that a bathroom would have been quite a handy thing for my parents to have, a useful thing indeed. But they did not have one, so they made do without. That's how they both had been brought up. Spend exactly all of your time making the most of what you have and exactly none of your time whining about what you don't have. After all, both my parents had lived with much less. They'd lived before the telephone, and before flush toilets, and before rooms with more than one light bulb, in houses with no running water or electricity, where seven or eight siblings would all sleep in one bedroom. As sparse as their present accommodation was, it was their own, and they were prepared to make it a home.

With no bathroom in their house, they would bathe my sister Kim and themselves with water that Dad would retrieve from the river behind our house and heat on the stove. An old plastic beef bucket with a handmade seat made a fine toilet, and the river behind our house served as a septic line that carried the effluent away into the ocean.

Mom and Dad say they were quite content with this arrangement, though Mom admits to noticing the vast differences of farm poverty versus fishing poverty.

"Back in Marystown, we had very little. Sure, you could starve to death in February. But we had a cellar and a garden and cows to milk and chickens to get eggs from. Those few things could get you through the winter. But living though the winter on the bare rocks of Petty Harbour, with not a barn to be seen—that was a whole different kind of starving."

They waited to develop the second storey of their house until they made some extra money. But as these things go, kids came quicker than money, and in a few short years, my parents, along with Kim, my older brother, Bernie, and me, all lived in that main-floor kitchen and one unfinished room in that little house on Skinner's Hill. Did I mention there was no plumbing? No water line in the house at all. And still no bathroom by the time I came along. No bedrooms. No cupboards or closets. I realize this arrangement sounds fairly poor, and I suppose in retrospect it was not lavish, but my siblings and I were always warm and fed and happy.

Most of my memories kick in around age five. I remember my new little sister, Michelle, coming home from hospital. I remember that upper floor finally getting developed so the empty space gradually became three small bedrooms—boys in one room, girls in the other, parents in the third. And a real bathroom down the hall, with running water . . . except for the four or five months in the dead of winter when the pipes would freeze and stay frozen till spring.

Me, Kim and Bernie in matching new PJs at Mom's family home in Marystown. Kim looks tidy and classy (typical). Bernie and me took off our pants for the photo op (also typical). Bern's chin is taped from a hard fall he took just minutes after we arrived. I'm sure our relatives were delighted to see us bruised-up, pantless boys.

We had an oil furnace in the basement. We frequently ran out of oil in the winter, which, of course, was cause for much celebration. We'd stay in the kitchen; we'd all play cards, and often some of my aunts or uncles would come over for an impromptu "out of oil" party, and after a warming drink or two, the adults would invariably start singing and playing guitar. It was on those nights that I learned that adults love it when kids sing, and if you do it well enough, you'll get to stay up later.

Before bed on "out of oil" nights, my folks would put heavy blankets across the doorway to the kitchen. They'd take the oven door off its hinges and heat up the room by turning the oven on. Then we'd warm home-sewn blankets in that room and bring them upstairs at night. Those heated blankets were enough to get us warm and falling into a cozy sleep before the real cold crept in. (To this day, my folks leave the heat off in their bedroom at night, and I cannot sleep with either heat or air conditioning in my bedroom.)

We had no car. My father hitchhiked twenty kilometres every day to get to his job at The Mental. And if he could get a ride for only part of the way, he'd walk the rest. But before leaving, if our plumbing was frozen, he would always go to the river behind our house. And in two or three trips with a five-gallon bucket, he would fill the sinks and kettles with water for our mother to feed and wash us for school.

We had a tab at the local convenience store that almost never got zeroed. We'd go there to get bologna or bread to have for lunch. "Tell Maureen at the store to mark it down," Mom would say.

With the exception of one new school outfit every September and maybe something at Christmas, I wore my brother's hand-me-down clothes till I was a teenager. The first time I ever slept in a room by myself was when I moved to St. John's to go to my second year of university. I was nineteen years old.

When my wife, Joanne, who was then my girlfriend, came to Petty Harbour for the first time in our early twenties, I showed her around the house I grew up in. I shared some of our stories, like the "out of oil" parties. On our way back to St John's, she casually mentioned she was not aware I'd come from a poor family. I had no idea what she was talking about. I honestly thought she was joking. It had never occurred to me that my family may have been less well off than most other Newfoundland or Canadian families.

Perhaps I should have clued in to our relative poverty when we visited my cousins in Marystown, as they had hot and cold water and even a shower in their house. I took a shower there for the first time in my life when I was about ten years old. It would have been around 1980.

It all seemed more than enough to me and to all of us at the time. Our little place on Skinner's Hill was all I really knew until I was a teenager. I'd never been in a house in St. John's and I certainly had never been on a plane or on a holiday to experience anything different. We were no worse off than most families in Petty Harbour. It was a childhood where we made something out of nothing. We always had three meals a day. Often, the slim pickings were bolstered by Mom's amazing homemade bread. And just about every supper had some meat or fish or chicken next to potatoes covered in some kind of rich and delicious gravy. Somehow, on a budget of a few thousands of dollars a year, my folks managed to house, clothe and feed themselves and four kids, bringing them up in a safe home full of music and love. I'll never understand how they did it. And I'll never be able to explain to them how grateful I am that they did.

The Doyle kids—Kim in the middle, with wee Michelle on her lap, me (left) and Bernie (right)—sitting in front of the only posh thing we owned, Mom's piano.

WHAT'S IN A NAME?

What's in a name? A lot, as it turns out.

Before our band settled on its current name, we were briefly called Best Kind. (I know, pretty bad name, right? Worse, it was my idea.) We had been performing under the name Best Kind for a couple of months. Fortunately, Bob Hallett talked us out of keeping that name.

"It sounds like we're bragging," he said. "Or worse, it sounds like it's supposed to be funny. Our band is not a joke."

This was right around the time we were producing our first record at Piper Stock Studios. The term "studio" only loosely applies, since it was just a couple of rooms in a basement—but that basement happened to be Dermot O'Reilly's, and Dermot was in Ryan's Fancy, an awesome traditional band (with a really good name, I might add). After the

Justin Hayward

That's me, Séan, Darrell and Bob in 1993.

week-long crash course of teaching ourselves to play and sing on beat and in tune, at least periodically, we were out of session time and out of money. That meant our record was as finished as it was going to get.

Our first album cover, featuring (you guessed it) a great big sea.

On that first record is a traditional Newfoundland song about a tidal wave. The song is often called "A Great Big Sea Hove in Long Beach," but we shortened that mouthful and amongst ourselves called it, simply, "Great Big Sea." We really liked the intro to that song, so we figured it should be the first on the album. Then we liked the name so much, we thought we'd call our whole album *Great Big Sea*.

But we were still very stuck on a band name. With the artwork deadline only hours away, we had to think of something. Lots of bands named their first albums after their band, but few ever did it the other way around.

"Guys, why not call ourselves Great Big Sea? We liked it for everything else."

"Better than Best Kind, that's for sure," said Bob. "And we'd have a cool three-letter abbreviation like the Wonderful Grand Band. WGB and GBS. Cool."

And so it was. Four guys agreed and our new band was about to be launched in downtown St. John's. It was only when we got some airtime on the radio that we realized naming a band, an album and the first song on that album all the same thing might be problematic. DJs certainly had an awkward time of it: "And now, I'd like to introduce to you a new band from Newfoundland, from their debut record *Great Big Sea*, here's Great Big Sea, with 'Great Big Sea.'"

Great Big Sea
NRA Productions Ltd.

BOB HALLETT, SEAN McCANN, ALAN DOYLE, DARRELL POWER

St. John's, NF

CHAPTER 2

The Way Things Were

When I was a young fella, my world was not a big one. I would often go many days or even weeks without seeing, much less meeting, a single person that I had not known for my whole life. Many people around me were happy with those boundaries, but even at a tender age, I would challenge "the way things were." I lusted for new faces and new stories. This attitude probably came from my mother, who always taught me to question everything and to be aware that there was a great big world beyond the confines of our tiny little town.

Now don't get me wrong. Petty Harbour was a wonderful place to grow up . . . until one got curious enough to want to see other stuff. And if I look back into my mind, I can see myself standing on that bridge and wondering what the world beyond was actually like, because at that young age, I still had no idea. And I also had to reckon with the fact that almost the entire town believed that Petty Harbour was truly the only place in the world to live. And by extension, whatever was the best in Petty Harbour had to be the best in the world.

One of my uncles was a bit of a cynic. He had travelled, so he was a bit more worldly than other types in town. He, too, liked to challenge "the way things were." If Granda said that Roger who worked at the fish plant was the best hockey player ever, my uncle would say, "If that were true, he'd be in the NHL, and he's not."

Getting angrier, Granda would say, "Yeah, but that's 'cause that crowd up on the Mainland never gave him a chance."

My uncle wouldn't leave it there. "Well, maybe he didn't try hard enough or he just wasn't good enough to make it in the big leagues, or maybe he just decided that the pro hockey life was not for him."

"No. Roger is the best damned hockey player in the world, no question. If he didn't make it to the big leagues, that's the fault of the f—king Mainlanders who never gave him a chance. Like I'm always tellin' ye, Mainlanders will take everything we got, but they won't put a Newfoundlander in the NHL."

"But Alex Faulkner made it to the NHL." My uncle was making a point about the first Newfoundland NHLer. "What, did he hide his birth certificate?"

"Go f—k yourself." Granda would always get the last word.

And so it went.

I remember thinking about this attitude as a kid, trying to work out the logic. I'd think to myself, that can't be right. Just because Roger is the best hockey player in Petty Harbour doesn't mean he's the best hockey player in the world. Not necessarily. Even then, without ever having left Petty Harbour, I knew the world beyond my town was bigger than I could imagine, the same way I knew it was possible that there was life on another planet. So maybe, just maybe, there were better hockey players elsewhere, too, like, say, in the NHL.

But whenever I tried to challenge the adults around me, I wouldn't get very far. "Jerry is bar none the best fish filleter in the world," someone would say.

"But are you sure that's right?" I'd ask. "I'm sure Jerry is the best fish filleter around here, but isn't it possible there's someone better in another place, like maybe someone over in Sweden or Russia? There must be lots of guys filleting fish over there. Is it possible that one of them might be better than Jerry?"

"You can wonder all you likes, but I'm telling you, Jerry is the best. That's it. No one's better at fish filleting than him."

I was often encouraged to look no further afield. But I could not help it. Whenever there was a foreigner passing through the town, unlike some of the other local lads who would point and jeer or run away, I was always curious. What on earth, I wondered, would bring people from away to Petty Harbour? It was as if by watching the outsiders in our midst I was seeing my community for the very first time.

When I was about eight years old, a painter came to town—an artist, rather. He was not what we called a painter back then—that was someone who whitewashes your house. This man was French. Not like Quebec French but from France. He would have been in his twenties, I guess. He'd been standing at the head of the wharf all morning in front of an easel like the one Mr. Dressup used on TV. Some of the other boys from Petty Harbour and I had been spying on him for a few hours.

"I wonder if he works for the government," I said to my cousin Benny.

"No, b'y. I'd say he's high or something. Just there drawing, whacked out of his head on dope or whatever," Benny surmised.

High or not, we wondered what this man could possibly be doing there in one spot for so long, not lifting or hauling or building anything. He held a long paintbrush in one hand and a flat piece of board in the other, which was dotted with reds and blues and greens. His longer than local hair lifted and fell gently in the spring breeze. As we often did when a new person showed up in town, we came to the unspoken yet unanimous decision that we should throw rocks at him and run up behind the church when he chased us.

But something about his peaceful progress at his labour got the better of me and I shocked the other lads by saying, "Hold on, b'ys. I'm going to ask him what he's at."

"What?!" Benny had already gathered a couple of real good throwing rocks—about half the size of your fist and round so they would not curve in the wind. He dropped them. "F—k sakes," he said.

I walked up the length of the wharf and the painter must have seen me over his easel but he did not speak. I stood in front of him, looking at the back of the canvas stretched over the wooden frame.

"Hey," I said.

In a thick French accent he replied, "Allo. 'Ow are you?"

I didn't waste any time with small talk. "Me an' the b'ys are wondering what you are doin'."

"I am painting."

"Painting what?"

"Painting what I see—the sun, the hills, the church."

"Why?"

"Because they are beautiful and will make a nice picture."

"What for?"

"I don't know. Maybe someone will want to hang this picture in their house."

"Why?"

"Because it will make their home a happier place."

I had no clue what to say to that. How could a painting make a room happier? I must have carried the question on my face, as the painter smiled and asked, "Would you like to see? I am almost done."

I walked around the easel and stood beside him in front of the canvas. I thought my eyes would burst when I saw what he had created. I'd never seen anything like it in my young life. He'd painted the water bluer and whiter than it really was, and the colours of the spring trees on the hill jumped off the canvas in thick ridges of paint. The white wooden church was slanted and tilted, and the cross on the spire looked like it was about to reach down and shake your hand.

"What do you think?"

All I could think to say was, "It looks like a dream."

He took his brush and made a diamond shape in the sky above the church in hazy, broken lines.

"What's that?" I had to ask.

"The sun."

"But the sun is round."

"Not my sun," he said and smiled a long-lingering smile. I knew I was supposed to learn something from what he'd said, but was not sure what it was.

I stood there for a half-hour or so and watched him put the finishing touches on his picture. When he said he was done, I said, "See ya."

And he replied, "Au revoir," which I'd heard on *Sesame Street*.

I looked around for Benny and the boys, but they must have gotten bored and left.

I walked up around the bend on Skinner's Hill and went in the back door of the house. Mom was at her usual pre-supper station, bent over a pot of gravy.

"Mom, I talked to a painter fella."

"That queer-looking fella on the wharf?"

"Yeah. He was painting a picture of the church."

My mom looked up from the pot she was stirring. "The Protestant church?"

"Yeah."

"Why?"

"He thought it would be a nice picture that would make someone's home happier."

My brother walked in then, having heard our conversation. "What a pansy," he said as he dipped a slice of homemade bread in the gravy pot. I was not sure if he was talking about me or the painter.

Mom gave him a smack for the bread-dipping and for his crass tongue.

She said to me, "Honey, I'm sure he made a nice picture. Did you see it when it was finished?"

"Yeah. It was cool, I s'pose. But none of the stuff looked like it do in real life."

"Maybe he's just learning," Mom said and turned back to stirring the gravy.

In my adult life, I came to know this painter I met on the wharf. His name is Jean Claude Roy. He made frequent visits to Petty Harbour in the 1970s. In my mid-thirties, I bought one his paintings of Petty Harbour and the Protestant church. And guess what? It does make my home happier.

There were other CFAs—Come From Aways—who I talked to as a child. I recall speaking with a tourist couple down behind the Bidgood's lobster pound. (Note for Mainlanders: a lobster pound is an onshore holding tank for lobsters, where sea water is pumped in to keep the creatures alive and kicking until they're sold and moved. I was shocked when my editor told me I had to explain this.) Bidgood's pound was perched on a three-storey-high granite ledge that stuck out into the open bay on the northernmost side

Jean Claude Roy's stunning painting of Petty Harbour, making my kitchen a happier place.

of the harbour. Easily the windiest spot on earth. There was not a blade of grass or so much as patch of moss on that spot. Bone rock. This tourist couple had been sitting on that rocky ledge for hours as the wind nearly beat the faces off them. Yet they looked so content with their picnic lunch and camera ready at the hip. I had to find out what they were up to, so I asked.

"We want to see a whale," the woman answered.

I was stunned. I was confused. I thought she was an absolute nutcase. I had to clarify my question.

"You want to see a whale *do what*?"

They just giggled. I never got an answer to my question.

It was the same with the tourists who were bused in to look at the icebergs. Who in their right mind would spend all day or even longer on a bus, come all the way to a tiny town in the middle of nowhere and go out to sea on a boat to watch a chunk of ice?

These encounters always gave me pause, because the people from away, the people from these interesting far-away places my mother assured me existed, saw the world in a totally different light. These moments made me even more eager to understand the perspective of people from away, one that was obviously not widely shared around Petty Harbour. In my little fishing town, folks were quite content with looking inward at the inexhaustible supply of characters and world views we had locally. And who could blame them when we had such a colourful cast. Consider Frank Brake.

Fisherman Frank Brake was as old as the hills when I was a kid on the wharf.

"The face on Frank is like a catcher's mitt," my brother, Bernie, used to say. I always thought it was more like well-worn saddle leather. The skin on his hands was even rougher. His sausage-sized fingers were twisted and ripped from years of cuts and injuries that were left to heal—or not—in whatever shape or misshape nature desired.

Unlike most of the other fishermen in town, Frank spent much of his life away from Petty Harbour and Newfoundland—and away from Canada, for that matter. He was a sailor and had sailed around the globe a few times and worked in various capacities as a deckhand or in whatever job aboard whatever vessel he found himself.

He would regale me and the other young fellas on the wharf with tales of storms at sea and the countless times his ship and crew were nearly lost. He'd tell us of fights he had in foreign lands where a man's throat was cut or neck was snapped at the hands of another sailor. He told us of brothels in French and Spanish ports, where dark-skinned beauties would come down by the dozen to "welcome" the crew. He told us of a shipmate who regretted his time in the brothel as he itched and scraped his infected crotch till it bled.

Listening to him talk over a fishing table, with an ever-burning cigarette hanging from his lips, was for a ten-year-old boy nothing short of mesmerizing. Jack Walsh, the respected weighmaster at the wharf who was responsible for recording each fisherman's official catch, best described Frank as an old workhorse: "Frank was rode hard and put away wet."

As if Frank's experiences were not enough to make him a source of fascination, he lived in the most remote and strange dwelling I've ever seen—an old wooden Canadian National Railway car. How that railway car got to the wharf on Petty Harbour is beyond anyone's imaginings. The closest railway line to the harbour was at least twenty-five kilometres away, but still, there it sat on the edge of the wharf tucked underneath the steep bank. It had always been there, for as long as anyone, including the all-knowing Jack, could remember. To this day, no one has been able to propose a scenario about how the railcar could have possibly wound up on the wharf.

Frank's boxcar had a single sliding window. What was in that boxcar was the source of much speculation, so much so that me and my ever-present accomplice and friend Perry Chafe decided we'd investigate. When Frank was out on the water, we'd hoist a littler fella to look in and report back to us. There were always a dozen or so younger boys hanging around, being baptized into life on the wharf. Mostly, these kids were scared stiff by the things us older boys said and did. But the eager ones wanted in. Mikey was my favourite of all the little fellas.

"Mikey, what can you see?" I asked as we hoisted him up for a peek.

"Can't see all that much. Pretty dark in there. He's got a kitchen table set up under the window."

"What else?"

"There might be a moose head, and that could be an accordion or a suitcase. Not sure."

"You're useless, Mikey," Perry declared. "Look harder. Is there anyone dead in there?"

"I can't see, b'y. There's not a light on in the place. Wait! Is that a rifle on the wall?"

And that's about as clear a view as we ever got, leaving lots of room for all of us to use our imaginations.

"He sleeps on old sails," Perry decided. "From an old shipwreck he was in just off of Spain or Africa."

"I heard he's got a trap door in there that leads to a hole in the wharf where he can get out to his boat without anyone seeing. He smuggles rum from St-Pierre and he sneaks it out to hide it."

But my favourite rumour was one the Hearn boys started about Frank being a pirate.

"He's got treasure in there. That's why he never lets anyone in and why he don't have a real address or a phone. There's Portuguese sailors after him. He's got gold church mugs and that stashed away, but what everyone's really after is the map to where the motherlode of treasure is."

"What?! Have you seen any of this gold stuff?" I asked.

"No, but I heard Father say that Frank was looking for some metal polish that was good for brass and gold. Ya knows that's what he's at in there—polishing gold church mugs and hiding from Portuguese pirates who wants to cut his throat."

I suppose Frank could have just been a lonely bachelor who wanted to polish brass fittings for his boat, but what was the fun in thinking that?

The truth of Frank's place, much like the man himself, is lost in darkness. I tried many times to be around when Frank hauled open the massive sliding door that occupied about half of one side of the boxcar, but I never got to see in. Most times, Frank came and went through a normal house door that he had built into the narrow side of the car. But he was so large and imposing that even when he entered and exited, we never got to see a single thing inside. Where did he sleep? Did he have a bathroom in there? A fridge? We could see smoke coming from a makeshift chimney pipe, so we assumed he had some kind of wood stove, but there was never any firewood lying around outside. What was he burning? Was there electricity or an oil lamp or what? The mystery of Frank's abode made for hours of curious speculation.

The other thing that made Frank so amazing was his ability to ignore his advancing age and the myriad of health issues that came with it. Frank was so hardened by years at sea that he had no time for illness.

"You can stitch that up yourself as good as any doctor," I heard him tell one of the boys on the wharf who was going home after slicing himself with his knife.

Frank fished alone and really had no one to take care of him. As he aged, Weighmaster Jack asked us kids to watch after Frank.

"You boys keep one eye on the fish and the other on Frank, you got that?" he'd say to me and Perry while we helped Frank gut his fish and clean his boat.

One day, Frank's boat came through the breakwater on a particularly busy afternoon on the wharf, and he pulled up his boat all the way down at the last station. Me and Perry had dibs on cutting out Frank's cod tongues and we went directly to catch the lines as he tossed them up. Within a few moments, we noticed two things odd about Frank. First, he was uncharacteristically quiet. No stories, no ramblings about how lazy and soft everyone was getting. No discussion of his day at sea. More telling was that Frank was gutting his daily catch using only one hand, jamming the not quite dead fish down with his elbow. The other hand had been inserted into an ice cream tub and covered with a plastic shopping bag, the whole thing tightly tied around his wrist. He held the whole contraption close to his chest, careful not to let anything touch it. Frank never mentioned it, which meant we were all sup-posed to ignore it, too, which we did as best we could—until it became apparent that we would be there forever if Frank had to gut all those fish by himself with one hand.

"Uh, Frank," Perry said sheepishly. I was glad he was the first to speak because I was afraid that my tongue might get cut out if I asked the wrong question. "What's up with your hand?"

Frank looked at us for a moment. "What?" he asked, as if he had no idea what Perry was asking about.

"You know . . . the bag, the bucket?" I said.

He looked down at the rather conspicuous white knight puppet he'd constructed on his hand. "Oh Jesus f—king Christ," he began, as he continued to gut his fish. "I reached down to haul in the handline earlier this morning and friggin' forgot I had two hooks on the line, and one of 'em caught me in the palm of the hand on the way up. Foolish thing. Hook's still in there. After we finishes with these few fish, I must get Jack to see if he can get at the hook with a pair of pliers."

Now we had known Frank long enough to know that a small hook in the finger would not cause him any noticeable discomfort. We were also very familiar with the hooks that were used in the inshore handline fishery in Petty Harbour. The smallest one was about eight inches long and about as thick as the laces in a men's dress shoe.

I leaned in to Perry, who was looking every bit as nervous as me. "Go get Jack," I whispered.

Moments later, Jack came striding with purpose down the full length of the wharf.

"Fine day, Frank," said Jack casually. Then he said, "A'rn?," the Newfoundland fisherman abbreviation for "either one," meaning "Any fish today?"

Frank replied with the customary "N'arn," meaning "Not a one," which was said no matter how good or bad the day's catch might have been.

With the small talk out of the way, Jack figured he could get to the real question.

"What's on the go with your hand and the ice cream tub, Frank? You got something jammed in it?"

Frank repeated the "small hook" story and assured Jack that it was nothing of any concern. He would have a look at his hand later when the work was done. But Jack knew better and insisted that Frank take off the ice cream tub and plastic bag and show him the minor injury.

Frank slowly untied the plastic bag and winced a little as Jack slid off the ice cream tub. All of us boys were standing around Frank, waiting to catch a glimpse of his hand. And when that tub came off, I almost fainted. The only thing that kept me upright was the fact that I was not totally sure what I was seeing. I saw a reddish purple mass of flesh. It was somewhat like a human hand but more closely resembled a misshapen hockey glove. The appendage was curled into a fist, and I could just make out the closed fingers and knuckles. The hand seemed to be holding a long, galvanized nail with an eyehole at the top, some three or four inches above the thumb. Of course, it was not a straight nail but a fish hook, an eight-incher, and when Jack gently turned Frank's hand over, we suddenly realized the galvanized steel hook and barb were not being held at all. The hook had pierced right through Frank's hand and three inches of hook had cleared the other side. The entire area around the puncture wound was swollen to bursting.

Jack shook his head like he'd seen this kind of thing before. "Jaysus Christ, Frank. When did you do this?"

"Ah Christ, b'y, 'bout four thirty this morning, I s'pose. Just after I got out past Tinker's Point. Didn't want to waste all the gas to come and go for nothing, so I started fishing and got in a good spot, so I stayed. Sure, there's nothing to it anyway," he said, studying his hand. "As long as you don't bang it off anything, you'd barely notice it."

Jack sighed. The rest of us stayed dead quiet. "Frank, you could lose your hand, you old fool. Hold on. I'll phone someone to take you to the hospital."

"To the hospital? For this? Don't be so foolish, Jack. Get the pliers and cut the eye or the barb off it and pull the bastard out."

"Frank, you're going to get an infection and drop dead

in your sleep. You at least need to go to the Goulds and see the doctor."

"The hell I do," said Frank as he walked past Jack and strolled right into Jack's office in the weight shed. We all watched as he grabbed a set of rusty vise grips with his good hand. He had them half set on the eye of the hook before he got back over to where we were standing.

A few more strides and we heard a click and watched as the eye and about an inch of the hook hit the top of the wharf and bounced a couple of times.

"Now," Frank said to Jack, "yank that out and I'll pour some iodine on it and we can all get back to work."

"Are you sure, Frank?"

The answer was wordless and clear.

Jack fixed the vise grips over the hook and barb and was about to pull.

"One second," Frank said, using his good hand to brace himself on the fish-splitting table. He looked around at us group of wincing boys. And then he saw me.

"You, Young Doyle. Hold my arm steady for Jack."

I shook my head, but Frank curled me in next to him and whispered, "Come on now, don't let the boys see you shakin'. It'll only take a second. Don't be so gutless."

With my two hands holding Frank's wrist, I pressed his upper arm and bicep into my chest.

"All right, here we go, Frank," Jack said calmly, and then he counted backwards in preparation. "Three, two—"

"Jesus Christ, b'y. We're not launchin' a f—king rocket. Yank it out!"

With that, Jack made a short, quick pull and the hook slipped out rather easily. It was not that big a deal at all. But what followed was far worse.

The moment the hook left Frank's hand—which was right in front of my face, because I was still holding on for dear life—a stream of liquid squirted out of his palm. If it had been red and red alone, I think I could have handled it. But the liquid was more yellow than red, and the thick, jaundiced pus made the whole mixture resemble bloody snot. A lot of it.

But even that was not the worst part. When the injured hand released its fluid, the smell of infection was forced out as well. This rank stench and the fact that the hand's swelling went down instantly before my eyes—a fleshy hockey glove transforming back into a human hand—put me over the edge.

I released Frank's arm. I stepped over to the edge of the wharf and barfed my guts out into the harbour.

Lucky for me, most of the boys had already turned away so they did not see me. They would have laughed at me for days. But Frank saw, and he was none too pleased by all the fuss about a "little hook" in his hand.

"Jesus, thank Christ that's out." He turned to me and the boys. "And ye crowd are as soft as shit. Someone wipe the puke off that young Doyle fella so we can get back to work."

Even later in his life, Frank was determined to go on about his day however he saw fit. He developed angina and should have been on heart medication, but that required too many trips to the doctor and pharmacy. One day, I noticed Frank was in pain and I asked him about it.

"Jesus, Jesus, Jesus. Me chest feels like it's going to bust. I must go to Fred Stack's and get some of them nitrogen pills, or whatever he calls 'em." And up he'd stroll to a house on the harbour where he would ask for a top-me-up from another aging heart patient.

As his condition worsened, he relented and eventually got a pacemaker. When he returned from the surgery, he was supposed to take a few months off to recover and rest. He was back on the water in four days.

"You boys need to pay special attention to Frank now, you hear me?" Jack told us.

That same day, Frank arrived back at the wharf uncharacteristically early. I could tell from hundreds of feet away that something was not right with him. He was hunched over and was sitting on the gang boards as he steered the boat. When he got up to the wharf, he had trouble climbing the ladder. I ran and got Jack right away.

Jack met Frank at the top of the ladder. "How are you, Frank? You're looking a bit pale."

"Ah frig sakes, b'y. I slipped in the boat this morning and fell right down on that foolish thing they put in me chest. I'm gonna have to go back to town now and have that looked at, ain't I."

"Let's have a look, Frank," Jack said. A crowd of boys and even some of the other fishermen were gathering around, partly out of concern and partly out of morbid curiosity. Jack asked Frank to sit down on the bench, but of course he refused.

"Sit down? Why, are you a dentist now or something?" Frank snapped, winking to all the younger boys.

Jack opened Frank's coveralls. There was a bloodstain just above the left pocket. Jack unbuttoned Frank's plaid work shirt. I'll never in my life forget what my young eyes saw when Jack pulled the shirt down a bit over Frank's shoulder.

Frank's chest had been recently shaved for the surgery, and the stubble of re-growth was dense and white, with trails of dried blood running in every direction. There was a hockey-puck-sized bump over his heart, closed with a few dozen stitches. But more than half of those stitches had broken open, revealing the fleshy pink insides of Frank's incision. But that was not the worst of it. Busting through the stitches, beyond the surrounding dried bloodstain of the gaping chest wound, hung a black electrical wire with a frayed silver metallic end.

Frank looked down at the wire, completely unfazed. "I s'pose if we got a bit of black tape we could rewire it and save a trip to town," he said. Then he casually started to push the wire back into the pink incision in his chest.

"Frank!" Jack and a few other fishermen who'd gathered around shouted. "For Christ's sake, Frank! Stop!!"

Frank was startled. "What is wrong with ye crowd? Shut the shouting and bawling. Ye're gonna give me a heart attack!"

Jack called an ambulance, which came quickly. I remember Frank agreeing to get in it, but refusing to lie down. He sat there, shirtless, with his coveralls rolled down to the waist, as the driver closed the rear doors and drove up the road. Last thing I saw through the windows was Frank, with a grin on his face and a wire hanging out of his chest, offering the paramedic a cigarette.

CHAPTER 3

Breaking Bread

There was a time when every weekday at the Doyle household started with the Bathroom Ballet. We were a large family living in a small house: two adults, two boys and two girls and our aging little black mutt, Pal. For years, we went to the bathroom in a bucket in the back porch, but by the time I was around six or seven years old, we had indoor plumbing and a fully operational bathroom. The bad news was that by the time I was about eleven, my brother, Bernie, was a teen, as was my sister Kim, and that added extra chaos as we all vied for some private time in the can. Meanwhile, Pal ran up and down the stairs barking and spinning and scratching at the door in a canine fit that meant "I am going to pee on this floor exactly right now unless someone comes downstairs to let me out!"

Our bathroom was small, with a tiny tub. There was a curtain around the tub, which was used for privacy, not for showers, because the tub didn't have one. There was a small sink and vanity with a mirror on the wall just above it. Across from the sink was a toilet that sat directly under a little picture window. My father is not a particularly tall man, and when he sat at the toilet, his knees touched the vanity doors. And when we flushed the toilet, the contents were funnelled down the drain, through the house, under the ground and into the river a dozen metres or so behind our house. You could flush the toilet, close the lid, hop on top, look out the window and watch your own poop come out the other end of the pipe in the river a few seconds later. But there wasn't much time on a weekday morning for this kind of entertainment.

My folks very sensibly tried to organize the chaos of the daily Bathroom Ballet.

"What we got to do," Mom decided, "is wake each of you ten minutes apart, so that everyone has their chance in the bathroom." It was a great idea, but like many great ideas, it worked very well in theory and not so well in practice. If we really wanted our own bathroom time in the morning, one of us would have had to get up half an hour before we even went to bed. I know this sounds like a bit of a poor man's situation, right? But please remember that in very recent family history, we'd had no bathroom at all, so sharing one seemed like a great leap forward.

It was not at all uncommon for the entire half-dozen of us to be jammed in the bathroom at the same time. The first one to almost make it to the bathroom every morning was my dad. I say "almost" because he was invariably intercepted by some of us kids who'd bolt around him and get in there before him. He'd be left standing in the hall in his underwear, with one hand on his hip and the other high on the wall, leaning so hard on it you'd swear he thought it would fall if he weren't there to hold it up. Every now and again, he'd take his hand off his hip and rub his sleepy eyes and whimper over the din of all of us kids packed in the can.

"Probably I'll just sneak in there for a quick sec before ye crowd gets goin'?" he'd ask. But we'd ignore him, cramming into the bathroom till it was most certainly a fire hazard.

My sister Kim was usually the first one in. She'd run a tub full of water, get in and close the curtain around her. Once she was settled, she'd shout, "The coast is clear!," which meant it was safe for Bernie and me to go in and make use of the toilet. But there was a rule, and it was this: only number one was allowed while someone was in the bathtub. Kim could suffer her brothers peeing on the other side of the curtain, but she would not allow the dropping of a number two bomb. But Bernie and I being mischievous young fellas, we were known for taunting Kim by feigning disregard of this rule, often as loudly as possible.

"Oh my Jesus, I think I'm having a baby," Bern might shout.

"Bern, you better be fooling, or that'll be the last time your arse is able to sit on that toilet."

Other times, I'd be the rule breaker. "Aw frig, Kim. I musta got the stomach flu or something. Sorry. Can't hold back!"

"Ye are just friggin' around, right? 'Cause if yer not, I'm putting my head underwater!"

Meanwhile, poor Dad was still in the hall holding up the wall. "Just give me one quick sec in there and then I'll be gone altogether," he pleaded, head down like an old dog, while Pal, the real old dog, scratched at his bare legs and barked "Emergency!" in dog speak.

A while later, Mom would stroll in with my baby sister, Michelle, who was just a tiny little thing at that time.

"Alan, Bernie!" she'd say as she ushered us away from the toilet. "Stop torturing your sister." Mom would pop Michelle on the toilet and then go to the mirror and begin fixing her hair.

Bernie and I would move on to brush our teeth. "I'm using your toothbrush, Kim! And I'm not going to tell you what for."

"Aw, gross! Mom, are they serious?"

"Ye lot can work it out amongst yourselves," Mom would say, not even looking over at us.

Then another distant whimper from out in the hall. "If I could just nip in there right quick." By now, Dad had given up holding the wall and was pacing up and down the hall.

Michelle would finish her pre-school pee and we'd congratulate her as she got off the toilet and washed her hands.

Bernie would rustle the bathroom curtain. "If you don't get out soon, Kim, I'm lookin' in. I'm gonna do it."

"No!" Kim would shriek.

"I'm friggin' doin' it!" Bernie winking to me as he raised his voice.

Then, right when Kim was most panicked, I'd lift up Michelle and poke her head through the curtain, her perfect little smiling face greeting Kim's and saying, "Kim's in the tub!" The discovery of Kim behind the curtain never ceased to amuse Michelle, even though it happened almost every morning.

When Kim could not stand the harassment any longer, she would call for a towel and we'd pass it to her through the slit in the curtain. She'd dry and wrap herself before coming out and heading to the girls' bedroom to dress, but not before smacking both her brothers. Once she was gone, Bernie and I high-fived each other for another job well done.

"I'm next," Mom would say, much to our disappointment, and she'd kick us all out so she could use the toilet. But Michelle would protest—"I want to brush my hair like a big girl"—so Mom would give in and let her stay. When Mom finished and opened the door, Dad would finally see his chance to get in there, but by that time Kim would be dressed and would bolt back in to curl her hair for school.

"But I just wants to dart in there for a tiny second. I'm friggin' bursting here," Dad would plead, as Pal wailed and wrapped herself around Dad's leg in a last-ditch effort to get his attention.

"Sorry," Kim would say. "You can't pee next to me, Dad. I'll be scarred for life."

Mom would defend her teenage daughter. "Jesus, Mary and St. Joseph, Tom. Put some clothes on, will you?"

And I'd watch Dad huff and puff back into the bedroom and slip on a pair of pants, cursing the whole time about how he'd "built the G-D bathroom" that he was never allowed near. Then he would give up and trudge downstairs with Pal in hot pursuit. From the window at the top of the stairs, I'd see him down below, standing shirtless in the freezing wind, peeing off the back step, with a most contented little black mutt squatting next to him doing the same.

Most mornings that would be the end of it. Bernie and I would be washed, dressed and running downstairs to an awaiting mound of toasted homemade bread and jam.

But the Bathroom Ballet didn't always go so smoothly. I recall one Sunday when we were all up and getting ready to go to mass, when Bernie insisted Kim give him a quick loan of the one hairbrush in our house. Kim, for whatever reason, outright refused. The argument grew heated and Kim ran out of the can and down the stairs with the long wooden-handled brush. When they reached the living room, Kim jumped up on the couch, spun around and cracked him as hard as she could on the head.

"Kim, give me the friggin' brush."

"No. I'm not done brushing my hair. Don't you touch it."

Whack. She cracked him a second time.

"Kim, if you hits me with that brush one more time, I'm gonna punch you right in the—"

Bernie did not even have the words out of his mouth when she whacked him hard again, right across the cheek.

I was getting worried. Mom and Dad were upstairs. So was Michelle. I was the only witness.

"Give him the brush, Kim, or he's gonna punch you in the face," I begged.

"He won't do it," she said.

Whack. She hit him a fourth time, the hardest smack yet.

Bernie's retaliation is better described as a hard shove rather than as a punch, but either way, Kim went flying over the couch and out of sight. Total silence followed. I thought she might be dead. But no sooner had I thought it did she squeal, not in pain but in anger, and she jumped back up, ready for blood. She was on Bernie like a wrestler and they were both going for the belt.

I ran upstairs and got Mom. "Quick!" I said, when I found her in the bathroom. "They're gonna kill each other!"

Mom came running down the stairs and separated her warring children. Mom's presence could not quell the rage. She had to pry them apart as they both kept swinging.

"That's some way to be getting on when we're on our way to mass. Ye crowd are not fit to be in the church! Get up the stairs and get back in bed before I drowns the two of ye!" she ordered.

I stood there, not believing what I'd just heard. Surely, Bernie and Kim, the two combatants, did not get to go back to bed to sleep, while I, the innocent messenger, had to go to mass!

My face must have said what I was thinking.

Mom said nothing. She just pointed towards Skinner's Hill and the road to the church.

"No way!" I protested.

"Yes way. Up the hill. Now!"

This was one of the rare times when me staying out of Kim and Bernie's constant warring did not benefit me in the least. I am certain my patience for refereeing other people's conflicts came from watching my sister and brother get nowhere with theirs. I was constantly rewarded for being the peaceful and easygoing kid, so I just kept doing it. I had no idea how well this quality would serve me in years to come. If a band is going to stay together for over twenty years, it's got to have some decent referees in the mix.

There were times when all of us siblings worked together, and now that I think about it, one of the memorable moments of teamwork amongst us centred once more on that bathroom. As teenagers, Bernie, Kim and I had a party at our house in Petty Harbour while Mom and Dad were over-nighting in someone's trailer. They'd be away for the evening, so we could sneak in a few people and more than a few drinks. We invited this girl we knew who, oddly, had false teeth. I know what you're thinking: a teenage girl with false teeth? Is that possible? All I can say is yes. Unfortunately for this gal, she was behind the locked door in the bathroom when it is presumed that she bent over the open bowl, most likely to rid herself of an overindulgence of alcohol, and then acciden-tally barfed her teeth into the can. Of course, no one knows for certain how her teeth were lost, but what is certain is that somehow her dentures ended up in the toilet and ended up flushed down it. Word travelled quickly through the party that a rescue mission was required. She was desperate to get those teeth back. She begged us for our help.

"They might still be in the sewer pipe," Bernie suggested. "I mean, it's possible." The girl's face lit up with hope. But the sewer pipe ran a dozen metres or so behind our house into the river. No sober person would have taken this mission on, but as we were all well lubricated, we launched Project Recover Dentures. The Daemon Liquor made us do it. Or at least he convinced us that it was not a totally crazy idea.

We all went outside, and Bernie and I stood knee-high in the river. I was armed with a spaghetti strainer, which I pressed up against the end of the drain pipe. Meanwhile, Kim was upstairs in the bathroom, and when we gave her the thumbs-up, she started flushing the toilet repeatedly and shouting through the open window: "Anything yet?"

"No! Just toilet paper and water. Keep going!"

After an hour or so of flush-and-check—which beyond the spaghetti strainer also involved peering up the pipe with a flashlight and digging up it with a bamboo trouting pole— we gave up. To this day, I cannot pass that drain pipe behind our old house in Petty Harbour without thinking that the poor girl's teeth are stuck in an elbow. Or maybe there's a strange-looking marine creature lurking in the river in Petty Harbour with one sweet-looking set of false teeth.

Once the Bathroom Ballet was behind us on any given day, it was time for breakfast. Our family almost never had what you would call a normal breakfast. Sometimes on Saturdays there might be bacon or ham or my favourite, bologna with eggs, but most times there were unlimited mounds of Mom's homemade white bread and butter. And that was just fine with me.

Two or three times a week, Mom would bake six to eight loaves of fresh bread. She would start early in the day and add the white flour, salt and butter to a massive white Tupperware container. She's start gently mixing and kneading the ingredients by hand, and in no time at all, the loose water and flour became a baby-sized wiggling living thing that seemed to protest her every touch. She'd punch and stretch and tear its flesh until she broke it into submission. Once it lay willingly under her hand, she'd soothe and smooth it into a perfect shiny mound and cover it with a damp cloth to let it rise and swell.

A while later, she'd pull bowling-ball-sized chunks from the mound and press two of them side by each in rectangular baking pans. She'd toss them in a warm oven and in no time at all, the greatest smell I've ever known would be wafting through the house.

At breakfast, the six of us would inhale slices of toasted bread and wash them down with one of the two other dietary staples of our young life, Nestlé's Quik and Tang orange-flavour crystals. We invented ways of recreating these drinks every morning. What would it be like to make cold Quik with no milk, just water? And what would happen if you put two packages of Tang crystals in one glass? Breakfast was a constant chemistry experiment.

I would venture to guess that I ate at least two slices of Mom's bread every breakfast of my life from the time I was one year old to when I moved out at the age of nineteen. That adds up to about 730 slices per year. This means I ate 13,870 slices of Mom's bread from the time I was old enough to eat till the end of my teens. And that's just for breakfast. I won't bother with the math of the remaining meals, which were all based around or bolstered by Mom's magic bread. If I had to pick one thing that was responsible for my joyous and completely satisfied childhood, I'd say it was my family. If I had to pick two things, I'd say my family and Mom's homemade bread. And while it was the North Atlantic cod stocks that fed the Napoleonic armies, Mom's homemade bread fuelled the Doyles on Skinner's Hill. Our delicious but often Spartan meals were always well rounded with heaps of it.

How to Make My Mother's Bread

"How do you make a loaf of bread, Mom?"

"Alan, honey, I don't know how to make a loaf of bread. I only knows how to make eight."

ALAN DOYLE: Mom, I'm trying to put your recipe in my book. Can you help me out? What ingredients do you use?
JEAN DOYLE: I use a bag of flour.

ALAN: A whole bag?

JEAN: A seven-pound bag. And about a cup of butter. And some salt in the palm of my hand.

ALAN: Some salt in the palm of your hand?

JEAN: Yes. Just some salt in the palm of my hand. I mix it all up, dry.

ALAN: In a bowl?

JEAN: In the pan I'm making the bread in. Then, I make like a hole in the centre of the flour, the flour and the butter and the salt that I just mixed up. In the hole there, I put in two tablespoons of dry yeast and two tablespoons of sugar.

ALAN: Sugar?

JEAN: Got to have the sugar for the yeast to rise.

ALAN: I didn't know.

JEAN: And then, what I do is use the whisk and just pour in the water.

ALAN: How much water?

JEAN: I don't know. It's about . . . I'd say probably seven or eight cups. And you got to get the feel of it. I pour in the water and I whisk it. And then when it gets too heavy for the whisk, I get my hands in there. I whack it.

ALAN: You whack it.

JEAN: Yes. And I knead it, until I gets it right nice and doughy. And then I make it into a ball in my pan and put some butter on it and cover it over and let it rise until it's double what I had when I started. And then I knead it down again—well, *I* do, but some people don't knead it down a second time. After, when it rises up again, I put the dough in the pans. This batch will make eight loaves.

ALAN: How long do you cook it for?

JEAN: I cook it at 415 degrees for thirty minutes. And take it out and then I brushes it with a bit of butter. And yummy.

ALAN: You make it sound so easy.

JEAN: Oh, it is.

We never really sat at the table as an entire family until suppertime, but we did that every single evening. Our suppers were delicious, simple and very consistent. Most often the fare was roasted beef, pork or chicken or fried fish, with piles of potatoes and gravy. My mom can make gravy, incredible gravy, from anything. I'm fairly certain that if you gave her a bucket of rocks, an onion and a cup of water and told her she had to make a gravy out of it, she'd find a way. And it would be awesome. From waking to sleeping, Mom is in a constant state of movement, always was. If you can get her to sit in an armchair, she'll reach to one side, grab a knitting project and in no time at all, a sock or hat will materialize in her hands. Magic.

Usually the smell of something roasting in our oven started in the late afternoon. By five, we'd all be salivating at the thought of that roast and the gravy Mom would make from it to pour over boiled potatoes and some canned peas or corn. I would venture to say that we had potatoes and some kind of gravy for supper more than 250 times per year. Which was nowhere near enough for me.

There wasn't always as much meat as we wanted, but there was no shortage of bread. "That's all the roast we have. Fill up on bread," Mom would say—a common refrain in our house. Mom would say it like it wasn't a good thing. But it was. It still is. Ask Mom what she did today, and she'll probably reply the same as she always did: "Nothing at all, honey." But if you look in the kitchen, you'll see eight fresh-baked loaves of bread on the counter and a large boiler on the stove full of recently jarred homemade preserves. And there's sure to be a pot of beef stew simmering away somewhere, and every flat surface in that house is so clean, you could eat off of it.

When I was growing up, I always sat in the same place at the table. We all had our spots. Not sure if they were strategically set up by my folks, or if in true Petty Harbour fashion, I sat in that place simply because I always had.

Our table was just barely big enough to fit six people. Dad sat at one end with Mom immediately at his left, closest to the stove so she could be cooking right up until the last second. Next to her, my little sister Michelle was in a high chair and later in a regular chair, with my sister Kim on her left. Mom and Kim would split the duties of helping Michelle eat her food. Bernie and I sat on the other side of the table. Bernie was next to Kim, I suppose so they could harass and abuse each other more conveniently. I sat between Bernie and Dad, both a challenging and advantageous place to sit.

There was no grace or any formality to our meals. It was load and go. To this day I eat like I'm in imminent danger of my food being taken away. At fancy dinners and restaurants, I've devised strategies to make myself look less like a total savage. I take a few forkfuls, lay my fork down, put my hands under the table and count to fifty, or sing a verse of a song in my head before I pick up the fork again. I'm serious. I have to or I'll be staring over an empty plate while others are still buttering their bread.

At the supper table of my youth, Bernie and I almost always got our food first, most likely because we were the most vocal about how hungry we were. Bernie would often have his plate emptied by the time the others had been served their first plate. Dad would follow close behind. I learned to eat fast because if I didn't, either Dad on my left or Bernie on my right would snatch something from me.

Kim would help Michelle with her plate, then attempt to eat her food at a sensible pace. But I imagine it was hard to do that with me staring at her like a starved gull and Bernie literally circling his fork over her food. Kim would guard her plate from Bernie with a sharp knife, and he knew she would use it.

At the supper table of my youth—(*around the table from left to right*) Kim's hand, Bernie, me, Dad and Michelle. (Mom must have moved Michelle into her seat so she could take the photo.) If you look carefully, you'll see the two little shining eyes of our dog, Pal, under the table awaiting droppings from me and Bern. Mom's gravy was so good, Pal never got much.

Mom would have two bites of her meal and scrape some of it off onto mine and Bernie's plates, much to Dad's disappointment.

"Go on, Tom. You had enough grub to do you the winter."

If in some lucky twist of fate there were leftovers, they got shoved to the boys' side of the table. As long as I was quick, I could get them first. So I was quick. Real quick.

Every once in a while, Mom would get adventurous with a meal and try something "exotic," like a sausage casserole she found a recipe for in the newspaper.

"Sorry, Mom. This is gross. Can we go to Maureen's and get bologna for sandwiches?"

"Ye crowd never wants to try anything different. All ye wants is meat and potatoes and gravy." It was true. Mom would get so upset with our attitude that she'd sometimes go upstairs by herself. But as I said, this was very rare, and most nights we inhaled every last bit of whatever was prepared. I have no memory of leftovers in our fridge. Ever. We ate everything immediately and loved it.

I discovered a funny thing when writing this book, something I have no explanation for. My long-suffering editor, Nita, asked me to describe what we talked about around the table. I did not know what to say. This, you may not be surprised to learn, almost never happens to me. I told Nita I'd ask my family. I asked my brother and sisters and parents what it was we talked about at mealtime. They gave the same look of surprise. None of us could remember many, if any, topics of conversation. This is truly amazing because I can guarantee you we did not stop talking to eat. No Doyle on Skinner's Hill in Petty Harbour ever has. So what did we talk about with our mouths full?

There were never any niceties or the polite "How was your day, dear? What did you learn at school?" For sure, we talked about how much we wanted to eat the leftovers and who would get them. In fact, I suspect most of the talk was jockeying between Dad and Bernie and me for the last spud.

Apart from that, we rambled on about nothing in particular. Does the fact that the topics of conversation aren't memorable mean that they were not nearly as important as the fact that we were there together every night? I don't know for sure. I just recall feeling more at ease at our table than anywhere else. I never had to entertain or be entertained there. Maybe that's what Home is.

I can still feel the sting of Dad's hot tea spoon on my forearm as he would playfully touch me with it immediately after stirring his hot tea. He did this every night just to watch me jump and to make everyone else laugh. I remember my sister Kim wiping the food from little Michelle's face and imagining what an incredible mom she would be herself one day. She is. I can still hear Michelle, just a toddler then, but singing in remarkable pitch. I suspected all along that she would one day become the best singer in the family. She is. I remember Bernie and me sneaking the fat from the meat down between our chairs to feed our old dog, Pal, under the table. And I remember the satisfied smile on Mom's face when all her kids were around her, happy and fed.

The cleanup was most often done by either Mom and Dad or Mom and Kim. There were many attempts over the years to get me and Bernie to help, but I'm not sure any of these attempts were successful. We'd fight over the dish drying and break a plate and eventually we'd be kicked out of the kitchen and ordered to bring in wood or perform some other "man duty."

Once cleanup was done, we kids would take the same places in the same chairs at the table. Part of the Do Something Golden Rule was that we had to do homework, even if we weren't assigned any. This rule was mostly in place for us boys, since Kim always had her perfectly organized exercise books out and her assignment checklists ready to be ticked. Bernie and I would have preferred to run outside after supper and take hockey shots at each other till bedtime, but Mom and Dad insisted we do our homework. Bern would help me with math, my least favourite subject. If not for his tutelage, there's no way I'd have passed a single math course after Grade 8.

"Hey, Bern, you know that thing about the sides of a right triangle? How does that go again?"

"Fer frig sakes, b'y. The square of the hypotenuse is equal to the sum of the square of the other two sides."

"Right, right," I'd say. "Now, is that every time?"

"Yes. Sorry it's so boring, Alan, but yes, every time."

Poor Bern, he was so good at numbers and equations that he would later get an engineering degree and a master's in business. Yet in our young life he was saddled nightly with the task of teaching me to add and subtract.

Mom and Dad would stand over our shoulders for a half-hour or more to ensure we did something. Anything.

"I wants four pictures of ye on the wall with them sashes from the university around your necks, you hear me?" Mom was adamant we'd all get post-secondary education, and Dad agreed. Their insistence paid off. Kim, Bernie and Michelle all were high honours students, and my grades were often described as "good enough." All of us graduated from university. Of course, I finished the last few of my courses towards a bachelor of arts degree from the back seat of the Great Big Sea van. But the point is: I finished. We all did. These days, pictures of grandchildren have replaced many of the photos of us kids on Mom and Dad's wall. But Mom and Dad still proudly display the four photos of us with them sashes on.

All four Doyle children "with them sashes," just like Mom always wanted. These photos are proudly displayed in my parents' home.

When homework was done, me and Bernie usually played some kind of sport. If there was enough daylight still, we played catch or he would take shots on me in our make-shift net out on the gravel driveway. We'd use a tennis ball or whatever we could find. The trick was to not only stop the ball but to do so while dodging the many small rocks and bits of gravel that would come flying with every shot. In the dead of winter when the after-supper skies were too dark, we'd set up a game of spoon hockey in our short hallway on the first floor of the house. We'd get two spoons and make a ball out of tinfoil and blast each other with it. You'd be surprised how easy it is to cut your face with the sharp points of a tinfoil ball.

Inevitably, fights would break out. Me and Bernie had some wicked ones. Once, he threw a pellet gun at me so hard that it went right through our bedroom wall and landed in Mom and Dad's bedroom.

"Bernie," Dad asked, "what in the Jesus do you think you're doing throwing a gun at your brother?"

"Alan won't die!" was his answer.

The worst fights occurred when we decided we would take on the roles of our favourite professional wrestlers. Off came our shirts and away we went with swings and kicks in a mock-wrestling match in the kitchen. Once, I decided to try to compact my brother into a small package, a wrestling move made famous by pro wrestler Jimmy Superfly. To my complete surprise, it worked quite well. Like, really well. Bernie went down like a neat ton of bricks and gasped in pain on the floor. He was acting it out perfectly, just like they did on TV. I climbed the kitchen chair and onto the table like I was about to finish him off from the top ropes with a flying elbow, but I paused when I finally noticed the realism of his acting was a little too perfect.

Me and my brother, Bernie, circa 1978. Don't let the clean clothes and angelic smiles fool you.

Bernie turned white as a sheet and pointed to his shoulder without saying a word. I got down and helped him to his feet. His shoulder was not where it was supposed to be at all. It had been forced down around his right nipple. The look on my face must have scared the shite out of him because his eyes widened with mine. Of its own accord, his shoulder started to migrate back to its home, slowly at first as it drifted up his right side, then it quickly clicked right back in its place. The bones and muscles made a grotesque snap. Bernie fainted and hit the ground like a man who'd been shot. I was not far behind him. To this day, his shoulder pops in and out of place with alarming ease. The kitchen wasn't used as a wrestling arena very often after that incident.

But these rows and mishaps were not as frequent as you might imagine. My brother and I got along fairly well. We often retreated to our room to listen to the radio or records. I learned so much about music from Bernie, as he had such a keen ear and appreciation for good tunes. To this day, he is one of the most musically literate people I know. Most nights as a kid, I'd sit on the bed and he'd DJ, explaining why he thought one Boston song was way better than the other. Or why the Little River Band must have at least two awesome guitar players as there were always complementary parts happening simultaneously. We practically memorized Billy Joel's *The Stranger*, Supertramp's *Paris*, Meat Loaf's *Bat Out of Hell* and Pat Benatar's *Crimes of Passion*, just to name a few.

Ever-resourceful Bernie rigged a wire clothes hanger out our bedroom window and up to the eaves and back down to an old radio we got from one of our uncles. Late at night, we could pick up stations broadcast from Detroit and Upstate New York. We'd lie there for hours listening to American soul and rhythm and blues, music we'd never get to hear on any local station.

Later, in his very early teens, Bernie saved up enough money to actually buy his own TV, which benefited me tremendously as we could lie in bed and watch hockey till Mom and Dad forced us to turn it off and go to sleep. That TV came in especially handy when we figured out that the French-Canadian station had a program called *Bleu Nuit* that came on after midnight. Use your imagination.

Most days ended with Bernie in his bed and me in mine across from him with my head up against the footboard. This made throwing a tinfoil ball easier and allowed for more

Bernie and me posing in our fancy front entrance.

important question-and-answer sessions. Lob and catch. Wonder. Lob and catch. Suppose. Lob and catch. Repeat.

"Bern, do you think Barbara Ann Chase would go out with me?"

"No. I really don't. Do you think this Gretzky fella is going to be as good as everyone says?"

"No, he's not on the Montreal Canadiens and they have all the good players. They'd have him if he was as good as everyone says. You think Pat Benatar would ever play here in Newfoundland?"

"Not a chance. We're going to have to get on a plane to see her, I'd say."

"Yeah, some chance of that. We'll probably never see her."

"Probably not."

"Frig, b'y, I'm starving. Can't wait for breakfast. Did Mom make bread today?"

"Yeah."

"Deadly."

And sometime after that, we'd fall asleep.

Part 2

CHAPTER 4

Ye Bastarding Doyles

For most of my young life, there were two convenience stores in Petty Harbour. At different times a third or even fourth one came and went, but mainly there was one on the Catholic side and one on the Protestant side. The Protestant store was run by the Weir family, and it was called Herbie's. We Catholics had Harbour Grocery, or Maureen's, as we all knew it. I'm not sure if the owners' religious affiliations had anything to do with the fact that their stores (and the shopping experience in them) could not have been more different.

Herbie's, the Protestant store, was—and still is—a traditional local shop with real showcase crystal-clear windows and freshly marked specials handwritten in white letters each day. It was like Christmas every day in that shop. A lovely older couple, Herbie and his wife, Marguerite, were always neatly dressed. They kept their store in tip-top shape, inside and out. One or the other would always greet me with a smile as I walked in, the pleasant *tring* of the door chimes ringing out after me. "Hello, Alan Doyle. We rarely sees your happy face over here!"

The long, straight softwood floor in that store reminded me of a fancy ship's deck. The boards ran perfectly parallel from the coolers with chilled milk, juice and pop to the counter, which boasted a neat wooden top with a glass showcase underneath, where rows of candies and chocolate bars were displayed right at a little boy's eye height. Behind the counter were impressive high shelves with vertical dividers displaying perfectly ordered cans of soup and plump bags of flour and rows of fancy molasses.

To the right of the counter, a few large bins held fresh carrots, potatoes, onions and so on. A small hallway led to the back of the store, where there must have been larger coolers and freezers, as that's where Herbie or Marguerite would go to retrieve the large hams, bolognas, turkey loaves or roast beef.

"I'll have six slices of ham, please," I'd say to Herbie and I'd wait for the show. He'd put the meat on a perfect wooden cutting board, and despite his shaky hand, he cut every slice himself. When Herbie was done, he'd tear a square of crisp brown paper from a wide horizontal roll and he would wrap the cold cuts into a tidy package. On the top, with a wide carpenter's pencil, he'd write, "Ham $1.10."

The final touch was my favourite, as Herbie would reach

for a length of white string. If you traced the end of the string with your eye, you'd see it hung from a small metal loop in the ceiling, where it turned ninety degrees and ran just below the white-painted ceiling boards all the way back to the very top of the wooden shelves. There, a large, magical, pyramid-shaped spool of white line sat, never seeming to increase or decrease in size no matter how much string Herbie used.

He'd take the end of the line and wrap it around the package of ham. He had this cool way of making a knot without needing to cut the line to tie it. Then, with a quick double flick, he'd snap the string exactly where the knot ended. There was not a millimetre of twine wasted in the entire

Herbie's Store in Petty Harbour, present day. The store is as perfect as it ever was. Note the string that runs from the ceiling (*top right*) and the roll of brown paper wrapping (*right*), both ready for tying up neat little packages.

process. He'd pass me the finished package, and I'd feel like I was holding a grand gift in my hands from Santa himself.

"Thanks, Alan Doyle," Marguerite would say with a lovely smile. "Bring your happy face back soon, honey."

I loved Herbie's. Too bad I almost never got to go there as a kid.

As noted, Herbie's was on the Protestant side and we almost never shopped there. No one ever told me I shouldn't. No one ever said we had to stay on the Catholic side to spend our money. We just did. Like many things in my young life in Petty Harbour, we did things one way because they had always been done that way.

This portrait of Herbie and his daughter, Sherri, still hangs in the shop.

When my mother sent me to the store, I didn't even think to ask which. I knew she was sending me to Harbour Grocery, or Maureen's. I only got to go to Herbie's when Maureen's was closed, which was never, or if I went to Maureen's and she didn't have what Mom asked me to get, which was almost never, or if word got around that a health inspector was banging on Maureen's door trying to get in, which happened more than I care to say.

Maureen was old when I was young. She lived alone in the back of her store. She had a son, but by the time I was about ten, he had moved away to go to school. I confess I don't know for sure what kind of living arrangements she had at the back of her store, but I suspect she had a kitchen and a bedroom. She never spent a lot of time back there anyway. Instead, she spent every waking hour behind the counter of her store, watching a small black-and-white TV about eighteen inches from her face. Most often, customers who walked in and stood in front of her counter were greeted by her right ear, because she was always facing that TV. Harbour Grocery was manned, or womanned, by Maureen and Maureen alone. I must have seen her in the store thousands of times, but never once did I see her outside of it.

To enter Maureen's store, you had to climb a set of uneven, broken grey concrete steps. They were in such a state of disrepair that it was tough to find a tread that was level. In the winter months, the holes and crevasses in the steps filled with water and froze into patches of treacherous black ice. This would have been far less of a problem if the steps had a handrail of any kind to hold on to. Slipping on Maureen's front stairs was a common event. One false move and you were flying feet first over the side of the steps and down, arse first, onto the rocky ground below. If you happened to break a glass bottle on your landing, there was no sense asking Maureen for a replacement or a refund.

"That's yer own stupid fault. Sure ya knows the steps are slippery. Now get out of my store, ye bastarding Doyles!"

Ye bastarding Doyles. That's what she called me and my whole family, cousins and all, from as early as I can remember. What she meant by this christening I cannot say. Did she mean we were all bastards? That our parents were not married? This was clearly not true. Maybe she was making reference to the generations of musicians in my family who she perhaps presumed went around knocking up gals and making piles and piles of bastard children. I don't know.

Maybe her crankiness towards us had something to do with the fact that my uncles, the town musicians, once made up a song about her to the tune of "Goodnight Irene." I won't provide the entire rendition here, but towards the ultimate verse, there was mention of a "sex machine," which rhymed quite nicely with "Maureen, Goodnight Maureen."

Yeah. This song may have had something to do with her apparent dislike for us Doyles.

In any case, for many reasons beyond the fact that Maureen was not a fan of the Doyles, it was no fun going into her store. Once atop the concrete steps, you often found the door locked if Maureen was in the kitchen or washroom. There was sometimes a handwritten sign stuck with a dart into the thin-panelled door. It read: KNOCK HARD. But when you knocked hard, you'd be greeted a few moments later by Maureen, unlocking the door while shouting, "Jesus, Mary and St. Joseph, don't beat the door in!"

And when she saw me, she would roll her eyes. "I should have known that if someone were beatin' down my door, it would have to be one of ye bastarding Doyles!"

I'd silently follow Maureen inside, careful to stay a couple of paces behind. The floors were dark, and what they were made of, I could not say. The walls were dark-grey panelling—or so I suspected. They were so covered in ancient, torn posters for Hostess Chips or Vachon Cakes or Pepsi that it was hard to say what was underneath it all.

Like Herbie's, the front wall of the store had a big picture window, but almost no light penetrated the old beer posters covering the panes. Duct tape snaked along the windows, masking the cracks. The whole place was dimly lit, and a layer of dust coated everything. It would've been tough for anyone who was claustrophobic, germophobic or anything phobic to spend any amount of time in Harbour Grocery.

And then there was the counter, which the door hit every time you opened or closed it, eliciting the same complaint from Maureen every single time: "Mind the counter! And close the door! Were you born on a raft or what?"

The counter occupied an entire wall. The glass cases underneath were either empty or filled with old newspapers or single rolls of toilet paper, or other things a young boy would never find appealing. Behind the counter, cardboard boxes were haphazardly stacked up to the ceiling, some cut open on the sides so you could see they held aging cans of tomato soup or dish soap. Some boxes were tipped on their sides, flaps torn in the cardboard to reveal grubby Kraft Dinner boxes or dusty ketchup bottles. Everything was in a state of disarray but also within just a step or two of Maureen's stool, which was permanently positioned next to her glowing black-and-white TV. She would sit lording over this mound of stuff and somehow she knew exactly where to reach when you asked for something.

Request a bar of soap and she would slide the box of paper towels to one side, lift the tins of Vienna sausages and take a bar of soap from a plastic bag underneath. Ask for a can of condensed milk and she would lean back a few inches and reach behind some playing cards for a hidden can. She'd slide it across the counter but often had to pull it right back to wipe the layer of dust off the top of it with her shirt or apron.

"So, what are you in for now?" her right ear would say.

"Mom wants a half-pound of bologna cut thick for supper," I'd say.

"I'll get you your half a pound, but you got to slice it yourself. What, do ye want me to come to your house and fry it for ye too?" I waited, not sure how to proceed. And then she'd say, "Go to the back cooler and get me the bologna."

I'd creep along the back wall of the rectangular room, which was lined with coolers and old fridges and a deep-freeze or two. Near the back was an industrial-sized cooler with pop and beer, and in the bottom of it was an open shelf for meat. Next to a mailbox-shaped processed ham cube, a roundish roast beef and a turkey loaf, I located a long tube of bologna. I lifted it out of the cooler and walked it to the front of the store. I had to stand on my tippytoes to roll it over the top of the counter.

Maureen would take the bologna, grab a huge butcher's knife from underneath a pile of something and hack off a piece about twice as thick as a hockey puck. She rarely stood to do this, using only her arm and wrist to push the knife through the wax coating on the meat. All the while, she'd bite down hard on her tongue as it poked out the left side of her mouth. Then she'd push the severed chunk of meat into some plastic wrap or tinfoil, jam it into a used plastic shopping bag and slide it back to me across the counter.

"That's around a half-pound, I suppose," Maureen would say, though she always gave a bit more than that.

I'd pay her and carefully say, "Thank you, Maureen."

"Finally, a bastarding Doyle with some manners," she'd say as I'd turn to leave. "Now close the door behind you! Were you born on a raft or what?"

FORTUNE'S FAVOUR

Great Big Sea is a Bastard.

So reads the press release for the band's *Fortune's Favour* album.

And it is true. We know who our mother is, but who is our father? Your guess is as good as mine.

We are a band forefathered by the Clancy Brothers and Def Leppard; we are the progeny of the Pogues and my uncle Ronnie's band; we're the love child of Freddie Mercury and the Catholic Book of Worship. As for the mother of Great Big Sea, there's no doubt she's the Wonderful Grand Band.

The Wonderful Grand Band was a musical variety group and a TV show in Newfoundland in the late 1970s and early '80s. WGB played contemporary versions of traditional songs and the amazing original compositions of Ron Hynes, the greatest songwriter in the world. The band's TV show, which aired once a week on CBC, was by far the most popular show on the air in Newfoundland—and it was homegrown through and through. Kids as young as toddlers and their grandparents alike watched every episode. The whole island came to a halt for thirty minutes when *The Wonderful Grand Band* was on. *WGB* was one of the only things that united Baymen and Townies alike in Newfoundland. I watched it in Petty Harbour and Séan and Bob watched it in St. John's, all of us laughing and singing along, none of us with the slightest clue how the musical foundations of our lives were being laid.

While WGB is the mother of GBS, she had quite a few

suitors before her baby was born. When my teenage years hit, I, like so many young fellas my age, fell under the spell of hair metal bands like Van Halen and Whitesnake as well as sexy rockers like Pat Benatar and songwriters with gun bands like Billy Joel and John Cougar. Meanwhile, when Bob Hallett became a teen, he loved early British punk and its near antithesis, new wave. And not too far down the road in the East End of St. John's, a young Séan McCann idolized Christy Moore, Bob Marley and the Police.

We had no idea at the time, but when the three of us finally met in 1992, we would bring all these improbable musical roots together—traditional shanties and Catholic hymns, hair metal and punk, Celtic folk and reggae—to produce the wave of sound we came to call Great Big Sea.

Cutting Out Tongues

P etty Harbour fell quiet, like many other fishing villages that were victims of the cod moratorium in the
early nineties. On that day in 1992, one of the darkest in
Newfoundland history, in an effort to conserve fish stocks,
the Canadian government effectively forced the extinction of
a Newfoundland way of life that had persevered through centuries. The government of Canada declared inshore cod fishing illegal. And with that declaration, Petty Harbour, along
with much of rural Newfoundland, was forever changed.
The deep rumbling sound heard in my town that day was
my Granda spinning in his grave. I was glad he wasn't alive
to experience that tragic moment the way the rest of us did,
but we could still hear his cold corpse booming up to us from
six feet underground—"I told you so!" he said.

I wish everyone I know today could have seen the Petty Harbour of my childhood. Let me try to paint for you a picture of what the inshore cod fishery of the mid-1970s till the late '80s looked like. When I was a kid, the fishery was going full bore. Petty Harbour was a twenty-four-hour town for more than half the year. At one point, three fish processing plants operated around the clock, employing hundreds of folks from town and down the shore. Workers began early and finished late; fishermen got up at the crack of dawn and headed to the wharf; trucks came and went at all hours of the day and night.

I remember lying in my bed hearing the sound of the offal chutes from across the harbour, as guts and gurry (the leftovers of fish processing) slid down aluminum chutes to an awaiting hopper that fed it all up to a huge container perched on two-storey-high metal posts. I remember the *psshht* of a truck's air brakes carrying a load of fish out of town, and the unmistakable *putt-putt* of the one make-and-break engine, the shouts and laughter of plant workers ending their night shift and drinking beers pulled from a fish pan filled with ice in the back of a pickup truck. I remember the slam of the screen door of our neighbour—a fisherman—who at four every morning left his missus in bed, closed the door behind him and started his old truck. This was the soundscape of our town from May through October. To this day, I can hear it in my mind.

One of the unfortunate aspects of being a mischievous teenager at this time was that it was nearly impossible to sneak around in the middle of the night during the summer months. There was always someone awake to see you.

Winter nights were quieter, but the days were almost as busy. Fishermen and plant workers who worked during the busy summer season collected decent unemployment insurance cheques throughout the winter—not that this stopped them from being busy in the cold months. Their skidoos towed sleighloads of firewood, which were loaded onto pickup trucks and hauled to homes all over town, where logs would be cut and split and split again. Then there was the hauling and stacking. And eventually, those split logs would be lugged piece by piece into wood stoves in homes and sheds and garages and makeshift boat shelters all over town, where fishermen sat close to the hearth as they mended nets, rebuilt gear and patched holes in their boats. Petty Harbour, summer or winter, was a busy place, with no end of good and bad a young lad could get up to.

All through my childhood, there was a larger section of covered wharf that jutted into the harbour perpendicular to the breakwaters. It was called the White Wharf. It resembled what most North Americans would call a covered bridge. It was my favourite section of wharfage in Petty Harbour. The White Wharf was a magical place, and I was saddened beyond belief years later when the local council decided it was too much of a liability to restore. It was demolished sometime in the late 1980s.

The White Wharf was an excellent place to sit and fish for tomcods or sculpins or to ride a bike, if you were lucky enough to own one, or to try to kiss a girl.

You could easily grab a few large nails and build a perfect ladder up one of the posts to the attic-like space in the roof. The kids in the harbour would often "borrow" a few planks from boats and line them along the lower trusses to make a walkway from one end of the White Wharf to the other. Some of us even made vertical walls to create our own hideouts high above the harbour. It was like having the best tree house in the world. Kids would bring ghetto blasters and old couch cushions up there and we'd listen to the radio or to the rain hitting the roof. If you were quiet enough after dark, you could go up there and spy on unsuspecting couples who'd stolen away behind one of the posts for a smooch . . . or whatever else.

All young male fantasies aside, the best thing that happened on the White Wharf was the Blessing of the Boats. Late in the spring, early in the summer, the boats from both sides of the harbour, yes, Protestant and Catholic, would gather at the head of the White Wharf. There, the priest and the reverend would lead a unified Petty Harbour congregation, joined for the one and only all-denominational event held in the town all year. It was beautiful. A choir comprising both churches sang songs of the sea and offered prayers to the North Atlantic for her to send our boys and men home safely. It was by far my favourite religious service, and it seemed so sensible to have the whole town gather to wish and hope for the same thing: *Give us lots of fish and don't let anyone drown this summer.* That was a prayer I could believe in.

The inshore fishery consumed the town from top to bottom for six days a week, nearly six months a year. The men fished for as long as they could stand it, then slept for a few hours on a daybed in the kitchen, and then jumped up the next day to do it all again. The women and girls had their work cut out for them keeping families fed and in clean clothes and houses. And most boys between the ages of ten and fourteen started cutting out tongues.

Cutting out tongues. I realize that phrase requires a bit of explanation. I have never met a Mainlander from any-where on earth who had the slightest clue what I was talking about when I've made reference to cutting out tongues. Even people from New England fishing towns, Scandinavian fishermen and folks from other great fishing cultures like Portugal all draw a complete blank whenever I use the term. Knowledge of cutting out tongues seems restricted to the small fishing towns along certain coasts of Newfoundland.

And now for a working definition. Cutting out tongues refers to cutting out the tongues of codfish, along with the triangular bit of flesh that lies beneath the actual tongue. Cod tongues are a bit of a delicacy in Newfoundland and a really big delicacy in parts of Europe and Asia. They are very labour intensive to harvest, as it requires someone to handle every single fish and cut out the tongue by hand. In the modern world of super trawlers and mechanical process-ing, fish come out of the water and into a processing boat where the meaty fillets are machined off the bone and into a store-ready package without ever touching a human hand. But when I was a kid, most of the fish that landed in Petty Harbour were caught on hand-held, single-hook lines, and those fish were carried to shore daily on small twenty-foot boats. Each fish was individually lifted from the boat to the wharf and from the wharf to a table, where every last one was hand-gutted and bled. Of course, the fillets were the choicest parts, but there were all sorts of other bits of the cod that were valued, including heads, livers, britches (roe), sounds (the fleshy liner of the spine) and tongues. The rest of the offal was shipped to a plant to make fertilizer. There was very little, if any, waste.

A typical summer day for me and most other teen and preteen boys meant rising around seven thirty, eating a toast-and-butter breakfast and dressing in the oldest, most wrecked clothes we owned. Around eight, I'd get on my rubber boots and avail myself of two very important tools in the tongue-cutting trade—the bucket and the knife. The bucket was generally an old white plastic salt-beef pail with a wire handle. The bucket was important because it held your cod tongues, but it also served as your seat for the early, sit-around-and-wait part of the day. The knife was usually a hand-me-down fish-filleting knife that had a full-size handle, but the blade had been worn too small for any kind of full-size fish work. When brand new, a Russell knife had a six-inch blade, but the constant razor sharpening wore them down to half that size. They would then be useless for filleting and perfect for cod-tongue cutting.

If you were lucky enough, one of the professional fish filleters from the fish plant would be throwing away his well-used Russell knife and you'd catch him and ask him for it before he ditched it. I got one from a fella that lasted me almost my entire four-year tenure on the wharf. Most young fellas around the harbour became adept at sharpening knives with a file or a steel or a stone. It was one of the services you could offer the fishermen in exchange for access to their catch.

Once my old clothes were donned, my toast eaten, my knife and bucket readied and my rubber boots pulled on, I'd head for the wharf. On the Catholic side. (Yes, Petty Harbour had Catholic and Protestant cod-tongue cutters.) Most of the gang would assemble around eight to wait for the boats to arrive after their morning "spurt," as the fishermen called their first outing of the day. These fishermen would have been up since four. Depending on the catch and the weather, they would head back to shore as early as eight thirty or as late as two or three in the afternoon.

Between six and a dozen of us boys would gather and wait on the harbour side of the grey plywood weigh house.

I'm not in this awesome photo taken by Robert O'Brien, but it totally captures the joy and fun of cutting out tongues.

Jack Walsh, the weighmaster, let us nail an eight-foot-long two-by-eight piece of lumber to the side of the weigh house to serve as a makeshift bench. He was even nice enough not to ask us where we had "borrowed" it from.

Jack was the unpaid, unofficial supervisor of us boys. The principal of summer school. The Fagan to our Oliver Twist gang of hooligans. The boss. A poor report from Jack, and you were off the wharf—out of work and out of spending money for the rest of the summer. Jack insisted we keep the place clean and the language, too. "No shagging around, lads," he'd say. "No bullying, no fighting, no cheating—and no stealing cod tongues from your buddies." He was constantly keeping us from falling overboard from boats or from electrocuting ourselves with some car battery that we found in an old boat. He was also quick to show us how to sharpen our knives or how to properly fillet a codfish or tie a half hitch knot or whatever else we needed to learn.

Jack had mystical superpowers. Apart from the fact that he never seemed to age and had that same youthful twinkle in his eye summer after summer, he could also forecast the weather forty-eight hours in advance—and he did it better than the meteorologists from the CBC.

"You won't be out tomorrow. It's gonna be blowin' a gale." The fishermen knew not to challenge Jack's forecast.

Jack Walsh was so familiar with the fleet of small boats around Petty Harbour that he could tell which boat was approaching just by the sound. A distant hum of an engine would drift along the water and up to the wharf.

Weighmaster Jack Walsh, who always kept the harbour in order when I was a boy.

Notice how Jack looks almost the same today, whereas I have aged considerably.

"That'll be Jacob Chafe," Jack would announce. And he was always right.

As if that wasn't enough, Jack could also look at a boat coming into sight through the breakwaters and estimate the weight of its catch to within a hundred pounds.

"I'd say Jacob's carrying twenty-six hundred pounds today, give or take a couple." And right he was.

Jack would greet us every morning as we took our seats on the bench. "There's the b'ys, ready to work for a few dollars like the big fellas. 'Attaway. Keep your knife sharpened and your bucket clean."

Sometimes we'd wait on the bench for just a few minutes

before we'd see the boats coming to shore; other times, we'd wait for hours. Sitting there on the long-wait days were some of my favourite times during my childhood. Perched on the narrow bench, rubber boots on the wooden edge of the wharf with a bunch of friends around my age. We passed the time talking about sports and how Gretzky would never be as good as Lafleur and how Tiger Williams would never take Stan Jonathan in a fight. We'd argue over who was the best local softball pitcher or darts player and how Gordie Doyle was probably a good enough goalie to make the NHL but would never be given a chance by the scouts. Everything was up for discussion and debate.

We'd declare Mike Hearn the strongest man in Petty Harbour, replacing old Frank, who wasn't as strong as he used to be years ago when he apparently turned a Volkswagen Beetle over all by himself. We'd spend hours debating which boat could hold the most fish and which cost the most and which could go the fastest. We figured Benny was the fastest runner but Bobby could probably still hit him with a rock, as he had by far the best arm. We knew for certain Harry Chase was one of the richest men in the world as he had two cars and a job in town somewhere. We heard that Ray was on drugs and that's why he came home from Toronto. Another girl, Mary, was definitely pregnant, and the father of her baby was a fella from up the shore who owned a van and played the Doors as loud as his stereo could suffer as he drove up and down the shore.

The older boys would talk about girls and how someone's brother had seen more than half of Jenny's chest from the second-floor choir loft at church. Another fella would swear that Rhonda let him stuff grass down her top just so he could cop a feel. And yet another would share the hot tip that if you brought a certain widow a meal of cod tongues, she'd reward you by leaving the bathroom curtain open so you could watch her while she took a bath.

When we got bored of talking, we'd wander around the wharf looking for trouble. We'd make a kink in one of the long rubber hoses and stop the water flow till one of the boys would stick his face to it and check if the nozzle was clogged. Then we would release the kink in the hose and blast his face with water. We'd bring little bits of flour with us to scatter around the wood cribs below the wharf and wait for the hungry rats to come out for a feed. The moment a rat stuck its head out, we'd pelt it with rocks or even shoot at it with a pellet gun, if one of us had been sly enough to sneak a gun on the wharf without Jack seeing it.

We'd get a line and old hook or even a fishing pole, and we'd play catch-and-release with sculpins. The ugliest fish in the world, sculpins lined the harbour floor and ate anything. You could catch them with a piece of red rag on a line. You would not even need a hook. You could pull them up to the wharf, where they'd regurgitate the hookless lure. Awesome.

We did a similar thing with the seagulls. We'd take a cod liver and put it in ice for a few minutes so it was not quite so mushy. We'd wrap fishing line in and around it and let it float out to the middle of the harbour or even past the breakwater into the open sea, if our line was long enough. Some poor unsuspecting gull would spot his lunch and nosedive to it, swallowing the liver and line in one gulp. Then the bird would fly off and just before our length of line ran out, we'd yank with all our might.

Most times, the gull would turn mid-air with a very confused look, barf up the line and liver, and head for the hills. But if you were really lucky, the gull would bite down hard on the line and refuse to give up the liver dinner. Then you had a fight on your hands—pulling and yanking a flying bird out of the air or being pulled into the harbour yourself if the gull was stubborn and strong enough.

One morning, Mikey went head to head in an epic battle with a big gull. Mikey was a smaller fella, barely ten years old, and he landed one of the biggest seagulls I'd ever seen up close. He was trying his best to reel the bird in, but this particular gull was just too strong. We all got behind Mikey and started chanting his name and he swelled up with pride and held his own for a good minute or two. When it looked like he was gonna get yanked in the harbour, a couple of us took a coil of rope and lashed him to a bollard. He was going nowhere now, but the gull would still not give up. The avian terror got closer and closer to the wharf till it was about four or five feet above Mikey's scared little head. It looked like the bird was going to attack him, and Mikey, still tied down, was crying like a baby. But to his credit, he would not let go of the line.

"Mikey, Mikey!" we chanted, at a safe distance.

Mikey gave one final heave and the gull released the line about three feet above Mikey's face. Unfortunately for Mikey, the gull's surrender caused the creature to barf up the liver—along with the rest of the contents of its stomach—all over Mikey's face and shoulders. As the gull flew off, we caught a whiff of the half-digested fish innards and rotting capelin and who knows what else that made up the seagull's last meal.

We all ran away screaming, abandoning Mikey, left tied to the wharf. And that's when the guilt came over me.

"That's a friggin' sin, b'ys, leaving him there like that, tied up and full of bird vomit. We gotta do something."

"Yeah, we should hose him down," Benny said casually.

"For his own good, of course," Perry added.

"C'mon, Mikey," I said. "A fresh douse, for your own good."

"No!" he begged.

"This is the best thing for you, b'y." This was Wade, one of the older boys. "Fresh start to the day now, all that gull shite and guts behind us." This made perfect sense to me. And that's when Wade grabbed the hose and blasted Mikey with it on full crank, almost washing the poor kid over the head of the wharf.

"Lift up your arms, Mikey!" Perry added helpfully. "So we can get all the gull barf off you."

We all tried to act like we honestly were not enjoying this in any way.

But after the scrub down, Mikey wasn't looking so good. In fact, he was turning a wee bit pale. The weight of the epic adventure with the gull had taken its toll, and Mikey then made matters worse by barfing all over himself. Of course, all of us b'ys were deeply concerned and did the only comforting thing we could think to do: we put the hose on him again. After a brief drying period with a bag of Cheezies and a Coke, he was right as rain and back at it with us all.

There was always something fun on the go at the wharf—chats, games and mischief. But all that would end the moment we heard the *putt-putt* of a small boat coming around the point. Then it was all business. If Jack hadn't already told us whose boat was coming in, we'd be out on the top of the breakwater with our eyes peeled. The moment the boat came into view, someone would yell out.

"Yes b'y, Hubert Chafe! My boat! My tongues! He's loaded to the gunwales too! Ye can all blow me!"

Many of the boats and fishermen had long-standing arrangements with tongue cutters. In exchange for our help with the unloading and cleaning of their boats, and the loading and cleaning of the splitting table, the fishermen let us cut out their cod tongues. I had an arrangement with two of the twenty or so boats that came to the Catholic wharf, but there were always a few boats that were unclaimed for whatever reason—for instance, because their usual tongue cutter was away that day.

There were also times when many boats would arrive together, and then a boy would have too much work for just himself. When this happened to me, I'd ask Perry to cover my usual boats in exchange for the same from him the next time he got double-booked. Some of us teamed up, offering employment to a younger helper who was paid a commission of a little less than half the tongues.

There was always wheeling and dealing going on, some of it a little sketchy, if you could manage it out of Jack's eye.

It was like being in a union. A rumour would go around the wharf that Roger had agreed to cover Wade's boats while he was away at a softball tournament, and Roger would get 25 percent of the cut—or a few beers, or whatever. There was more bartering on that wharf than there was at the Grand Bazaar.

When a boat reached the wharf side, no matter if it was arranged or not, all of us would shout out the same thing every single time:

"Can I have your tongues?"

I expect that's a sentence that sounds strange to just about everyone, yet it was shouted hundreds of times on every summer day in Petty Harbour. How weird it must have seemed to any visitor from the Mainland who happened upon the wharf when a boat was coming in—this pack of young fellas in rags, waving buckets and sharp knives, shouting out to sea, "Can I have your tongues?"

Once a fisherman agreed to let you have his tongues, your first job was to get the fish out of the boat. If you were lucky, the fisherman had a webbed net in the hold of the boat. If so, all you had to do was hook the four corners of the net to a winch and hoist the entire mesh bag, containing as much as two thousand pounds of codfish so fresh that much of it would still be alive, and drop it on the wharf. But if the fisherman did not have such modern technologies—and about half of them did not—you had to heave the fish onto the wharf one at a time using a single-pronged pew. (For you Mainlanders, that's a pitchfork with half the U gone.)

It was a super drag when the quality control inspectors from the provincial Department of Fisheries were patrolling the wharf because they restricted how you could poke a fish—no punctures in the sides or belly because that would leave holes in the fillets. So instead of blindly plunging your pew into a hold of fish and flicking onto the dock whatever came with it, we had to carefully stick each fish in the head or gills or, best of all, in the eye. It was time-consuming to aim for the eye, but according to the inspectors, this was done in the name of "quality control."

I would never have admitted at the time how disturbing it was to poke a half-living thing in the eye. If I'd have admitted that, I would have been ribbed for the rest of my life. But I'll confess to you now that poking fish like this freaked me out just a little bit. At the end of a long, dreamlike day, I'd go to bed and have odd nightmares where those broken eyes and blank faces would be staring at me menacingly. But the nightmares never stopped me from going back to the wharf and pewing thousands of fish each day. I needed the cash.

Once all the catch was on the wharf, your next job was to keep the splitting or gutting tables stocked with cod so that the fishermen could gut and bleed them, one by one. Somehow, you also had to harvest the precious cod tongues in whatever spare moment you could find from the time the fish hit the wharf till they made it to the table. You had to be fast. And I got fast—nowhere near the fastest on the wharf, but I think I got up to more than a dozen cod tongues in a minute.

How to Cut Out a Cod Tongue

Step 1) Turn the codfish belly up, tail away from you.

Step 2) Place your left thumb in one set of gills and your fingers in the other (for right-handed cutters). Pull and spread the fleshy triangle at the bottom of the cod's head.

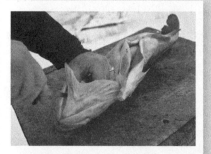

Step 3) Cut underneath the left and right jawline, leaving just a nip of flesh attached under the chin (if you can say that a fish has a chin).

Step 4) Slide your index and middle finger into the slit and pinch down with your thumb. Then cut along the bottom of the triangle.

Step 5) If you are a first-time cod-tongue cutter, use your knife to snip away the attached nip. If you are an expert, push the round gill bone and tear off the little nip. (This increases your speed and looks super cool to tourists and visiting cousins from the Mainland.)

Step 6) Repeat a thousand times per day, or until your fisherman tells you you're done.

Once a fisherman was done with his catch, he would accompany it to the weigh house with Jack Walsh. While he was gone, your job was to get the hose and clean the splitting table, the wharf and the holds of the boat. If you did a good and fast enough job, you'd be sure to get that fisherman's tongues the next day. If you shagged this part up and the fisherman returned from the weigh house and found his table and boat still dirty, or saw you buggering off to count your tongues before you'd bothered to clean up, he would not be happy.

"Well, look at this, Jack. Young Stack here cuts the tongues and shags off before the tables are washed. What do you make of that?" Hubert Chafe would say loud enough for young Stack and everyone else to hear.

"Hubert, I guarantee ya I knows who will not be getting your tongues tomorrow," Jack Walsh would say. He would always have the last word.

When I look back on this now, I'm grateful for the training ground that was the wharf. I learned a lot about effort and reward, about co-operation and about getting along in a group. About honesty and effort and commerce. About being a part of the community and sharing in its economic rise and fall. No fish, no tongues. No tongues, no money. Adult problems were understood by us boys from an early age. I also learned to have a blast with a bunch of idle dudes. (I had no idea these things would serve me so well in my adult life in a touring band.)

But the biggest lesson I learned on the wharf was that a job is not just an assignment or a task. It is something bigger than that. A job is an agreement, a deal you make with someone to do your part right, so everyone else can do theirs. If you don't clean out the boat right, the tired fisherman who just gave you his tongues is going to have to do it. He doesn't need that. He's been up since four in the morning. Far earlier than most, I learned that work does not do itself. What a lesson.

The boys and I made some good dosh on the wharf, but it was not just the money that made me love cutting and selling tongues. Con O'Brien, from the Irish Descendants, grew up a couple of towns down from Petty Harbour, in Bay Bulls on the Southern Shore. A while back, we were talking about cutting tongues as kids. Con lamented the fall of the inshore fishery and the fact that our sons would not have those summers that we had. He had written some verses about it and we added to them to make a song—a song about cutting tongues. To my knowledge, it is the only song in existence on this particular topic.

> *It was the thrill of my life*
> *When I first held a knife*
> *And was told I could join in the gang*
> *Making cash of my own with a bucket and stone*
> *Makes a lad feel like more of a man.*
> > —from "Not for the Money Alone,"
> > Con O'Brien/Alan Doyle, 2006

CHAPTER 6

Selling Tongues and Picking Capelin

I've outlined for you, dear reader, what it was like for us as kids to be working on the wharf and harvesting cod tongues. But the whole point of gathering them was to sell them and make a profit, and once the boats were in, usually by early afternoon, all of us young lads would do our best to sell our buckets of tongues as quickly as possible—and for as much money as we possibly could. Some days, we raked in quite a mountain of cash for wee fellas, and other days, not so much. And through it all, we learned about the markets available to us and how to squeeze the most out of them.

From worst to best, here were our vending options.

The very worst option, which we'd only consider if we'd considered everything else several times, was to bring the cod tongues home and give them to Mom to either cook for supper or put in the freezer. Mom would be delighted.

"Well, look at this. Alan, my son, bringing home the supper like the man of the house."

I was still hoping to be paid in cash. "Do you think I could get something for the tongues, Mom?"

"Yes, honey. You can get your supper."

The next-worst option to giving your tongues to your mom was selling the tongues to Bidgood's Fish Plant. We hated selling our tongues there because we could not fool the Bidgoods or their man on the ground, Lewellen, into paying more for the tongues than they were worth. The Bidgoods weren't cruel people, not at all. They just knew everything about the fishery and were way too smart to swindle.

Lewellen would pay around a dollar a pound for really fresh tongues. That meant that for your bucketful, which took you all day to collect, you'd earn about twelve dollars by selling to Bidgood's. Perry and I would constantly debate the pros and cons of this. We resented Bidgood's because the fresh cod tongues we had worked so hard to harvest and sell were then resold at the fish counter in Bidgood's supermarket for $5.25 and higher per pound. That was more than four times what we got paid for the tongues. We always resented seeing any kind of markup on our tongues, believing we deserved the bulk of the money.

The fact that the Bidgood family took all the risk in this supermarket endeavour and bore all the costs for the fish plant and the store, including paying the dozens if not hundreds of local employees, was a fact that was lost on us boys. We focused on one hard fact and one hard fact only:

Bidgood's bought our tongues for too little and sold them for too much, ripping off the local fishermen and getting filthy rich in the process. It was all we ever heard from local fishermen a couple of generations older than us: merchants are all bad; fishermen and plant workers are all good. Our little cod-tongue exchange was all the proof we needed to confirm what we'd always heard.

We'd do anything we could to avoid selling to Bidgood's, and naturally, we felt totally justified in trying to con them in any way possible. We'd try things like selling day-old or two-day-old tongues to Lewellen. But Lewellen could tell in a heartbeat if the tongues were more than a few hours old.

"Go on, Alan Doyle. The stink off them tongues would knock you down. When did you cut them? A week ago? Get out before I tells your father."

We were even known to freeze some tongues we couldn't sell, and then we'd defrost them and try to pass them off as fresh to Bidgood's. This ploy never worked very well either.

"Couldn't find a buyer for your fresh tongues, b'ys? Back now with frozen shite? How stunned do ye think I am? Go throw them out back for the cats."

Me, my brother, Bern, and Perry heard from Burt, the best tongue cutter in the world, that soaking your fresh tongues in water for twenty minutes or so would increase their weight by as much as 10 percent, turning your twelve-dollar bucket into a thirteen- or fourteen-dollar bucket. But you had to be careful.

"If ye makes it too hot," Burt said, "the tongues will cook a little bit and turn grey. But too cold and the water won't absorb into them." Burt shared his formula. "Hold one finger in the water and one in the air. Make sure the one in the air is a little bit colder than the one in the bucket. That's the right temperature."

"These lot smell all right, b'ys. Not trying to scam me this time?" Lewellen would ask when we brought the water-logged tongues around.

"No, sir," we'd say.

"I'll give you thirteen-fifty for this lot." And because we had no other options, we'd accept.

But here's the worst part of all and yet another reason why we hated Bidgood's. As a tongue seller, you did not receive cash on the spot for your goods. No way. You received a receipt, and a week to ten days later, a cheque would be made in your name, which you'd have to pick up at Bidgood's. Then you'd have to deposit it in the bank or hope one of the local stores would cash it for you. Added complications. This is how I learned that cash in hand is an unbeatable way to do business.

But a far better way to sell tongues was to avoid Bidgood's altogether and first try a buyer from one of the restaurants in St. John's. Buyers from restaurants could occasionally be spotted trolling the wharves to stock up on fish. Those guys did not come that often, maybe once a week, but when they were in town, they wanted a lot of tongues quickly and would pay top dollar for them. There was one fella who owned a fish-and-chips place in St John's. He came every Tuesday and would pay us a dollar fifty or more a pound. Not only that, he would buy every tongue he could get. And he would give us cash right away.

"Who got some, b'ys? Big and small, as long as they're fresh. I'll take whatever you got. Fifteen cash for a bucketful. We got a tourist dinner for a hundred people tomorrow night and they wants fresh tongues for appetizer. Who got 'em?"

Some of the kids on the wharf got their parents involved in our little business. Someone's dad would pile us into the back of his truck and we'd go to the richer parts of St. John's, knocking on doors and asking, "Would you like to buy some fresh tongues?"

The results were generally good, and Townies would pay whatever we asked. A dollar a dozen was the common asking price for doorstep delivery, and there were often a couple of dozen in a pound, so you were selling for double the price you got at Bidgood's. If you got lucky, you could make a real killing. But I never enjoyed this kind of selling. I learned I was not a salesman or a negotiator at heart. I always felt like I was intruding on people's afternoons, and I often felt that the Townies only bought tongues from us because we looked so damn pitiful. We were a bunch of ragamuffins from Petty Harbour, hanging out the back of a truck dressed in dirty tongue-cutting clothes and smelling like fish guts.

One time, a boy my own age answered his front door wearing a brand-new soccer jersey and holding a Pepsi. For no obvious reason, I wanted to punch him right in the face. The kid did not say anything to me, but for a second I resented how clean and fun his summer morning was compared to mine. At the time, I didn't know I was embarrassed. I felt poor and unsophisticated. In retrospect, I had no reason to feel embarrassed. Me and the boys were doing honest work, but sometimes on these trips, I felt like people laughed at us, or worse, pitied us. And I wanted no part of that.

Well, kind of. Funny to consider it now, but I have to admit that while being seen as a poor ragamuffin by the Townies infuriated me, it never kept me from using that as a sales tactic, provided the image was intentionally projected by us.

And playing out stereotypes was exactly what we learned to do when one of the best options for selling your tongues rolled down the hill—via a bus full of seniors on a scenic day trip to the cozy town of Petty Harbour, Newfoundland. They'd come only once or twice a summer, but when they showed up, it was a jackpot. Imagine: fifty or sixty well-off seniors starving for a slice of the old times, a meal of tongues the way they used to have so many years ago.

At first, when we saw that bus, we'd go running like rabid dogs to the bus door and assault the folks as they got off, shooting each other in the foot as we did so.

"Would you like to buy some tongues? Two dollars a dozen!"

"His tongues are maggoty! He cut them three weeks ago! Buy mine!"

"Hey, my Nan knows you! You should buy *my* tongues!"

But later, we got organized and figured out that teaming up could really pay off. Wade led us in the con.

"B'ys, there's a busload coming in soon and they all wants tongues. They're gonna buy every tongue on this wharf if we plays our cards right. They're old and easily shit-baked, so we can't be too loud or we'll scare them away. They loves the cute fellas, so Patty"—he was the youngest and most perfect Irishy-orphan-Oliver-Twisty-looking fella in our group— "will go to the bus once they all gets off. Patty, you know what to say?"

Patty had obviously practised. He doffed his tiny salt-and-pepper hat and with his voice cracking perfectly, said, "How are you gettin' on? Welcome to O'Brien's wharf in our town of Petty Harbour, Newfoundland. Would you like to buy some fresh cod tongues from me and the b'ys?"

The con worked like a charm. The ladies would gush, he was so damn cute.

Then another Nitzy Pumpkin (that's what we'd call a cute little Irish-looking kid with red hair and freckles) would sidle up to the tourists, eyes wide and smelling like a rotten cod, and he'd say, "Me and the boys have been here on the docks since five a.m. We're trying to raise money for school clothes."

And that would be all it took. "Oh my honey, I loves tongues. How much are they?"

"A dollar," Nitzy would say.

"A dollar each?"

"Uh-huh."

We rarely got a dollar each for them in the end, but when the orphaned Nitzy Pumpkin starts the bidding there, you know you're gonna do well.

Once all the tongues were sold and all the Nitzys' cheeks were pinched, we'd walk down to the head of the breakwater, where we'd sit down in a circle and divvy up the money between the big boys and the little ones.

I remember piles of dollar bills and fives and even twenties, and I remember Wade counting out six even piles for six boys.

"There are six pots of money there. I counted them even. You guys pick your pile and I'll take the last one."

We all trusted Wade. He was the oldest and the biggest—the enforcer in our lot. He would bully us occasionally if he got out of Jack's sight, but never too bad. He respected you if you stood up to him and even though he could have beat the crap out of us, he never did. (It was a lesson I never forgot: Don't be afraid of tough guys. You need them and they need you. Let them have their moments in charge if it buys you order and civility where there might be madness. To this day I always make friends with the security guys and bouncers at gigs and concerts.)

Wade never rigged the piles and always took the last one. Everything he did was transparent and fair. This taught us who was honest and who was not. It was simple: only the kids who might one day try to rip you off counted their money; the others never did. I quickly learned never to count my cash in the circle and never to rip off any of the other kids. To this day, if someone hands me a handful of money, I won't count it. And if I hand money to someone, I always invite them to double-check the amount just to see if they will.

Later in my life, Ed McCann, Séan's dad, explained to me his notion of what work is. He said, "Nobody works for you and you don't work for nobody. You only work *with* people." Selling tongues drilled that lesson home for me at a very early age.

When the selling of tongues was done for the day, by late afternoon, I'd amble home with my hopefully empty bucket and my knife. I'd be looking forward to the rest of the day swimming or playing softball or scheming with Perry about how to get girls from the Goulds to like us. I'd be sopping wet, full of guts and gurry and fish blood and dirt. Mom would always make me get undressed on the back step. I'd strip in full view of my grandparents and uncles, usually. They always got a great kick out of this. I'd walk into the house with my stinking clothes in my hands and I'd jam them directly into our ringer washer. (If you did not wash tongue-cutting clothes right away, they'd stink up the house for days.) My sister Kim hated having to wash any of her clothes with my tongue-cutting clothes, as she swore they made everything smell. I'm sure she was right, but Mom would never let us use the washer for just a couple of things.

It's true that the work was hard, the hours long, leaving me tired, dirty and smelly, but at the end of a good day, I'd head home with as much as twenty to forty bucks in my pocket.

"How much did you haul today?" Mom would ask when I arrived.

"Made just twenty today, Mom," I'd answer, with thirty dollars in my pocket.

"Well, that's not bad, Alan. You can save fifteen in your bank account for school clothes or for hockey in the fall. And you can spend five."

"Good plan, Mom," I'd say, and then head out that night with fifteen dollars in spending money. Pretty good dosh for a twelve-year-old kid in the early eighties. I could get into plenty of trouble with that much money burning a hole in my pocket. But getting the money in hand was often the trickiest part of the whole day.

Tongue cutting was a young man's game. By the time you hit fifteen years of age, you were expected to be out of it and to search for other summer work. When I was that age, I heard they were hiring over at the red plant on the Protestant side of town. Picking capelin. There's another phrase that looks so strange in type and must be so foreign for most people to read. Yet when I was a kid in Petty Harbour, "picking capelin" was as easily understood as "washing the dishes."

During certain weeks in the Newfoundland summer, millions upon millions of small fish called capelin washed ashore in Petty Harbour and the nearby coastal towns. Capelin look pretty much like sardines, but bigger. You can catch them from a boat in larger nets, as you might codfish or any other schooling groundfish, but the real fun was that magical time of year when you didn't have to fish for them at all. All you had to do was collect them as they rolled ashore.

The rolling of the capelin was a joyous event that happened only for a few days at most, but not every summer. Like some kind of Old Testament miracle, those fish would roll ashore as part of their spawning process. Dads and moms and kids and grandparents all flocked to the beach to grab the free catch.

Some folks cast nets and would haul them in, load after load. Others would wade up to their waists and scoop the fish in plastic buckets with a few small holes punched in the bottom to let out the sea water. Kids would stand in the rise and fall of the surf and let the fish wash over them. The whole town would gather on the shore when the capelin were rolling.

I recall tales of older times when the rolling of the capelin was known to cause courtships to blossom. I suppose fellas were made randy watching the gals hike up their long dresses and enter the water. A fella could get a very rare glance at a gal's bare ankles and calves. No wonder so many birthdays are nine months after the capelin season.

There are many traditional Newfoundland tunes about the rolling of the capelin, including "Brent's Cove Capelin Song," which commemorates the strange event this way:

Now when it's caplin time down in Brent's Cove with
    the women on the wharf,
And they wipes their runny noses in their scarfs,
All the girls are having fun as they pick them one by one,
'Tis a lovely place to be when the caplin comes!

And it is lovely. It remains an amazing sight to behold to this day. Capelin are pretty good to eat when salted or smoked and roasted. Some folks fry or dry or pickle them. When really plentiful, they are also used as fertilizer in the few gardens in town.

But the capelin also had two commercial uses when I was growing up. The males were used for bait in the hook-and-line fishery, and the females were harvested for their roe, which was quite valuable. For a couple of weeks each summer, fish plants hired extra hands to separate, or "pick," males and females.

To pick capelin, first you had to know the difference between the males and the females. This isn't as easy as it sounds. It's not like the males have a full frontal crank and berries and the females wear bikinis. But once you pick for a few hours, you get the hang of it. The males are usually larger than the females, but it's the variety in the fins that is the big difference.

In the Protestant fish plant in Petty Harbour, you stood at a conveyor belt in a long line of pickers. The fish would be loaded onto the belt, and as they passed, you'd grab a bucket of capelin from the belt and dump it into the middle pan of your three fifty-pound fish pans. Then you'd sort through the pan, grabbing each fish and tossing it left (male pan) or right (female pan). Once your middle pan was out of fish, you'd refill your bucket from the conveyer belt, and then you'd do it all over again. All day long. Not hard, just boring.

The only enjoyable part of picking capelin in a fish plant was the eavesdropping. I used to listen in on the conversations between women and men older than me. There was lots of innuendo.

"Hey, Connie. This capelin is stiff and wet. Remind you of anything?"

"Nothing comes to mind, Jimmy. I have not had anything in my hand as big as that in quite a while. Now I could tell everyone about something much smaller and wiggly I had in me hand in your truck the other night."

"No, girl, that's all right."

Much laughter followed.

Inevitably, I'd be included in the ribbing somehow. "Hey, Janey," one guy would joke, "what about our little guitar player here? Why don't you take him out behind the lunch-room at break time."

Janey would pretend to put a capelin head in and out of her mouth. "Don't worry, Little Alan. I won't hurt you."

I didn't get it, but the fellas all laughed and the girls wailed a "Wahoo!" Stuff like that went on all the time. (Note: I never did go out behind the lunchroom with Janey. Probably should have.)

The worst thing about picking capelin was the sound fatigue. The conveyor belt on the line groaned and weaned and squeaked in an endless twelve-second cycle.

Groan. Wean. Squeak.

Groan. Wean. Squeak.

Groan. Wean. Squeak.

. . . eight to ten hours straight. After my shift, I'd lie awake in bed and hear it well into the night. Bernie worked in the plant with me, and we learned to sleep with the radio on to drown out the noise in our heads.

The mental and eye fatigue was even harder after a week or so of picking capelin. The sight of pan after pan of the skinny silver bodies, each with that single unblinking eye staring back at you—it was a bit more than I could take. At night when I went to bed, I'd close my eyes and instead of seeing darkness, I'd see beady-eyed capelin, hundreds of them lying on their sides staring their one-eyed stare at me.

I'd drift off to sleep and dream of a million capelin turning to me and asking, "Am I a boy or a girl, Alan? Are you sure I'm a girl?" And as the fish flopped in the pan, I'd suddenly realize it had lipstick on. I kid you not. I had dreams like this all the time while I picked capelin. Sometimes, the dream fish would cross-dress just to confuse me.

Lucky for me, the capelin picking was seasonal and brief enough that I never completely lost my mind. After about eight or nine nights over a couple of weeks, the run was over and the plant was on to another species.

I was out of work for only a few days or a week before I'd be on to the next summer job, like laying sod with a landscaper in the Goulds or baling hay with a local farmer. I never liked these jobs very much. It was backbreaking labour, but it kept me busy until school started. By the end of the summer, after all that work, I'd actually be happy to hear the school bell ring, a graceful exit from hard labour. I've tipped my hat to manual labourers ever since. I'm nice to the garbage man. I say hi to the room staff at the hotel. I know first-hand what it's like to work hard, and all those thankless jobs have to be done. So I'm always kind and grateful to folks willing to do work that most of us don't want to do.

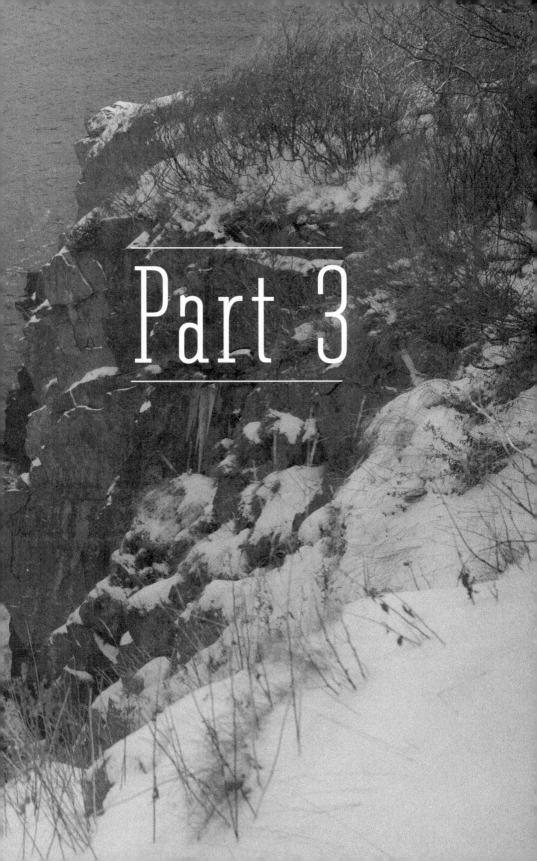

Part 3

CHAPTER 7

Old Woman's Gulch

It started innocently enough. I was at the post office with my mother. She was working there temporarily sorting mail into slots. She was chatting to one of her friends who'd come in to gossip and get the mail.

"My dear," Mom's friend said to her, "don't turn that magazine over or you and your b'y will get some eyeful."

"Why's that?" Mom asked.

Mom's friend held a rolled-up magazine close to her chest and said, "This here's for Simpson. Skin mag. Crowd of skinny women with not a tack on."

This intrigued me. A lot. Of course, I pretended not to listen and kept leafing through the hockey equipment pages of the Sears catalogue. You have to understand, this was long before the internet or even cable TV. If you were curious about girls, you had to work hard to satisfy your curiosity. I had many unanswered questions.

Later that evening, I consulted a higher authority, a guru of sorts, about what I'd heard in the post office. I was lucky to have such an authority living close by, so close in fact that we shared the same bedroom.

"Bernie," I said as we were in our bunks about to go to sleep. "Simpson gets skin mags delivered to his house." Of course, I was not really entirely sure what a skin mag was.

"Yeah, I know," Bernie said. "Orders them by the dozens. Looks at them and then gets rid of them. He's afraid of putting them in the regular garbage because Uncle Eddy might find out and make fun of him, so he chucks them over the guardrail down into the Old Woman's Gulch."

"But . . . what's in the mags?" I really wanted to know.

"Women with no tops on. Women with no bottoms on. Some missus kissing some other missus."

That's what I suspected, but if I wasn't absolutely certain beforehand, this confirmed it. It also confirmed the fact that my brother, Bernie, knew everything about everything.

"Too bad you'll never set eyes on those mags. You'd have to be cracked to go down Old Woman's Gulch," the guru continued. "Jack says two fellas drowned trying to scale down the Gulch and catch capelin a couple years back. And some other idiot tried to get to those skin mags and nearly fell from the rocks. No one goes into Old Woman's Gulch and comes out to tell the story. No one."

Perhaps now is a good time to describe for you what the Gulch was like and still is like today. It's is a jagged, high precipice that leads down, down, down to the sea. It's flanked by treacherous pointy rocks on each side, and the water that finds its way into that steep cavern blasts against those craggy cliffs. It's about a hundred feet wide, but the mouth of the Gulch narrows in one section to just a few feet. If you did not know about the Gulch and found yourself upon

Old Woman's Gulch, just outside of Petty Harbour.

That's me last winter jumping over the guardrail to get a photo of the gulch. (Kids: Don't try this at home.)

it, a single misstep and you'd careen down several storeys of rough cliff face, past a maze of sharp-toothed ledges and dangling branches before the Old Woman below swallowed you whole.

I was terrified of the Old Woman's Gulch. Perry and I once dared each other to peer over the guardrail that separated the road from her terrors.

"I'll hold the rail and you grab my arm and look over the edge," Perry kindly offered.

"I've got a better idea. *I* hold on to the railing and *you* look over the edge."

Gripping firmly to that rail, we'd often examine the Gulch as though she were a puzzle we had to solve. We'd stare down her and wonder if there was a safe way to make it, step by slow step, to the bottom. But it was no use. Every possible path we could map was blocked by an obstacle—a pointy rock, a slippery face, or worse, a giant chasm.

One Sunday morning, the altar boys were all gathered as usual in the church locker room before mass when the topic of Simpson's captivating reading material in the impossible-to-breach crevasse came up. There was much speculation as to what kinds of pictures were contained in those mags, and the conversation did very little to quell my curiosity.

Later, as the congregation left the church, Bart, one of the boys who had been most interested in the locker room talk, whispered to me as he carried the cross out, "You wanna see the skin mags?"

I nodded.

"I knows how to get down the Old Woman's Gulch. Meet me after mass."

This news came like a clap of thunder, and my eyes went immediately to the figure on the eight-foot cross that Bart was holding. Was the man nailed there weeping at me?

I immediately recruited Perry and we waited near the entrance to the church basement. A few minutes later, Bart came around the corner, lighting a cigarette as he approached.

"If ye arselickers gets the shit beat out of yerselves trying to get down the Gulch, ye can't say who told you what I'm about to say. Deal?"

We nodded. Bart continued.

"My uncle Jerry came home from the navy last summer and wanted to catch some capelin. We all knew there was a ton in the Gulch, but no one knew how to get in there. Jerry and me, we went down to have a look and in five minutes he figured it out. He says he saw some cliff just like it in Gibraltar or some place, and he and a bunch of Spanish sailors stashed some rum barrels there once.

"So here's what you need to know. You have to find some way to bridge the biggest gap between the rocks or you'll fall to your deaths, but you can't carry anything with you as the ledges are too narrow. Here's the trick. Get a twelve-foot plank and about thirty feet of rope and hang the plank down over the side of the gap. When you make your way down the bank to that empty space, the plank will be there waiting for you. Use it like a bridge. Cross it, and off you go. From there, you'll make it to the bottom. Easy." Bart took a long drag off his smoke. "But you didn't hear this from me."

Then he was gone.

Perry and I were gobsmacked. It seemed so simple. Why hadn't we thought of this?

Later that afternoon, while the rest of town slumbered after Sunday dinner, we "borrowed" some rope and a plank from a fisherman's stage on the wharf and made our way down the main road out of town. What a sight we must have been: two ten-year-olds carrying a twelve-foot plank between us and trailing a long tail of rope. Cars passed us and we got a look or two, but no one stopped to ask what we were up to. Petty Harbour was that kind of place, a place where boys roamed and got up to God knows what kinds of adventures. It was perfect.

We arrived at the spot along the guardrail where the Gulch was the closest and the deepest. Without hesitation, we popped over the guardrail and lugged our gear down to the cliff's edge. I tried not to look down. Instead, I looked to the first step only, the pine tree on a nearby ledge. Sure enough, there was a ring worn out of the bark—rope burn. This was relieving—Bart was not shagging around. Someone had been here and found a way down.

We fed the rope through a knothole in the plank and tied it securely with three half hitches around the pine tree. Then we slid on our backsides and pushed the plank to the edge of the ledge. With our legs outstretched, we gave it a kick to send it over the chasm. But it got hooked on debris at the very lip of the gulch. We would have to go closer.

We looked at each other without saying a word. We flipped over onto our stomachs and pulled ourselves away from the safety of the pine tree and towards the edge of the cliff where the plank was lodged. We reached forward gingerly and laid our hands on the rough wood. Then we gave a quick push. But the plank did not budge. We had to move closer still, close enough that we could peer right over the horrifying edge.

We had never had the guts to fully hang over that edge and stare down into the hole, the hole that dropped straight away to cragged rocks and the whitewash of the cold, angry Atlantic below.

"Look!" Perry said as he pointed to the churning waters beneath us. The surf was violent, but we could make out two plastic kitchen garbage bags. One had landed intact on the rocky shore, just out of the reach of the water. The other hadn't fared as well. It had ripped to shreds on the way down, probably catching on the sharp rock faces, and the full-colour pages were strewn along the mossy ledges at the bottom of the Gulch, the pages dancing in the wind. We couldn't make out images from that distance, but we were certain: these were skin mags.

And once we were on the edge, we could see the problem with our plank. It was caught on a small twig. We wiggled the board and the twig broke instantly, sending the plank careening into a free fall and the two of us scrambling backwards as fast as we could, trying not to get tangled up in the rope. For the first time in our lives, we realized the true danger of the Old Woman's Gulch. But we realized as well the treasures she held.

We were going in.

We assumed the early steps in the path would be easy to navigate. We were wrong. The narrow stones and worn cracks were slimy with moss and mist. At times we faced the rock wall and inched along the ledge; other times, we pressed our backs to the wall and were paralyzed as we watched the crashing waves and foam beneath.

"Don't look down," Perry said, and we continued our descent until we reached the gap where the plank awaited us at the impasse. There was a wide enough spot for us to stand next to each other and catch our breath. And we needed to, because the gap in the rock ledge in front of us was well over ten feet, with nothing below but white water and foam. From this vantage point, there was not even a glimpse of shore or rock. One slip here and you plunged into Davy Jones's locker for sure.

We gathered ourselves and hoisted the rope till the plank peeked through the chasm. We carefully levered it up and across the void until, *clunk*, it caught the edge of the far side. We gave it an extra push for safety but then realized we didn't have much extra length to play with. The plank barely spanned the gap, less than a foot touching ground on either side.

Perry evaluated the situation. "This is crazy," he said quietly. "Circus crazy."

I coiled the rope neatly in a circle as I had been taught to do by Jack on the wharf. It was still attached to the plank. I looked at Perry. "We are walking this plank. I'll go first."

I took one step onto the plank and it bent ever so slightly. I kept my gaze straight ahead at the target of terra firma. A step or two later, I was past the point of no return. The plank was bowing quite a bit at the midpoint, so I made the decision to hurry it up. I should not have. I pushed a little hard with my left foot and slipped. Down I went on one knee.

"Jesus Christ!" Perry shouted.

I outstretched my arms like a tightrope walker as I lifted myself and carefully took the last few steps to the other side.

"Nothing to it!" I yelled across to Perry, who looked doubtful. And terrified.

"I don't know, b'y!" he shouted. "You were almost shagged!"

"Too scared? Fine, then. I'll go see the skin mags myself."

With that, Perry took one step back and ran as fast as he could at the plank. It was as if he was a lizard and was crossing the entire length without touching the board at all. The wood barely bowed, barely moved.

"Hmm," I said when he made it across, triumphant. "Looks easy if you do it that way."

We slid down a couple of easy mossy ledges till our feet finally touched beach rocks. Our rubber boots were washed with sea water each time a wave made its way up the small shore, but we had arrived, safe upon the shore. And the treasure lay before us.

The full bag of Simpson's magazines was within arm's reach. But instead of starting with that, Perry got caught up by the stray pages that had been cliff-battered and were now wet and clinging to the rocks. It didn't matter to us that they were tattered and soaked, not if there was a naked lady somewhere on them.

And that's when Perry's eyes went wide. He found a whole series of photos of a lady strewn across boulders on the bank. In the first one he came upon, she was on all fours and had more makeup on than we'd ever seen before. She stared right off the page with her mouth slightly open and her eyes kind of sleepy-looking.

"She's got a friggin' nightie on!" Perry said.

He was right. And it was a small nighty, a frilly see-through housecoat kind of thing covering what appeared to be dark underwear and high socks with a garter, kind of like the garter we wore playing hockey but way more flimsy. I scoffed. "They wouldn't last two games," I said.

Perry and I followed that series of photos up the rock. Even though the pages were torn, we could see there was some kind of progression happening with each new photo. The lady seemed increasingly surprised by something, as her eyes and mouth opened wider in each shot. To be honest, her expression was a bit confusing. She seemed amazed and even shocked but at the same time uncontrollably curious about whatever was being presented in front of her just out of the frame. Also odd was the fact that she seemed to get less comfortable in her nightie and attempted to tear it off herself, picture by picture, until . . . we made it to the last photo in the series.

This was the photo we wanted to see the most, but it was also the photo most damaged by the rocks and sea. Perry picked it up, puzzling over the shapes.

"Is that a boob?" he asked.

We were transfixed. We moved our faces closer and closer to the page. We put our fingers on the outline of the undefined body part and tried to trace what we thought we saw.

"Not sure, b'y." I said, as we stared blankly for what could have been ten seconds or ten minutes, I really could not say.

Perry finally broke the spell. "Forget this. Let's get to the real goodies in the bag."

We took one step towards the bounty when a scraping of wood on rocks turned us back to the side we'd scrabbled down. To our horror, the plank had slipped and was now suspended by the rope. But that wasn't all. It appeared the plank was floating back up towards the top of the cliff. We traced the rope with our eyes and there at the highest edge stood Bart, heaving and hauling for all he was worth.

"Two arselickers!" he called down, cigarette in his mouth. The plank now lay at his feet. "Bring me up one of those bags right now or I'll take this plank and go home with it, ye friggin' idiots!"

"That's not fair!" I yelled.

"All's fair in love and skin mags, b'y! Bring me up a bag or I'm gone. And I'll tell your fadders that ye're stuck down there up to no good. Can't wait to hear what ye tells your mudders about what ye were doing down there in the first place."

We knew he had us. Perry didn't say a word. He just grabbed the intact bag of treasure and started up the path. I followed. We slowly made our way back up the mossy ledges while Bart lowered the plank once more when we arrived at the chasm. Our walk across the plank seemed easier this time. We were back up to the top in minutes, even though we were laden with a garbage bag full of magazines, the magic fading in a hurry.

The moment we reached the top, Bart grabbed the bag.

"Thanks, arselickers," he said.

"Let us see one," Perry said.

"Nah, ye're too young for this stuff. Might rot your minds. Sorry."

"We were friggin' old enough to send down the Gulch," I said.

"Yeah, sorry about that. To be honest, I wasn't even sure the plank business would work. Dreamt it up one night but never tried it. I'm not so stunned as ye, apparently."

"But what about the rope burn on the tree?" I was sure that part of Bart's story was true.

"Oh, that. It's from a fishing seine Dad ties on there every summer. Nice touch, isn't it?" Bart laughed, as if congratulating himself.

"You don't even have an Uncle Jerry, do you," Perry said.

"Not that I knows of, b'y. Not that I knows of." Bart flicked his cigarette at our feet, turned and was gone up the path and down the road. And so was the treasure.

Perry and I walked back towards Petty Harbour. Barely a word was spoken the whole way. When we arrived at Perry's house, we didn't even exchange goodbyes.

"Frig sakes" was all Perry said as he climbed the steps to his house, his wet boots leaving dirty footprints in his wake.

I walked home with only two thoughts in my head. The first was "I'll never trust another story about someone's Uncle Jerry."

Turns out I was right about that.

The second was "I'll never work that hard to see a girl again."

Turns out I was wrong about that.

Petty Harbour was a tough place for a boy to be indoctrinated into the wooing of the fairer sex. This difficulty was partly due to the isolation and innocence of the place and also to the fact that almost all the girls my age were out of the courting market because they were my cousins. And, of course, there was no texting or Facebook to hide behind; no internet to consult; no virtual ways to locate, approach or eventually land a date for the Hockey Dance. On the other hand, the courtship mystery of my young life in Petty Harbour also smashed headlong into grown-up, capital-A Adult territory thanks to a few of the town's more colourful characters.

Consider Billy.

Billy was an older fisherman, in his late fifties. He stood out physically for two reasons. First, he was much taller than most. He stood around six-foot-five. His ever-present rubber boots and his orange toque made him seem even taller. Second, he had a very large bulbous nose, rounded at the tip and longer than average. When Billy drank, which was always, his nose turned a reddish purple and even seemed to grow. It looked like the long neck of a bottle, one which started between his tiny beady eyes and ran down, ever widening, till it reached just above his upper lip. Bottle-Nosed Billy he was called, and we younger fellas abbreviated that to "The Bottler."

The Bottler was a great source of entertainment for the young lads of the wharf, myself included. He regaled us with stories about the prostitutes he regularly hired to come to his little house in Petty Harbour and avail of their services. There was no shame in it at all as far as he was concerned, and he was quick to tell us little fellas what services the ladies provided. He had a slight lisp, so his *s*'s sounded like *th*'s. This, combined with the usual Petty Harbour accent, made for some fascinating pronunciation: "girls" became "girlth" and "wonderful" became "wanderful." And "wanderful" was the adjective he most often used when detailing his adventures, many of which involved more than one lady for hire and all of which involved these ladies giving him a good scrub in the tub first. "Jethuth, if thath not the betht wath ye ever got in yer life, I don't know what ith," he'd tell us kids as we helped him carry his catch from his fishing boat to the gutting table.

We were in awe of The Bottler, at once captivated and terrified by his vivid accounts of what he got up to on one of his nights in the company of prostitutes—or "the "whorth" as he called them (I kid you not). But at some point, the stories weren't enough anymore and we grew very curious about the facts.

"Perry, you think The Bottler really gets them women from town to wash his pickle?" I asked during a break in the action on the wharf.

"Tough to say, b'y. They don't come out for nothing. Dad saw a taxi from town dropping them off one night. Imagine! A taxi come all the way from town."

Perry looked at me. I looked at Perry. "We're gonna have to check it out," we said simultaneously.

The next time word got around town on a Saturday evening that The Bottler had ordered up whorth, Perry, me and a bunch of the other boys defied our mothers' warnings to stay clear of Bottled-Nosed Billy and we crept over to his house. Once outside, we began negotiations.

"All right, Mikey, you're the smallest," I said. "Get up on Perry's shoulders and look in the window."

Perry hoisted Mikey till his face touched the glass of the bedroom window.

"What's on the go?" Perry asked, balancing Mikey like a Cirque du Soleil gymnast.

"I . . . I don't know." Young Mikey's eyes were as big as saucers.

"Come on, b'y!" the rest of us down on the ground said. "Tell us something!"

"They, uh, probably got their shirts off and are, uh, lyin' down and dancing, or something I s'pose, I don't know. I just don't know. Let me down. I wants to go home."

Mikey jumped off Perry's shoulders and ran back across the bridge to Catholic safety.

I was determined. "We gotta get up there," I said.

"The beer bottles!" Perry was always smart and had come up with a great plan. The Bottler stored empties in a nearby shed, so we broke in and grabbed four or five cases, building a makeshift ladder up to the window. Two of us scrambled up.

"Frig! The friggin' steam!" Perry couldn't see a thing, the single-pane glass was so fogged by the action inside.

My turn. I scaled the beer-case ladder and peered in. I can't truly say I ever saw anything other than shadows, but there's no doubt we could hear things going on in there, even over the Elvis Presley records with the volume maxed.

Smack!

Out of nowhere, two sweaty hands, a big Bottler-sized one and a small woman-sized one, slapped against the steam on the inside of the window and pressed hard on the glass about a millimetre in front of my face.

"Ahhh!" The two-handed monster frightened a loud squeal out of me and I tipped backwards and sent empty Dominion Ale bottles crashing down the bank.

We were had, and we did what any respectable young kids would do in a situation like this. We threw rocks at The Bottler's house and shouted, "Ye bunch of whores!" and ran as fast as we could back home, fortunately without getting caught.

Billy enjoyed his company on a weekly or biweekly basis. Everything seemed to go well for him, except for one small ongoing problem: he was married. And it turns out that his scandalous adventures took place only when his wife was away in the Goulds tending to her ailing mother. The moment she was out the door, The Bottler would call in the ladies. It was a regular occurrence to see The Bottler walking on the main road on Monday with his recently returned wife behind him screaming and yelling and pointing in protest of his weekend escapades. Billy all the while strode casually in front of her and seemed to not even notice her ranting. My mother would sometimes run into The Bottler and his shouting wife in the post office on a Monday, and The Bottler would immediately include my poor mother in the conversation.

"Listen to her going on like that, Jean. Now what do you think of that? Ranting like a savage 'cause some fella found a little bit of pleasure in this hard life. Is she cracked or what, Jean?"

My mother would collect their mail and try to get them out the door as quickly as possible.

When I was in my twenties, I met Paul, a friend of a friend in St. John's. I got to telling some stories, and eventually The Bottler came up.

Paul's eyes went wide. "Holy frig! Are you talking about Billy?" Paul explained that he'd been sent to Petty Harbour when he was a student in fisheries college. At one point, he had an appointment with a fisherman to see about a loan application for a modification to a fishing boat. Paul was to go to the fisherman's house at the appointed time, one o'clock in the afternoon on a Sunday, but in his eagerness he arrived a little early. He knocked on the door just after twelve thirty. Paul described the man who smiled at him, a man with a fiery-red, bulbous nose—The Bottler. They exchanged a few pleasantries, and Billy invited him to sit on the front porch. Then, *whap*, something golden and shiny struck the wall just behind The Bottler's head.

"You lousy prick!" a woman shouted from inside the house, and then *whap*, another golden tinfoil bomb just missed The

Bottler's head. Paul had no idea what he'd just walked in on. Then the woman came to the front porch. Paul smiled and said hello, but she barely took notice of him. All her rage was directed at The Bottler, and she carried something in her hand, another golden package.

"I told you to never bring them dirty whores into this house again!" the woman yelled.

The Bottler didn't even turn around. Paul was terrified.

After more yelling and screaming, the woman turned to Paul and said, "You know what I came home to find this morning? My husband putting two whores into a St. John's taxi in front of my f—king house!"

Billy calmly said to Paul, "Isn't that shocking? A woman her age using language like that with a *guetht* in the *houthe*. And on a *Thunday*! Tsthk tsthk."

And that's when a third gold-foil-wrapped projectile met The Bottler's head and stuck there for a moment, before sliding down his bottle nose and falling to the floor with a thud.

The Bottler quietly turned back to Paul, who was speechless, and without so much as wiping his face, he said, "*Jethuth*. Look a' that now. She'th gone and wathted another perfectly good block of butter."

It's a wonder we ever learned to court girls properly with role models like Billy leading the way. But there were other role models in town who were a tad more upstanding.

Harry Chase was a tall, handsome man who lived in a house on the Protestant side of town even though he and his family were Catholics. He was always very well dressed in a suit or jacket, and even when he was working around the house or shovelling snow, his clothes always looked new and clean and properly tailored. He had a moustache that made him look a whole lot like Magnum, P.I.

The Chase family was the first in town to replace their old clapboard siding with the new shiny vinyl stuff that never had to be painted. They always had more than one cleaned and polished car parked in the driveway, and beyond that, as a sign of total affluence, their driveway was paved. A paved driveway. Wow. Can you imagine?

Harry and his lovely wife had six children. An older daughter and two sons had moved on to work or to go to school elsewhere by the time I was about eleven. The remaining children living at home were three daughters, all of them a few years older than me. They were the most beautiful creatures I had ever seen in my life.

At mass, all eyes would turn when the Chase family entered. They would parade up the centre aisle led by Harry in his perfectly pressed suit and overcoat, if the weather required. The daughters always followed in order of age. The oldest, about seventeen, had the lightest hair and slimmest waist; she was followed by her slightly younger sister, who was the athletic type; her youngest sister, who was around thirteen, had olive skin, and her jet-black hair framed her massive, amazing dark eyes. Mrs. Chase, who followed last, looked like she could have been the oldest sister, so youthful and pretty was she. All the gals wore dresses, flowing, flowery dresses, sometimes covered by snug sweaters or blazers with fancy crests.

As I said, all eyes turned to the Chases when they entered, and some in town rolled their eyes and exchanged sniggers or whispers. But not me. I thought the red carpet covering the centre aisle of the church was a perfect runway for the Chase ladies, and I enjoyed the pageant every single Sunday.

The Chases sat five rows back from the altar, on altar left, every Sunday. Harry would stand by the pew as his daughters and his wife filed in. Then he'd slide in last, nodding at his wife as he sat. All of us boys tried to get our altar boy assignments on altar left, or pulpit side as most of the priests called it. From altar left, you had a clear view of the Chase girls. You might even catch a whiff of their shampoo as they walked past after communion. You might pick out their voices as they sang in perfect unison, with Harry an octave below. If you were really lucky, the youngest Chase daughter, who I fantasized was the most rebellious, would throw you a glance and maybe even the slightest smile.

As we were taking off our robes after mass, one of the boys swore she'd winked at him. "Bull," we all said, though for months to follow, Father Maloney looked puzzled when we all lined up on the Chase girls' side just before the mass began.

The Chase daughters were the first girls I clearly remember having crushes on. I may have been too young to even know what that meant. But I knew that they were as pretty as pretty could be, and the fact that they barely knew we were alive made me and my brother want them even more.

But we also knew they were unattainable, and eventually we turned our sights elsewhere.

For Bernie, this meant crossing the bridge. Literally. He began looking to the Protestant part of town for ladies. My grandmother was none too pleased but would never say so directly.

Once, when we were over at my grandparents' house for supper, Kim said to my grandmother, "Nan, Bernie's got a new girlfriend." If looks could kill, Bernie's laser eyes would have cut Kim's life short at that moment.

"Oh have ye, honey?" Nan said to Bernie. "Who's that, now?" Nan asked while serving french fries and pretending to be only mildly interested.

"Lisa Clarke," Kim offered. Nan's serving halted just enough for us to notice.

"Lisa, you say? Now where do she live?"

"Down the Southside, Nan. WAY down the Southside," Kim said, grinning from ear to ear, knowing full well that she'd just revealed to Nan that Bernie was dating a Protestant.

"Is that right?" Nan paused and just nodded, while some others of her vintage would have run straight for the holy water.

The rest of the meal was noticeably more quiet.

Protestant girls were a source of mystery and fascination to all of us b'ys. They attended school in St. John's and knew people from all over town. They went in cars to dances at their schools and always seemed way more worldly and outgoing than the Catholic gals. You can only imagine how amazing it was for us young fellas to find out the Protestant girls were all on the pill, which definitely meant they would have sex with you just about any time at all . . . or so I heard Wade say on the wharf. I remember watching them on the other side of the bridge on Sunday mornings as they walked to church in their Sunday best. They always wore pretty dresses and sometimes hats.

"Who's that one, Bern?" I'd ask as I spied.

"That's Mandi. Way above your skill set. Wade says she goes out with a fella from town who's gonna play pro hockey in Quebec."

"How do you get Protestant girls to go out with you, I wonder."

"Like anything else hard, Alan, b'y," Bernie said. "Practise. Don't be afraid to shag it up a few times before ya gets it right."

And so I did. My chance to socialize with these gals came in the summer months, when the foolish religious division of the school system was lifted. We'd all play softball together and then go walk up the Long Run to the greatest swimming hole in the world, Lee's Pool.

Lee's Pool was across the road from the Lees' house, the last house up the Long Run. It was really a large crevasse in the rocks behind the tubular wooden flume that carried water from the dammed pond above to the hydroelectric plant below. Lee's Pool was out of sight from the adult world, and when the dam overflowed, it filled the crevasse with water. Some places got up to twenty feet deep. In the shallow parts, you had to be careful not to hit the rocky sides or bottom when jumping in, but it made for a pretty amazing space to clean the wharf off you, to cool you down and to hang out with all the kids in Petty Harbour, Catholic and Protestant alike.

I'd watch the older boys showing off for the girls, jumping off the highest rocks into the pool, narrowly escaping some life-altering injury just to impress the ladies. The older girls would spread towels over the rocks and lie there in their bathing suits, occasionally asking one of the fellas to sit with them or even go for a "walk" down the river.

I'd always try to keep up with the older fellas and impress some of the Protestant girls. This resulted in a few near-drowning experiences and in me splitting my head open on the sharp rocks in the pool. But in one of the greatest conquests of my life, I somehow managed to get Mandi to talk to me.

We were walking back from Lee's Pool and the two of us were lagging behind. I was telling her how pretty she was, repeatedly and in every way I could possibly imagine, and she in turn kept saying things like, "Oh my, Little Alan Doyle. Chatting with one of the big girls. How cute."

I wasn't about to let her comments dissuade me, not when she was still walking right next to me, which was a huge achievement in and of itself. Eventually, I came right out with it. "You know, you should give me at least one kiss. I've never had a real one."

"A kiss? You're too young to be kissing teenage girls. You might pass out."

"No, I won't. And I've seen people do it on TV."

"How old are you?" she asked.

"Almost thirteen," I said. That was about two years off the truth but close enough.

Mandi looked ahead and saw the rest of the gang was far off. She looked behind us. No one there either. Then she said the words I'll never forget: "Come here, Little Alan Doyle. Don't make a big deal out of this or you'll never get another one."

Next thing I knew, she turned me to face her and she put her wet lips on mine. I could taste her sugary lip gloss on my mouth and I could feel her press her whole body against mine. Her tongue parted my lips, the sweet taste of bubble gum coming with it. It was over as quick as it began. She pulled away from me and walked away with a sly smile I can still picture as I type. It said, "You lucky bastard." And I was. To this day, Perry still refers to this as one of my most ambitious achievements.

My first real girlfriend came a few years later and was a Protestant girl named Stacey. I met her while playing street hockey by the fish plant. She was from Maddox Cove and she knew a lot of the Catholic fellas. She had blond hair. After much cajoling, she agreed to go to the Hockey Dance with me. The Hockey Dance was the social event of my young life and that of all the b'ys in the Goulds minor hockey league. At the end of the playing season, in early spring, there would be an awards banquet and a dance.

On this particular year, I was going to be one of the only fellas my age to have a gal accompany me to the dance. To make it even more amazing, I won top goalie in the league that year. (To be fair, there were only two of us. Greg Hawco, the other goalie, had won the coveted title the year before, and the next year he won the title back.) But awards were the last thing on my mind that night when the dance got going and Eric Clapton's "Wonderful Tonight" blasted through St. Kevin's Parish Hall.

I asked Stacey to dance, and as soon as we were on the dance floor together, my right ear touching hers, I felt her head drift back slightly. My ear was now against her cheek. Her cheek came ever forward and I turned my head into hers and pecked her as gently as I could. A question of a kiss. The answer came hard and fast, and the next thing I knew we were full-on making out on the dance floor. This was no quick intro like Mandi had offered. This was the real deal! After the initial shock wore off, I opened my eyes and shot a glance around the room. Others were grinning or pointing at us. I was not too concerned about what they thought, though I really did enjoy the wink and hearty thumbs-up offered by Frankie Packman, who was dancing with my cousin not too far away.

After a few girlfriend-confirming kisses, the song ended. I was in a daze in the beautiful darkness. I felt for the hand next to mine and proudly led the way back to our table. Something felt odd, though. I was expecting a hero's welcome, but instead everyone looked puzzled and amused. I got to the table and my teammates were not looking at me with envy at all. I turned around and discovered the source of everyone's amusement. I was not holding hands with Stacey. In the fray of the bodies in the dim light, I had grabbed the closest hand to mine, which turned out to be Frankie Packman's. We looked at each other in horror and quickly unhanded each other with a look that said, "We'll never speak of this again." That should have been my first lesson that courting can be a minefield.

CHAPTER 8

The Taste of Salt

F rom kindergarten to Grade 8, I went to the very Catholic St. Edward's School in Petty Harbour. When I walked into my kindergarten class, there were nine boys and four girls. When I graduated from Grade 8, the exact same boys and girls graduated with me. Not a single new classmate entered our school in nine years. And not a single classmate left either.

The one-room schoolhouse was not a common institution in Newfoundland by the time I started school. The era of the split-grade classroom ended in most of Newfoundland after my parents' generation. By my day, just about everyone in the province went to school in a more typical North American fashion: in a classroom with a bunch of kids your age in your same grade in a great big school with lots of

Me at kindergarten graduation. I'm thinking, "I must be wicked smart by now."

different classrooms and a library, a gym, a schoolyard to run around in at recess, a staff room, an office, a computer room and a whole bunch of other resources, too. Not so for Catholic kids in Petty Harbour. St. Edward's was a tiny school with five small classrooms, a boys' washroom and girls' washroom and a principal's office. The only other rooms were the staff room and what was supposed to be a makeshift science lab, but I never saw either of them used by anyone for either of those purposes.

Our little white wooden school, perched right next to the Catholic church, was more notable for what it did *not* have. St. Edward's had no paved parking lot or groomed grounds or any playground of any kind. It had no gymnasium, no library, no cafeteria and no music room. There were no lockers lining the two narrow hallways and there was no sweet, maternal reception lady waiting by a desk to greet students when they came through the door in the morning and left at the end of the day. In fact, there was no reception area at all.

It was a skeleton of a school, but as I heard my Catholic parents say many times, "At least we've got a school and don't got to bus little children to town in the winter." The

St. Edward's Catholic School in 1977.

Protestant kids, of course, didn't go to school with us Catholic heathens. They went to school in either the nearby town of the Goulds, twenty minutes away, or in St. John's, a forty-minute bus ride away. Bus rides in winter were something my parents swore were unsafe, and they had a point. The roads leading out of Petty Harbour were treacherous most winter days. The snowplows were no match for the amount of snow that fell, often in no time at all, and those hills were always white with snow and ice. The local council would spread salt on them, but that didn't mean the roads weren't dangerous and occasionally deadly. And my parents knew it.

"Wouldn't mind if it was in a new safe car or something," Mom would say, "but them buses are not fit to carry the mail around, never mind our children." I am sorry to report that her fears would be realized when a student died in a bus accident one very sad winter day. But the fact that I didn't ride a bus to school every day didn't mean I was safe from all other dangers. Far from it. I had to dodge daily disaster before I even made it to class. My house was on one side of Skinner's Hill and our school was on the other. Climbing snow-covered Skinner's Hill in February was an undertaking for a seasoned Sherpa accustomed to Everest, never mind for a young fella trying to keep up with his older brother and sister who were cold and tired of waiting for him. You needed Arctic-grade spiked mountaineer boots to navigate Petty Harbour's impossibly steep inclines—and that's on a spring day. When those slopes were covered in ice, the short trek to school became a treacherous adventure.

Bern was always an adventurous and sporting yet practical engineer kind of fella. "Alan, b'y. Will you walk on the sides in the snow and not on the ice in the middle of the road, please? Do you want to wind up back down by the house?"

Kim would usually object to the injustice of it all. "Whose job is it to keep these roads safe for us to walk on? I'm writing a letter to the town council complaining about this." (She probably did, too.)

And if that wasn't bad enough, as soon as we'd close the door of our house and head three steps up the hill out of parental earshot, Bernie would begin talking about things that he'd never get away with in front of Mom and Dad. I recall one time when he decided to enlighten both me and Kim on the topic of how to pleasure a woman. Keep in mind that Bernie was about thirteen at the time and I was about eleven.

"It's all in the wrist," he said as we started up the hill. "See, Alan," he continued, making a tight fist with his fingers but extending his long middle one, pointing it out stiff and straight. "Just like this." He bent only his wrist up and down in front of my face. I nodded, not really sure what it was he was demonstrating but knowing enough not to ask questions. Then Bernie repeated the demonstration to Kim, who rolled her eyes, pushed his arm away and said, "Gross, Bernie. Eff off." Bernie shrugged, and up the hill we went.

If Bernie's daily antics weren't bad enough, steps before the very peak of Skinner's Hill, for every day of our elementary school life, Bernie, Kim and I had to deal with Gabby the Beast. My brother and sister swear to this day that Gabby was merely a canine, a canine of the common German shepherd variety. But I swear to you that the evil primordial monster guarding the Kennedy house arrived in Petty Harbour straight from the Gates of Mordor. Even though all of us Doyle kids walked past Gabby's yard at exactly the same time and in the exact same configuration every day of the week, Gabby was always surprised to see us. His response? To launch with his fiercest snarl and growl and then to snap his hideous jaws directly at our tender calves, ankles and butts. He would grab a boot or a pant leg and pull his screaming victim back down the hill a step or two before getting distracted by someone running up ahead. He'd let go of his current prey and dash up to grab the next Doyle.

I cannot say Gabby ever drew blood during the daily attack, but he did bite all of us Doyle kids just about every day. Bern and I would make a dare out of it sometimes; other times, we'd strategize elaborate avoidance plans.

"Bernie, you go up first and get him going up the hill. You're the fastest."

"Yeah, and you come up the rear and see if we can lead him over the bank."

Kim, ever sensible, once again pointed out the injustice of it all. "This is not right, you know. They should have their dog on a leash."

Bern scoffed. "No one around here walks their dogs on leashes, Kim. Where do you think we are? California or something?" He was right.

"So? We shouldn't have to run for our lives every morning on the way to school. There should be a rule about this. I'm going to call the town council." (She probably did, too.)

So up the hill we'd go, and we'd be scampering in circles to distract Gabby, and if we were lucky enough, we'd cross that boundary visible only to Gabby, at which point he'd retreat to his front doorstep, pleased by another effective defence of his castle.

I'm not sure where you are right now, dear reader, as you are reading this book. But let me ask you this: Is there a place left in the free world where kids daily dodge a wild beast on their way to school? Imagine the parental and civic uproar if today in a typical Canadian town or city, a dog bit kids—every day, for nine years! I'm pretty sure Gabby, the Beast of Skinner's Hill, was the last of his kind.

You'd think everything after that on the trek to school would have been easy. But it wasn't. That was just the first trial. As they say in the mountain-climbing world, "The top of the mountain is only the halfway point." Once we made it to the top of Skinner's, we then had to descend the school side. We went from exhausting ourselves hiking up the treacherous icy slope to exerting every effort to keep from sliding down the other side. If you lost your footing on a particularly inclement day, you could slide out of control, hit the rounded snowbank at the school's entrance and find yourself hurtling past the school, down the hill, across the road and into the river faster than you could drop an anchor. I've often thought that the makers of Olympic luge tracks should have visited Skinner's Hill in Petty Harbour during one of those winters. They most certainly would have learned a thing or two about how the human body can speed along on ice. Whether those conditions could be replicated anywhere else in the world, we'll never know.

After scaling Skinner's Hill, crossing the dangerous terrain of Gabby the Beast and creeping down the other side of the mountain, we arrived at school, usually relatively unscathed. I'd say we were battered, bruised, bitten or frostbitten only about 30 percent of the time, which, given the circumstances, is pretty good.

The boys in our town were often called Petty Harbour Dogs. The history of this nickname dates back to the times when Petty Harbour folks used dogsleds to pull them and their cargo to and from St. John's. Townies in the downtown core of St. John's would hear the barking coming over the hills and announce, "Look out. Here come the Petty Harbour Dogs!" And eventually, men and boys from Petty Harbour became known as Petty Harbour Dogs, too.

Thinking back on this now, I believe the moniker was quite apt for us kids. We'd often sit in gangs on the bridge in Petty Harbour and eyeball the Townies and tourists who drove through on Sundays. And before school, it was the same thing. The second we stepped foot on school property, the boys and girls quickly separated. Bernie and I immediately went to the Dude Section of the yard, standing in a group right by the driveway, eyeballing every person and every car that turned into the dirt yard used as a makeshift parking lot. We must have looked like we were about to bark and defend our territory if they so much as stepped out of their vehicles. Standing around in our pack by the school gate, we'd reluctantly step aside only to let a teacher pass. I suppose we wanted the illusion that people got in only because we let them. We were cool like that, so cool that we needed to stay as far away from the school—and from the Girls' Section—as possible, until the bell rang. Did it matter that the Dude Section was where the wind whipped right up the hill, freezing our faces and hands off? Did it matter that we weren't always wearing hats or gloves? Of course not. We boys stood every morning on the most exposed part of the school property, wearing as few clothes as possible. The girls, much more sensibly than us lot, congregated in a little alcove close to the school and out of the cold wind.

Like a true pack, the boys in the Dude Section were all shapes and sizes, with pups as young as five to others in their teens. The quiet young ones were constantly studying the older ones, imprinting their words and actions into their young minds, whether they realized it or not.

Bern and I would sidle up to Wade and Donnie, two brothers who lived close to the school. Wade was a year or two older than the rest of us and hence was bigger and stronger, and Donnie was never far behind him. Both of them were tough as boots, as they had a few older brothers and cousins who kept them at the top of their game. Like in most of the families in Petty Harbour, Wade and Donnie carried a few strong physical traits from the previous generation. Wade was tall and good-looking with an olive complexion he shared with one of his older sisters. Donnie had the family freckles and red hair. In Petty Harbour, it was not difficult to pick out which family anyone was from. To this day, faces are handed down from generation to generation. I regularly visit Petty Harbour and can actually tell just by looking what family a young kid comes from. It is both odd and comforting to go there today and see a kid who's the spitting image of Wade or Donnie and who's riding his bike across the bridge just as we did a generation before. Same faces for generations.

Once the dogs assembled at the school gate, the banter often got going with a simple morning poke from Bernie.

"Alan, tell the truth, b'y. Did you comb your hair with a pork chop or what?"

"Yeah, Alan. Your head looks like a moose's arse," Wade might say.

Bernie would jump to my defence. He was allowed to mock me all he wanted, but no one else was. "Shut up, Wade. Your sister's arse is as big as a moose's and her butt cheeks probably hang down like two pork chops."

"Maybe so, but I can tell you exactly what *your* sister's arse looks like," Wade would counter.

"Oooh." All the boys loved when it got real dirty.

"Yeah. We've seen her arse so much we're all sick of looking at it," Donnie would chime in.

"You're confused, Donnie, b'y. That's Wade's arse you gets to look at all the time."

"Oooooh!" The boys loved it when the big b'ys wouldn't let it go. You see, in Petty Harbour, whoever zings last wins. As long as you kept upping the verbal jabs, you were still in the game. The moment you got sookie or threatened to make it physical, you forfeited victory.

"Feeling all brave this morning, are you, Bern?" Wade would say to test the waters.

"Yes, b'y, Wade. There's something about picturing your sister's arse that gets me all riled up. Funny, ain't it?"

While this verbal sparring went on, I and some of the others would be making bets about what would happen next.

"Bernie could take Wade in a fight if Wade's coat was open and he got a quick shot in the guts," my cousin Benny would say. He'd even act out the description to make sure we all got the meaning. Benny was thin as a rail with a head of hair as thick as a horse's mane. He was quick footed, which made his shadow-boxing demonstrations most awesome to watch.

"To take down Wade, you gotta punch him in the neck and cut off his breathing," Cousin Tommy would say. Tommy was Benny's older brother. He was stocky, with a freckled face. He performed a little demonstration, punching the air to make his point clear to us. We mimicked the action and commented on the effectiveness of this technique. Clearly, Tommy had given a lot of thought to how to take down Wade.

"You're both wrong," he said. It was a tiny voice, high-pitched and reedy. We all looked down to see young Mikey had arrived. The youngest of the gang, at around seven years of age, he was full-on Nitzy Pumpkin, with blazing red hair and a face and body covered in freckles. "You gotta boot him in the nuts."

"No booting in the nuts!" we'd all shout, but by this point Bernie and Wade were out of earshot and very involved in their banter.

Because he lived farther away, my friend Perry would arrive about fifteen minutes before school started and size up the scene in a few seconds. Never the loudest in the group but always the most observant, he remains to this day one of the funniest people I know. He walked and stood like an adult, even as a ten-year-old, but he had a perfect baby face that was always plastered with the same grin, like he knew something the rest of us did not.

"Alan, while the bulls are snorting at each other, you might want to pay particular attention to Miss Cindy's blouse today." Perry would then wink and touch his nose or perform some other gesture he got from a television character. "Miss Cindy passed me in her car as I was walking up the harbour, and even at top speed I got a fair look at her goods." He'd wink and touch his nose in that "just between you and me" kind of way.

It was a longer walk to the school from the Long Run, so Bobby, Stephen and Paul, Jack Walsh's sons, would arrive later than everyone else, and almost without fail, the entire conversation of the pack would shift to sports. All three brothers excelled at almost every sport. Between them, they had softball, bowling, darts and hockey championship trophies from Petty Harbour and beyond.

"Did you see the save Palmateer made last night for the Leafs? Best double-leg slide I ever saw." Bobby would be uncontainably excited. "He went post to post, skates up in the air. Robbed Gainey of the puck. Thought he had a goal for sure! Almost as good as the home run from Reggie Jackson that just nipped over the glove of the outfielder. Deadly."

Once these sports conversations got started, they quickly morphed from discussion to full-on theatrical performances. Bobby became a sportscaster, with more natural enthusiasm than anyone we'd ever seen on TV. When Bobby's show started, Stephen and Paul took centre stage, the rest of us gathering to watch. As Bobby narrated, Stephen and Paul did a slow-motion play-by-play re-enactment of every last detail they'd seen on TV, doing so with perfect accuracy. It was our very own amateur *SportsDesk* show, live every morning. It was better than TSN.

Bobby would channel Bob Cole's voice from *Hockey Night in Canada*. "Here goes the youngster Coffey, up the wing." The boys would act this out, skating down the invisible ice.

"Other wing, Youppi." (That was Paul's nickname, like the Montreal Canadiens and Expos mascot, because he often wore big baggy jerseys.)

"Wake up, b'y." Bobby would correct anyone who made the slightest error in the replay.

Back to Bob Cole. "Down the right side, around the defence. He can go, you know." Bobby would transform any spectator into participant if he needed someone to assume a role. This time, he grabbed little Mikey. "And into the centre with a quick look between the legs."

"Much like you'll do with Miss Cindy's attire today," Perry would say as an aside just for me.

"But Coffey looks upstairs and blows it past the out-reached glove of the goalie. And he finishes with the goal!"

Bobby would run to stretch Stephen's "glove hand" a little more so the re-enactment perfectly matched the angle and quickness of the actual save.

This broadcast would inevitably start debates about how Carbonneau was soft for the Habs, and Lanny McDonald and Börje Salming should retire from the Leafs. Every dog had his own opinion, and everyone would fight for airtime.

"I likes Wayne Gretzky," Mikey would say, gathering up a ton of courage to speak.

"Who the f—k is Wayne Gretzky?" we'd all shout.

Eventually the bell would chime and we'd file into school and we'd be greeted by Mr. Kelly, our principal, with his exact-same-as-yesterday, exact-same-as-tomorrow greeting, "Good morning, children." He was a tall, slender, Ichabod Crane kind of fellow who looked all the way down at you over his thin wire spectacles and long, sharp nose. And when I say long, I mean *loooong*.

"Mr. Kelly could smoke a cigarette in the shower," Bernie used to say. I was eleven or twelve by the time I actually got the joke.

"Straight to your classrooms now, children." I can still see Mr. Kelly standing in the doorway with one hand high on his chest, holding the two flaps of his blazer tight together while the other hand held his ever-present handkerchief, ready to catch anything that shot out of that almighty nose.

All of us kids would file into the school and hang our coats on the hooks in the hall, leaving our wet boots on the floor. Then we'd stream into our various classrooms. We had no PA system. Instead, Mr. Kelly would stand in the foyer area and ask all the teachers to keep their doors open. Then he'd raise his voice to what must have been a very uncomfortable volume and he'd yell out the announcements for that day. Any other person might have shouted like a referee at a sporting event or perhaps like a ringmaster at the circus, losing all formality. But Mr. Kelly was far too respectful and dignified for that kind of showmanship. He spoke exactly as he would if you were standing right next to him, not a word more or less, only about forty decibels louder:

"Today, children, there will be a mass to celebrate the Twenty-Sixth Day of the Holy Ascension of the Blessed Saint of Non-Rising Bread!" or something like that.

"Benny Stack, Perry Chafe, Peter Wells and Alan Doyle will serve mass and should go to confession fifteen minutes before the other students!

"Next Friday the Bookmobile will be back, so please have your library books ready to return!

"And finally, today is Day Three, so Mr. Pilgrim will be here this afternoon to take Grades 5 to 8 to play ball hockey. Weather permitting, this will take place up the road, but given that the weather rarely does permit, it's more likely that ball hockey will take place in the basement of the church.

"Now, children, bow your heads and let us pray!"

And the low hum of a hundred or so students from kindergarten to Grade 8 would follow. "Our Father, who art in heaven . . ." When we reached the "Amen," the classroom doors closed one by one and lessons began.

All classes were split grades except for kindergarten. I have no memory of the split-grade arrangement being an issue in Grades 1 and 2, or even in Grades 3 and 4. I suppose there was not such a delineated difference in curriculum for those levels. But as the grades got higher, sharing a class with kids doing a different curriculum became more and more difficult.

In Grade 5, for example, our teacher would teach Grade 5 math on one side of the room while the Grade 6s "read quietly" or did assigned work on the other side. When the teacher was finished, he or she would cross the floor at the front of the room and everything would switch. This meant there was always a group of idle kids in the room.

Imagine a dozen eleven-year-olds in a classroom. Now imagine asking them to stay intermittently quiet and work independently for about half an entire school day. When I was in the lower of the two grades in the room, it was conceivable for me and Perry and a few others to quietly eavesdrop on the lessons being taught to the upper grade. That would hold our attention for a few minutes at a time. But when we were in the older grade in the room and the teacher was teaching the lower grade, there was nothing at all to hold our attention. Naturally, we devised a whole array of quiet activities to engage in that were not quite related to the lessons we were supposed to be doing. But perhaps we learned a few things all on our own. Here are some highlights:

• *Perfecting paper airplane shapes.* I always found the classic shape could travel the farthest, while my cousin Benny made a smaller model that could not fly as far but was deadly accurate. He could fly it from the third row and have it land on the teacher's desk while his back was turned. Brilliant. We learned so much about aerodynamics.

• *Passing notes.* These notes primarily consisted of creative insults about each other's choice in hockey team. Me to Perry: Habs Rule. Perry to Me: Habs rule what? Or do you mean there is a Habs rule? We learned a bit about grammar.

• *Whispering* back and forth about the distinct possibility that Wanda may very well have grown breasts:

"Mr. Chafe," I'd say to catch Perry's attention. I'd cleverly taught myself to talk out the side of my mouth.

"Mr. Doyle." Perry was even more discreet.

"I believe there may be some new action in Wanda's upper underwear."

"Do tell, Mr. Doyle."

"If you lean forward about forty degrees and wait for the sun to bounce off the rocks, you'll see what I mean."

"Waiting for it . . . waiting for it. Yes sir. I can confirm a distinct outline through the white blouse."

"A degree or two back and you might catch a direct look through the arm hole."

"Yes, indeed. New gear, I see."

We could carry on a conversation like this for quite some time, proving that we learned a lot about ventriloquism.

• *Drawing.* If the teacher's lesson droned on too long with the lower grade, we'd sometimes turn our sizable artistic talents to drawing genital shapes in class dictionaries. You would not think there are over eight million ways to draw a penis and a vagina. I suppose the lesson here was in creative artistic design.

When, on the odd occasion, we actually concentrated on the school work assigned, I learned that I liked English and history and religion. And telling stories. I learned I did not enjoy math or science. I would not have put it in these words at the time, but I was never much for constants—you know, those things in math and sciences that never change . . . ever. Those things bugged me. Like water freezes at zero degrees, every time. A + B = C . . . every time. Boring.

But I recall the first time I really heard a poem and understood the function of that kind of language. It was E. J. Pratt's poem "Erosion." I found it very exciting that words arranged in a particular sequence and rhythm could make me feel a certain way. It made me start to think about songs. Was it possible that songs were really just sung poems? I learned that poetry can make predictable things a little more interesting.

My favourite class was gym, which was unfortunate because we did not have a gym. As Mr. Kelly mentioned in the announcements, once a week the phys. ed. teacher, Mr. Pilgrim, would come for a visit. He looked like a professional hockey player and honestly seemed to love coming to Petty Harbour to do sports with us kids. We had no gym or recreational facility of any kind, so we made do with what was around us. When the weather was fine, we'd go up on the hill and play softball or soccer. We'd go on hikes in the woods or walks around the harbour. Once a year, there'd be the National Fitness Program, where the older boys and girls would time their flexed arm hang or do other bizarre tests of strength. It didn't matter to us what the activity was. It was not in the classroom, so it was all fun.

When the weather was poor, we went into the only space big enough to hold us all—the basement of the Catholic church. It was a rectangular space about eighteen feet wide and about forty feet long, with a ceiling height of eight feet or so. Because of some posts and dividers, the room had about three thousand sharp corners, cast-iron radiators and pillars to look out for, and those corners are probably responsible for the facial scars on most Petty Harbour children of my generation. If those obstacles were not enough, there was also the perilous floor. It was old, crumbling linoleum tile that ripped your sneakers if you moved or twisted on the wrong spot. If you ran the wrong way, your feet could slide right out from under you and you'd land on your arse. The walls were covered in pressboard panelling that chipped and splintered and gouged your skin if you so much as lightly brushed against it. None of this was ideal for a ten-year-old. It was a hazard to walk around in that church basement; to play sports in it was a death wish. But that's what we did. And we did it happily.

The two most common games we played were dodge ball and floor hockey. Oddly, dodge ball was a fairly safe game, and we mostly escaped without serious injury. But floor hockey was another story. We played five against five. We had sticks. That's right—in a cramped basement with plenty of obstacles, it was decided that the best thing to do would be to give young children hockey sticks. Swinging in a space that small was, to say the least, dangerous. It was almost impossible not to get pushed into a stanchion or hooked in the leg with a pressboard splinter. It was rare that anyone would shoot the ball without also sending a projectile floor tile rocketing into someone's face. And we loved every second of it.

Adversity develops the strangest skills. That's what I learned about floor hockey in that church basement. Because the ceiling was so low, we used it like it was another player in the game. Hockey wasn't two-dimensional, a game in which a ball was moved from one end of the indoor rink to the other. Instead, we played all three dimensions, becoming experts at banking the puck off the ceiling and walls to avoid our opponents. We could rip the ball off the ceiling and into the net over the goalie's shoulder if we got the angle right. We played the ball in and out of corners the way a pool player manoeuvres the cue ball.

As with ice hockey, I played goalie as often as I could in street and ball hockey. I recall playing ball hockey in a real gym later in high school and noting how easy it was to stop the ball when I did not have to deal with bounces off the ceiling or shards of tile flying in with the ball.

After school, our hockey skills were put to good use and instead of playing in the church basement, we moved our games to O'Brien's Wharf, which boasted the only flat piece of pavement in all of Petty Harbour. It was behind O'Brien's Fish Plant, on the Catholic side of the harbour. The owners of the plant had paved the area to allow trucks to turn around when loading or unloading fish or offal. But for us, the pavement served a much more important function as the main ball hockey rink in town.

We played there for hours, in all seasons, in all weather. Sometimes we played pickup; other times, we organized ourselves for serious matches, pitting Up the Harbour (the Catholic b'ys) against Down the Harbour (the Protestant b'ys) in legendary contests of will and skill.

Some may think that our makeshift rink was lacking. It's true that it had no boards or lines, and no nets, and was far from regulation size and shape, but to us it was glorious. Did it matter that the giant stainless steel legs of the offal tank stood right where the blue line of one end would be? No. Did it matter that one edge of the rink faced the open water, allowing the ball to slip periodically into the freezing harbour? Of course not.

In fact, we always found ways to use these obstacles to our advantage. A few of the better players would run unsuspecting defenders into the offal tank, while others would ricochet the ball off the two-storey tank to clear the zone. We used that tank the way most hockey players use the boards, and it worked. But to be fair, most encounters with the tank's legs ended fine for the tank and very badly for the players. Often, one of the younger players would break out on a wing, racing ahead to prove to the older fellas that he was a good player. He'd be hitting his stick on the pavement and screaming for a pass, running backwards while his eyes were firmly fixed on the ball in play . . . instead of the rapidly approaching metal posts of the offal tank.

With all the focus on head injury in pro sports these days, I would like to do a study on how many concussions were inflicted by those posts. The worst case was Craig, who ran his head so hard, so dead centre, so directly into one of those posts that he was knocked completely unconscious. He lay on the pavement for minutes, immobile. It looked so serious. We almost stopped play.

"Is he breathing or is that just the wind in his sweater?" I asked, my plastic goalie mask lifted on top of my head.

"He's breathing. Game on!" Bobby yelled, already breaking down with the ball and whipping it up net.

"Hold on, hold on," Shawn said. "Mikey, run up and tell Maude to come down and see if Craig should go see Dr. Natsheh. Benny, help me haul him out of the way."

And so we laid Craig on a pile of coats behind one of the nets. But nobody could stand the wait, and soon enough, Bobby said, "Well, come on, b'ys! Maude's on the way. Game on, for frig sakes." And game on it was.

But the most challenging obstacle on the O'Brien rink was the sea, which, as I said, was inconveniently located right at the edge of the pavement, and there was no way to move it. The ball easily slipped over the edge of the wharf, quickly floating out into the water before we could reach it with our sticks. This became very aggravating.

"Frig sakes, b'ys," Bern might say. "Watch the passes on the left or we'll spend the whole day getting soaked."

"Yeah, b'ys," Wade insisted. "Next one to shoot the ball over goes in after it."

Over time, we devised several ways to retrieve the ball. The most primitive way was to throw a pile of rocks to the outward side of the floating ball and hope the resulting ripples would bring it back to us. This method was time-consuming and required a good supply of rocks, which, depending on the season were not always available, as for half the year they were buried under mountains of snow. Fortunately, we devised a better system. It all started when Bernie and I were watching hockey one night and a news break between periods showed an oil spill. The coast guard had placed cool-looking semi-circle buffers around a slick, and these were doing a good job containing the oil. Bern, the engineer-in-training, had a bit of a eureka moment.

"That would work perfectly for ball hockey on the wharf!"

And that's how we developed a sophisticated boom system where we'd effectively rope off a section of the harbour so that when the ball fell in, all we'd have to do to retrieve it was reel in the floating rope, which nestled around the ball and gently led it back to shore.

The ingenious boom system is a fine example of how a group of young boys can work together to solve a problem, especially a hockey-related problem. But our powers of co-operation were inconsistent at best, and when we weren't working together towards the betterment of all things hockey, we were beating the shite out of each other. You see, in Petty Harbour, scuffles of all kinds occurred on the wharf, and not only between boys. Fishermen who had gripes with each other would have a bit of beer or rum, and fisticuffs would sometimes follow. These brawls were generally harmless, often nothing more than shoving matches. In the worst cases, one party might leave with a bloody nose. But a common feature of all of these fights was the ending, where a tussle was punctuated by the inevitable launching of one combatant over the wharf and into the freezing water.

And that was that. The tradition was carried on by all us boys when we started playing street hockey on the wharf. Any serious hockey disagreement was solved by one kid throwing another kid over the side and into the freezing-cold water. We'd all watch as the boy went under and surfaced a few moments later, shivering and turning blue, much to our amusement. One of the bigger boys would reach an arm down and haul our sopping-wet teammate out of the drink, whereupon he'd most likely simply run up to his house, change into some dry clothes and be back in the game ten minutes later with no harm done.

Fortunately for me, I was mostly a dry player because I played goalie. I wore a lot of equipment and therefore considered myself safe from being thrown over the wharf. That was my first mistake. I didn't fight all that much, but one time, I got in a scrap with an older boy, David. I was about eleven years old; he was about thirteen. He kept successfully screening me and either scoring himself or helping his team score with his aggressive play in the crease area.

"If you don't get your arse out of my crease, I'm going to ruin you with my goalie stick!" I warned.

"What?" he said. "This is fair play, Doyle. If you don't like it, get one of your pansy defencemen to move me!"

When he succeeded again with his aggressive play in my imaginary crease, I lost it and whacked my goalie stick up between his legs as hard as I could. He dropped to the ground. I looked from teammate to stricken teammate and was met with blank stares. No taunts or curses or cheers followed. None of my defencemen sprang to my defence. Instead, the eyes of every face I turned to spoke the same wordless opinion. It was only then that I realized I'd broken the unwritten rule, a commandment so ingrained in everyone that it didn't even need to be said out loud: NO DRILLIN' FELLAS IN THE NUTS.

No one was on my side.

David stumbled to his feet, red with pain and tears in his eyes. He grabbed my goalie stick and hurled it into the harbour. "You're goin' in after it," he said quietly but with certainty.

No way, I thought. I'm the goalie. I'm wearing all these pads. If these pads get soaked, I'll be pulled underwater and drowned. But all the players around me were taking formation, creating a corridor to the opening at the wharf's edge. Justice and tradition had to be served.

David took me by the scruff of the neck and dragged me kicking and screaming to the lip of the harbour. I tried to make a fight of it and dropped my gloves, but with the pads and heavy coat, I was no match for him. And with one quick push, he flung me in—with my helmet and cage and my goalie pads on. The water was so cold it actually burned. I can still remember the feeling of searing heat on my legs and lower back and the taste of sea water splashing into my mouth. Fortunately, I managed to grab some of the cribbage on the way into the water, so I only went in about waist-deep. I was scrabbling and struggling like a lobster in a pot, and I somehow lifted myself and my soaking pads up the cribbage and back over the edge of the wharf. By the time I collected myself enough to look around, the game had resumed. I was glad to see that at least my own brother was still on the sidelines, eyes on the water, making sure I made it up and out of the drink.

David yelled out, "That'll teach ye to keep your stick down!"

Bernie said discreetly, "Go home and get some dry clothes on before you catches pneumonia."

Dripping with water, looking no doubt like a drowned kitten that had clawed its way out of a beef bucket, I had only one thing to say: "No." And with that, I walked back to the net to resume the game, bringing play on the rink to a halt.

"You ain't playin' now, b'y," David said. "I'm not having your fadder coming over here blamin' me for putting you in the hospital with pneumonia. Go home or I'll throw you over the wharf again."

My face was resolute. I looked at all my teammates, who were clearly not the least bit happy with me for causing this second disruption to the game. By this point, I'd lost most of the feeling in my legs, but that was irrelevant. What was more important was getting back out there.

"No," I said definitively one more time.

"F—k ya," David finally said. "Let the stupid little prick freeze to death if he wants. Game on!"

And with that, the game resumed, with me in net. We played for another forty-five minutes. My pads froze to my legs, but I discovered that if I kept moving I could stand it. I'm not sure why it was so important for me to keep playing. It wasn't pride or bravado. Rather, I suspect it was embarrassment about breaking a rule of conduct that was as clear to me as it was to everyone else. And sticking around in freezing-cold hockey gear and not complaining was my Catholic way of playing out the penalty. Amazingly, I never got frostbite. Or pneumonia. And never again did I drill an opponent in the nuts. Ever.

Will lived just up the road from us on Skinner's Hill. He lived in a small but very well-kept two-storey house that we had to walk past to and from school every day. Will was always around. He was a man with a keen appreciation for science, technology and progress. He often engaged Petty Harbour folks in conversation on these topics. "Everybody's always going on about the 'good ol' days,'" he'd say. "What a pile of bull. Back then, we were starved to death, froze to death, going around like savages looking for firewood. These are the 'good ol' days'—right now. Up to the house with your guts full, the electric heat on blast, hove off on the chesterfield, watching the hockey on the colour TV."

Will kept the gardens around his house as tidy and prim as the house itself. In his backyard, he had several rose bushes and a vegetable patch. Now perhaps to you Mainlanders that doesn't sound like a miracle, but believe me when I say it's a testament to that man's determination that he was able to

HELMETHEAD

I am a massive hockey fan. I've tried for years to write the ultimate hockey song for Great Big Sea. I've always known that a rowdy hockey song would fit very well in the GBS live show, both in Canada, because the game is a holy sacrament here, and abroad, for the sheer Canadianness. No matter where GBS plays, a great hockey song would rock the house.

Me in my all-star team uniform for the Goulds Minor Hockey Midgets in 1985. I believed this was a glamour shot that would impress all the ladies—ladies who really dig smelly goalie gear, over-sized glasses and peach fuzz.

Ironically, it is my passion for the game of hockey that has kept me from writing the perfect hockey song for the band. My attempts to discuss hockey in song are always too heavy-handed or desperately poetic. I wrote "Walk on the Moon" with a young goalie in mind as he stands in the crease before the puck drops at the top of overtime in game seven of the playoffs. I compared the moment to Neil Armstrong's moon landing, perhaps a bit grandiose a description for a hockey game . . .

Along with Séan and Bob, I wrote a small tune for *Hockey Night in Canada* called "Play the Game," which rattled through images that caught our eye while watching hockey. But the song was only ever played a couple of times on TV and never found its way onto a CD or into a live performance.

I was still looking for the perfect hockey ditty when Bob, genius man that he is, penned the perfect song. I was thrilled, of course, but also totally pissed off that I did not write it! After all, Bob hates watching hockey and never played a game in his life. I suppose it was his distance from the sport that enabled him to look at some of the more honest and human aspects of the characters in the game and write the now beloved GBS song "Helmethead."

This hockey ballad tells the story not of the hero captain who scores the winning goal or the rookie goalie who makes the big save, but of the fourth-line bruiser in the minor league who is a big hit with the ladies. He makes his way from town to town as women everywhere swoon—and he loves every minute of it. He says he'll never win a championship, but has lots of good fortune with the babes.

The song ends with a send-off and warning, one that always brings the house down when we perform it live. It simply advises that we probably should be wary of fellas wearing head protection.

Brilliant lyrics. Check them out at www.greatbigsea.com. I can't decide if I'm more grateful to count this as a GBS song or more jealous that I did not think it up.

grow anything in that impossible ground. And he was proud of it, rightly so.

But beyond Will's vegetable garden, his true pride and joy was his crabapple tree—a crabapple tree that had somehow managed to root and thrive on the indomitable rock of Skinner's Hill. That crabapple tree was massive. It stretched as high as the house. At the end of the summer, when the crabapples were almost ripe, my brother and I would set our eyes on them.

"By the frig, I'm getting those apples," I would say.

"What do you want with those apples?" Kim rightly wondered.

"We wants them because we are not allowed to have them." Bernie always had a way of keeping it honest and simple.

"Ye should leave them alone if ye're just going to flick them at each other. If I took them, I'd at least bring them home so me and Mom can make a pie." (She probably would, too.)

Dad also warned us to stay off Will's property. Will guarded his crabapples for weeks as they turned from green to a reddish hue, but forbidden fruit makes you want it all the more. Every time I'd see him, he'd be talking about how those apples were just about ready to be picked for jam or something. Jam? To us boys, that was just dumb. That's not what crabapples were meant for. They were clearly meant for throwing at people.

We would sneak round the back of his house and see Will in the window, standing there like a sentinel. If you rustled a bush, he'd be out on the back step, eyes peeled. When he let his guard down, leaving his window post to go to the bathroom, we'd jump the fence and make for the tree in a full-on assault. But we rarely got to the tree before Will's Irish setter would come racing down the back step, teeth bared for attack.

"Run, b'ys! Run!" Bernie yelled during one failed attempt. "Friggin' dog's got a scent of us!"

We hightailed it over the fence and narrowly escaped getting mauled.

But the dog was not the final defence measure Will was willing to take to protect his precious fruit. Will had a salt gun—an air gun that he packed with rock salt instead of BBs or pellets. If you were not careful and Will got you in his sights, you'd feel the sharp, jagged salt rip into you and sting like a bugger as it melted into your open flesh.

One benefit of going to school in Petty Harbour was that we got to have lunch at home (which we called dinner; what Mainlanders call dinner, we call supper). Mom would usually have sandwiches and soup or, my favourite, potatoes fried in the pan. Once, my brother and I were sprinting home from school for lunch when we noticed Will's car was gone and assumed he was in town. The crabapples were a perfect bluish pink. They were calling out to us. We had no choice. And with Will away, this would be a walk in the park. We didn't even bother going home to change out of our gym-time shorts and put on protective gear (meaning jeans and a jean jacket to drape over our heads as we ran away).

Bernie and I casually jumped the fence.

"Bern, are we sure there's no one here?"

"No car, no dog in the yard. Everything points to an empty house. Gotta jump at these opportunities, Al."

It was all too easy. Bernie and I strolled up to the tree and started grabbing apples.

And that's when we heard it. "Ye! Ye bastards!"

We turned, and there was Will on his back step, with his dog behind him barking madly through the screen door. Will's brother must have driven the car elsewhere and the dog had been inside the house the whole time. Frig. Frig. Frig. In one fluid motion, Will opened the door, never taking his eyes off us, and that rabid Irish setter sprang our way. Bernie and I made for the fence, but we were not going to make it. The hungry dog was just about to take a chunk out of my arse when the clinking of a chain being pulled tight and a whimper from the dog turned us around. Will had forgotten that the dog was on a leash tied to the back step rail.

As soon as we figured this out, Bernie and I started laughing and teasing the leashed dog from about six inches past where he could reach with his flared teeth. Will was scowling when he turned to go back in the house. We'd won! Victory was ours! All that was left was to claim our prized apples! I turned away from the house to high-five Bernie, but when I looked at his face I saw that he was not laughing. He was pale and his eyes were wide.

"Run," he managed to whisper.

"Why?" I asked.

And even quieter than before, Bernie said, "He's getting the gun."

I did not need to hear any more. We bolted for the fence. My brother was still in shock and his pause cost him a step or two. And that's all the head start Will needed. I jumped and cleared the fence, and as I landed I heard a single pop, like a balloon bursting. I turned to see my brother caught halfway over the fence, his arse and bare legs waving on the other side. His face was clenched in a wince and I could tell he was trying hard not to cry.

"I got you, ye little bastard!" cried Will from the steps. "Get away from my crabapples!"

My brother used all of his remaining energy to jump clear of the fence. Safe on the other side, he stood next to me, panting.

A few seconds later, once he'd caught his breath, he yelled out, "You didn't get me, Will! You're too blind and old! You couldn't hit a moose if it was sitting on your lap!" Then Bernie grabbed my arm and we bolted into the bushes and ran till we came to a clearing.

As we slowed, I heard Bernie fighting back tears. "Eff me," he said. I looked down and that's when I saw that the backs of both of his thighs were covered in red welts as if he had been bitten by a hundred giant mosquitoes. Not only that, there were two open wounds on his right thigh where larger bits of salt were lodged deep into his skin. There was no blood per se, but I could see the chunks of sparkling salt melting into the tender gashes in his flesh.

I leaned forward.

"Don't touch them!" he said. "You'll just drive the salt in farther. I just gotta wait it out."

And so, we sat in that clearing for about fifteen minutes as the salt melted and eventually the pain and most of the redness subsided. When Bernie was ready, we wandered home, defeated yet determined to take another crack at the apples the next day.

But when we waltzed through the door as usual, Mom saw the red marks on my brother's thighs. "Oh my Lord in heaven! Look at this child's legs! What happened?" she exclaimed.

"Nothing. Nothing. Must have walked through some sting nettles or something," Bernie said, wincing.

"Yeah, wild old stuff growing over behind the church," I added. "We'll stay clear of it next time. What's for supper?"

"That's no sting nettles. Ye were up after poor old Will's crabapples, weren't ye? Jaysus Christ, he never turned the gun on ye, did he?!"

Once she'd heard the full story, Mom called my father in from the shed. He raised an eyebrow and flashed us a look that clearly said, "What did ye two do to get your mother so riled up?" Then he saw the salt welts on Bernie's legs, sighed and shook his head. "Ye foolish bastards," he said.

"Jesus, Mary and St. Joseph, Tom. This harbour is full of goddamned hillbillies. Imagine shooting at little fellas over crabapples. This place is cracked altogether. I think we should phone the police," Mom decided. "Tom, what do you say?"

My father shook his head and crossed his arms across his chest. He looked at both of us boys.

"I'd say ye two fools should have listened to me when I told ye not to be up at Will's crabapples."

Then he turned and went back to the shed.

Apart from the odd mishap, I was quite content in Petty Harbour as a kid, and quite content at St. Edward's School, until I hit Grade 7. By that time, I was almost a teenager and wanted to play on a school sports team, which of course we didn't have. I'd heard that the Protestant kids who went to school in town played in school bands and performed in school plays. This sounded like a dream. I was also really eager to meet new people, particularly girls.

But more than anything else, I wanted to get away from my teacher, Mr. Gushue. Mr. Gushue had been transferred to St. Edward's to teach Grade 7 and 8 just as I was to enter that split-grade class. Unlike all the other teachers, Mr. Gushue did not seem to enjoy our town, our school, children or anything about teaching, as far as I could tell.

Early in September of Grade 7, just weeks after the start of what would be our two-year stint together, I asked Mr. Gushue a question in history class. Mr. Gushue did not know the answer, and for some reason he scolded me for speaking out of turn.

I was very confused. "Sir, if you don't know the answer, just say so. I'll look it up tonight in Granda's encyclopedia," I said. For once, I wasn't even trying to make all the kids laugh, but for some reason they did.

Mr. Gushue went red. "Being smart, are you?" he shouted. He walked down the aisle and grabbed me by the collar, yanked me out of the classroom and dragged me into the hallway. Once we were outside, he pushed me against the wall. I was scared, as I thought for sure I was about to be yelled at. But Mr. Gushue did not yell. Much worse, he whispered.

"You listen to me, you little prick. I did not come to this backward arse of a town to get laughed at. You embarrass me like that again and you'll feel my belt long before you gets to the principal's office. Got it?"

I was so terrified I could not speak. I just nodded and fought back tears.

And so the relationship with Mr. Gushue began. Some days were better than others, but generally I thought Mr. Gushue was a bully who was not very knowledgeable and was desperately afraid of being exposed. Mr. Gushue likely thought I was a know-it-all show-off who sought to humiliate him and win the class's favour at every opportunity. I'm pretty sure both of us were right.

By the eighth grade, I was getting increasingly bored in class. I had heard all the lessons for both the Grade 7s and 8s the year before and occupied myself by being the class clown. By this point, I was becoming quite a good entertainer and could sing and play guitar. This made me a really good class clown. I'm sure Mr. Gushue hated this and probably felt I undermined his authority, which I did.

Late in the school year, at a school outing to an indoor swimming pool in St. John's, there was a bit of tomfoolery in the boys' dressing room. After swimming, we had all dressed and were chasing each other around before going back to the school bus. Mr. Gushue came through the change room door

just as I was darting out. The
door bumped into him hard and
we both hit the ground. All the
boys howled with laughter and
pointed at us. I jumped up and
said, "Sorry, sir," but Mr. Gushue
was turning red . . . then redder.
He was so angry that I thought
he was going to hit me, right then
and there.

He got to his feet and yelled,
"Shut up! Now!" The room went
silent. He stood in front of me,
pushing a finger hard into my
chest, hard enough to leave a mark.
"You've just had your last laugh at
me," he whispered. "Get on the
bus and stay after school. Let's see

This is my Grade 8 graduation photo.
Photo-conscious even then, I took off
my glasses for the pic.

who laughs when it's just me and you in the classroom."

For the whole ride home on the bus, I tried not to show
how scared I was. We made it back to the safety of Petty
Harbour, the bus unloaded, and all the kids left to go home.
Except for me. Mr. Gushue grabbed me by the sleeve and
dragged me into the empty classroom, slamming the door
behind him. The whole school was empty. Not even the
principal's car was in the parking lot.

Mr. Gushue took off his coat as he walked to his desk at
the front of the classroom. I walked behind him, about to sit
down in front of his desk.

"Stand up like a man!" Mr. Gushue shouted. "You were acting like a big man earlier."

Then he reached into his desk and took out a long wooden ruler. It was the type that teachers used to draw long, straight lines on the board. It was heavy enough to hurt.

"You think it's amusing to make fun of me? You think you can knock me down and get away with it? Let's see who the real man is. Put your hands on the desk."

I had seen the principal's strap before but had never felt it. And I'd certainly never been hit with a ruler. I was so scared at that moment, but what I wanted most was not to cry.

"Sir, I'm sorry for what happened. I was running for the door. I didn't know you were—"

"Bulls—t," he said. "Put your hands on the desk."

I put my hands flat on the desk, palms up. Mr. Gushue laid the hard wooden edge on my palms.

"Thems your guitar-playing hands, aren't they? Shame to beat them up."

He pushed the ruler between my hands, separating them a few inches. Then, *whack*! He struck the ruler down as hard and quick as he could. He hadn't touched me, but the noise startled me and my knees buckled.

"You sure you're a man? Thought I saw you blink just then." Mr. Gushue was grinning. He was enjoying this.

Whack! Down came the ruler again between my shaking hands. My lips trembled as I fought back tears.

"You're not going to cry, are you? Men don't cry. I'm not crying."

Whack! Down came the ruler a third time. I felt one tear

escape my left eye. I couldn't stop it. Even now, so many years later, I can still feel the path of that tear on my cheek and taste its salt as it passed the corner of my mouth and travelled down my neck.

"What's this?" Gushue asked with a grin. "Are you crying? Well, that proves it. You're not a man at all. You're just a little boy. Go home to your mommy."

With that, he put the ruler away and walked to the back of the room and opened the classroom door. He had a wide smile on his face as I approached. At the door, he stopped me.

"This will be kept between me and you, right?"

I nodded and ducked under Mr. Gushue's arm. The moment the school door closed behind me, tears came like a river. I ran around the corner of the school where no one could see and I cried a thousand tears.

I walked home, a little later than normal, and went right up to my room until suppertime.

"What's your problem?" As soon as he caught sight of me, Bernie knew something was wrong. But I would not say what.

Later, when I came down for supper, Mom asked, "Everything all right, Alan, honey? You're some quiet."

"I'm fine. Just not very hungry."

I did not tell anyone about what happened. I doubt Mr. Gushue did either.

A few weeks later, at the end of the school year, I was graduating. I was so excited to leave St. Edward's and go on to a new school in the Goulds. There was a ceremony in the basement of the church. At the front of the room stood Mr. Kelly, our principal, the priest and Mr. Gushue. All of us graduates were called up front, where we were handed our diplomas and where we shook hands with the principal and posed for a photo. Then the priest made the sign of the cross over each of us as we passed him. Finally, Mr. Gushue shook hands with every graduate.

When my turn came to receive my diploma, I walked to the front and smiled for the camera as I shook hands with Mr. Kelly. I walked to the priest and stood, head bowed to receive the sign of the cross. Then I walked right past Mr. Gushue. Nobody noticed.

After the ceremony, as parents and graduates were milling about, Mr. Gushue came over to me.

"Not shaking hands today?" he asked.

I looked him right in the eye and said, "Shame to beat them up."

I never spoke to that man again. The following September, I went to Grade 9 in St. Kevin's High School in the Goulds. There were as many kids in my grade as there were in the entire school in Petty Harbour. Almost none of the girls were my cousins. It was awesome.

About a year ago, I was at a gym working out when an older gentleman approached me and said hello. He must have recognized me as the Doyle fella from Petty Harbour who sang in Great Big Sea. He was a nice gent and we had a lovely little chat. After a few pleasantries, he asked if I really had grown up and gone to school in Petty Harbour.

"I did indeed," I said.

"Oh. You must have had my brother, Mr. Gushue, for a teacher."

I wasn't sure what to say. I just nodded.

The man continued. "My brother was a bit of a hard ticket, but he was good to our mom when she was dying, and he was always really good to all of us. He passed away, you know. Died a hard, slow death with a long and painful illness. Nobody deserves that, do they?" He sighed, wiping his forehead. Then he asked, "So what was my brother like as a teacher?"

I looked into the sad eyes of Mr. Gushue's older brother. I paused. "He was great. Smart teacher and really kind to all the kids," I said.

And that was all.

After my workout, I walked to the gym's change room and paused for a second by the door. I read the sign: Men.

I pushed the door open, got showered and went home.

I could taste salt in the corner of my mouth the whole way.

CHAPTER 9

Transubstantiation

A day or so after my birth, I was baptized a Catholic in St. Joseph's Church in Petty Harbour, Newfoundland, and I suppose some or a lot of Catholic moral programming was installed from that moment. I'm sure I sat in a high chair or crib while Mom and Dad said prayers or the rosary. I'm also sure I was told as a toddler that misbehaving was a sin that resulted in a trip straight to hell and behaving properly would get me on the high road to heaven. But I have no memory of this.

I do remember noticing that religion dictated many massive things in my tiny town. Apart from literally splitting the town in half, people got up early on their one day of rest. They dressed up more to go to their respective churches and participate in a ceremony than they did at any other time of the week. I'd seen the Protestant ceremonies and the Catholic ones, and to me, even as a five-year-old, they looked really similar. When I was growing up, everyone seemed to take this religious divide as a given. Things in my town were a certain way because they'd always been that way. But I was a curious lad, and I had a lot of questions.

"Why do all the Protestants go to school in town when we Catholic kids walk to school here in Petty Harbour? Why do we have one small convenience store for the Protestant side and one for the Catholic side instead of one bigger, better one for everybody? Why don't we all use the same church instead of having two? What exactly is the difference between them and us?"

I asked all these questions repeatedly throughout my entire young life and I could not find a good answer. I still can't.

The first confusing religious tradition that I recall in our house occurred every Friday. Catholics of a certain vintage agree that eating meat on Fridays is a sin, and my family concurred. But here's the thing. We lived on the edge of the sea. We ate fish a lot. I mean, a real lot. You could walk down the road to the wharf and get a cod caught just a few hours previous. In fact, when Petty Harbour folk ask, "When was the fish caught?" they're not asking what *day*—they mean what *time*. And fish was free for anyone from the harbour. I got tired of it from time to time but mostly all of us kids loved fish. So did my folks. But if it was Friday, we were sup-posed to act like eating it was something special.

"Why can't we eat meat on Fridays, Mom?" I asked.

St. Joseph's Catholic Church, Petty Harbour. This is where I served mass and learned to play the difficult guitar chords in folk mass.

St. George's Anglican Church. Well-dressed girls I never met but admired from afar went here on Sundays. According to Catholics of my Nan's generation, this was the house of people unfortunately bound for hell.

"We sacrifice on Fridays to remember Jesus's sacrifice for us."

"How is eating fish that we eat every day a sacrifice?"

"Because it is. Now go run up and down the hill."

To make the whole situation more confusing, when we had access to certain fresh meat, we had the church's blessing to eat it on Fridays. When seabirds were in hunting season, for instance, we would eat turrs (seabirds) on Fridays instead of cod. Mom would roast them in the oven and serve them up with a delicious thick, brown gravy. One day, despite my better judgment, I asked why we were allowed to eat turrs on Friday when we weren't allowed to eat any other fowl on that sacred day. "Mom, aren't turrs a kind of meat?"

"They most definitely are not," Mom answered. "No meat on Fridays. You knows that."

"Mom, a turr is a bird. Like a chicken or a turkey," said my über-smart and equally perplexed sister Kim.

"No, honey," Mom said. "Turrs are caught in a fishing boat, so turrs are fish. Also, turrs eat fish. They aren't meat."

Kim went quiet for a moment, then said, "Mom, a cow eats grass, right? So therefore we should be allowed to eat beef on Good Friday."

Mom would get upset and put her fork down. "Ye crowd thinks ye knows everything. The priest said we were allowed to eat turr, and I am not stunned enough to argue with that. Not like ye crowd. Now go run up and down the hill."

I wonder sometimes if my mother really worried her children were destined to burn for their sacrilege. Every once in a while, Mom would insist we say a family rosary. For you non-Catholics, a rosary is a series of repeated prayers that corresponds to each bead on a crucifix necklace. You may have seen these in *The Godfather* or in Madonna videos. When a family rosary was called, we'd all gather around the kitchen table. We'd kneel on chairs that had been spun around so the seats faced away from the table and the backs served as resting places for our forearms in prayer position. We'd recite ten Hail Marys in a row, out loud. By the time we hit the third one, my brother would fart or I would say "Snail Mary" or something, and the whole thing would go off the rails. My mother would be so upset, she'd run upstairs crying. Then we'd all feel guilty about her having to raise children bound for hellfire. I don't know how Mom ever expected the family rosary to go well. Dad behaved only because his wife insisted. My sister behaved because she always followed the rules. Bernie and me: we were just hopeless.

I wonder if part of my constant suspicion and curiosity about religion came from the fact that I tested some of its most sacred certainties at a very early age. Consider the story of a boy who sold his soul to the Devil . . . or at least tried to.

When I was around ten years old, we had very little in our house in the way of fancy or modern things. There was no car in the driveway. In fact, there was no driveway. We had no colour or cable TV. No stainless modern appliances or heating or cooling. No closets full of nice clothes or coats or blankets or cups or plates. The floors had no expensive hardwoods or carpets. The walls held no glorious artwork. There were no crystal chandeliers, no grand staircases and certainly no servants. But there was a piano. Mom and Dad bought it used for five hundred dollars, a minuscule amount for a piano but by far the most expensive thing our family owned. The piano was Mom's only respite from the long and hard days of cooking and cleaning for a family of six. She loved that piano.

One night, while Mom and Dad were out, a babysitter was looking after us kids. Kim and Bernie were huddled around the hand-me-down black-and-white TV adjusting the makeshift antenna made out of an old, rusted coat hanger. Kim and Bernie had been trying to tune the set to *Little House on the Prairie* for far too long and I became bored. I turned my attention to the piano. I could play a few scales and chords and could even hum a few bars of a few songs. As my confidence grew, so did my volume, just as a clear enough picture emerged on the small TV screen.

"We got it!" yelled Kim. "Give it up with the piano and let us watch our show."

I refused. I thought I was entitled to keep enjoying myself at the piano.

"Give it up or I'll punch you right in the face," Bernie said.

But still I would not give it up.

The argument that followed grew so loud the babysitter came running downstairs from where she had been putting Michelle to bed. "Quiet, all of you, or you'll wake your sister!" she said. "Watch your show and stop at that piano right now!"

I did not think this was fair at all. I flew into a rage. "No!" I said, slamming my fist down as hard as I could on the keyboard. I expected to hear loud, discordant piano notes, but there was no clang, no sound at all—except the cracking of tender wood and the crashing of felt hammers inside the sound box.

The silence in the room was sickening. Kim's mouth opened wide as she drew her hand up to cover it. Bernie backed away and pointed back and forth between me and the piano. I was numb with disbelief. I pressed the three keys I had slammed. They were light, weightless. They dropped under the pressure like broken fingers or injured limbs. They made no notes at all, except the dull knock of ivory on wood.

It was the babysitter who finally spoke. "You broke your mother's piano. Get upstairs right now."

"Holy shit. Holy shit. Holy shit," repeated Kim, though she rarely swore, never once taking her gaze off the piano.

Bernie had a much clearer message and said it only once to me as I rushed past him to the stairs: "You. Are. Dead."

I ran to the small room where Bernie and I slept and slammed the door behind me. There was a single small window that let the moonlight in and some glow from Granda's porch light across the dirt road. There was barely enough room for me to fall to the floor and cry. But I did. I wept the sorriest tears a boy ever wept. I felt as low as anyone could feel. I had broken the one nice thing in our home and the only thing my mom had ever bought for herself.

After much anguish and still through tears, I got up. The door had drifted slightly ajar and through it, I saw the carved wooden crucifix hanging in the hallway. My days on the altar taught me that the Lord heard our prayers and performed miracles for those who prayed long and hard enough.

I slipped into the hall, took down the wooden cross and laid it on the floor. I made the sign of the cross on my forehead, lips and heart. Then I prayed.

"Dear Lord. Please forgive me for I have sinned. I got pissed off and broke Mom's piano. She'll be very mad and sad if it is not repaired. Please fix it and I will be your servant on Earth for my whole life. Amen." I said this prayer over. And over. And over.

After the tenth time, I figured that ought to do it, so I crept downstairs past my brother and sister, now near catatonic with worry. With some confidence, I approached the piano and pressed the broken keys. I truly expected a miracle. After all, I had said my prayer ten times in a row, like Mom insisted was worth doing in rosary. But when I heard nothing more than a dull knock, I ran back up the stairs and into my room.

Not one to give up easily, I started a second round of prayers, but this time repeated the plea twenty times. Surely *this* would do the trick. I went with a little more caution to the piano this time, but I'd always been told that this whole praying-to-God thing worked. I pushed the keys. No note.

I went back upstairs once more. I prayed again. I counted the prayers on my fingers. Fifty more prayers. But when I went downstairs, the piano was unchanged.

I was getting desperate. Prayer on high was not working. My parents would be home soon, and I was running out of time. I ran upstairs and closed the bedroom door behind me. I needed a miracle and I needed it fast. Tears came to me again, but I had no other choice. If God and the Angels could not help me, I had to turn to the one who surely would.

I knew from Father Maloney's homilies that the Devil was always watching, ready to win boys' souls at their weakest moments. And this surely was my weakest moment. I turned the cross upside down like I'd seen on TV when people want to call Satan forth. My voice was weak, but the words came clear enough.

"Dear Devil. Please take me for I have sinned. I got pissed off and broke Mom's piano. She'll be very mad and sad if she finds out. Please fix it and I will be your servant on Earth for my whole life. Amen."

I did not repeat the request. I suppose I was sure the Devil would hear me the first time around. I rose, and I swear I felt lighter, as if an invisible army of demons was hoisting their most recent acquisition onto their shoulders. I felt exactly like the damned souls Father Maloney had mentioned so often in church, damned to hell to live with the Devil for all eternity.

I descended the staircase. I remembered the mirror at the landing and turned slowly towards it. I was not sure what I expected to see, or not see, now that I was one of the damned, like that Dracula fella, but to my surprise and slight disappointment, I was fully visible in the mirror. Hmm. I walked to the piano, slowly, like the guys from Caul's Funeral Home did when they marched a casket up the church aisle in honour of the deceased.

"What are you doing?" Kim asked.

"Did you hurt your leg or something?" Bernie asked.

I ignored them and went to the piano. The damned were,

after all, special folks and need not bother engaging in idle chat with mere mortals. I was about to seal my contract with Satan. One fixed piano for one life of Devil Service on Earth. I took just a moment before pushing the keys down. I wanted to enjoy my last few seconds before being cursed for all eternity. I placed my fingers on the keys and pushed down to seal my fate.

Again, nothing but a dull knock. No chiming note to trumpet my passage to the dark side. No fire and brimstone leapt from the floor and no laughing cloven-hoofed fella emerging from the smoke to claim his prize.

I could not understand it. What was happening? Were my prayers and promises ignored on high and down low? Was it possible that not even the Devil would take me? This was depressing. And, worse, the friggin' piano was still broken.

Soon after, my parents came home and Mom was very sad and mad when she found out what I'd done. She sent me to my room immediately. I was made to understand that this was never to happen again and I would have to pay for the repair out of the money I raised working with the fishermen on the wharf. And that was all.

Sitting on the altar a few weeks later, I was glad that I remained undamned and glad that no Devil showed up to take my soul. In fact, I started to think that maybe there was no Devil at all. My daydreaming was broken by the shouts of Father Maloney. He preached a loud warning to all to behave or burn in the fire and brimstone.

"Ye shall be pulled into the depths of hell by Satan himself!" he yelled.

My friend next to me was shaking in his robe, scared half to death. I turned to my friend with a grin that comes from the confidence of experience in such matters and said, "No, we won't."

As an even younger child, I recall sitting on the floor in the choir loft of the church in Petty Harbour as my mother played the organ and led the singers. She let me hide behind the organ and sneak a comic book in with me.

From my secret hideaway, I heard the mass many times before sticking my head up to actually watch it. I remember the sound of the organ speaker puffing and sweating, the sound of Mom's foot pushing the squeaky pedal and the click it made when she released it. I remember the individual voices that made up the choir, the good singers, the okay singers and the ones who barely made a sound. There was the swish of turning pages as hymns were flipped in unison, the clap of the kneelers as they hit the floor, the booming voice of the priest through the speakers and the chant of the congregation's reply.

"Peace be with you."

"And also with you."

"Lift up your hearts."

"We lift them up to the Lord."

"Let us give thanks to the Lord our God."

"It is right to give Him thanks and praise."

By the time I was five or six, I could recite pretty much the entire mass from beginning to end. To me, it was like the words to a song, one long hymn from start to finish.

Later, when I came out from behind the organ, I started to notice the sights of the church—the massive wooden arches that began at the floor and met in the centre of the roof beam, the stained glass windows that were almost ten feet high and bathed the church in an ever-changing mix of soft yellow and red. I loved the altar with its shiny red carpet and multiple levels, a perfect place for a concert. Too bad it was used only for mass.

I also really liked the costumes worn by the people on stage. The priest always wore a long white vestment with a bright image of a golden cross down the middle. He looked like a magician, with all sorts of tricks hidden in that big cloak. I also really liked the plain white hooded robes that the altar boys wore with rope belts cleverly tied around their waists—magicians in training.

But there were sights in that place I found quite scary. The centrepiece of the church was a life-sized statue of a man nailed to a cross. His hands and feet were bleeding and tears ran down his face. He had a cut just above his waist that bled into a cloth, and that cloth was the only thing that kept him from being totally naked. Worse yet, someone had rammed a circle of thorny branches down over his head, and it had cut him in several places. And his eyes, those eyes, wide open and staring upward through the blood and the thorns. To me, he looked alive. He was alive and suffering through extreme pain.

"Mom," I said one day. "Why can't I watch cowboy and Indian movies where people shoot arrows and bullets but I have to watch Jesus on the cross every Sunday?"

"Because Jesus reminds us of the sacrifice He made for us. And pretend violence in the movies is not good for young boys, Alan."

"But, Mom, the movie is make-believe and the statue in mass isn't. Father Maloney pointed to it and said, 'Don't forget, this really happened!'"

"Alan, go run up and down the hill."

Equally troublesome to me were the Stations of the Cross that represented the arrest, torture and murder of Jesus. We were supposed to walk from the earliest arrest all the way to His death, pausing at each portrayal to consider the sacrifice and say a prayer of thanks. The trouble was that these images were graphic and horrifying—a bound man falling as He carries His own gallows past His own mother, all the while being whipped by men in uniforms. For any kid with open eyes, it was the stuff of nightmares.

The weirdest sight of all was the congregation on Sunday. I recognized every person in the crowd, but nobody ever seemed themselves. Fishermen who normally wore coveralls and rubber boots were neatly dressed in pants and sweater vests. Some of them wore full three-piece suits. Their heads were exposed in a way that made them seem kind of naked. Normally, their hair was covered in a wool toque or baseball cap. And they walked and stood differently, too. On the wharf or in town, people walked with confidence. Some even had a skip to their step and a real sense of purpose, heads up and full of pride. But in church, people walked slowly and tentatively, often with their heads bowed slightly. They stood awkwardly and looked around uncomfortably. The strongest men I knew cowered in this one place.

But church was the only show going on Sundays. And if there was a show going, I wanted to be part of it. I would have loved to have jumped right in the choir, but Mom said I was too young to join. There were only two other parts to be played: priest and altar boy. The position of priest was out of the question, but by the time I was about ten years old, I got the part of altar boy and I was in the show.

Now, when I say "show," I don't mean any disrespect. I'm not suggesting that the ceremony was phony or dishonest. Not at all. What was amazing was that if the songs came and went at the right place and people hit their marks on time and no one dropped the baptismal candle, there was a better chance that the congregation was more engaged and better able to consider the message the priest was trying to impart. Any smart Catholic knows the show is an important part of Catholicism. If you don't believe me, just go to St. Peter's Square in Vatican City. Again, with no disrespect, it's the greatest show in history.

I should also note that the desire to put on a show come mass time varied from priest to priest. I served under some that were very shy or studious, who did not see themselves as the centre of the mass but rather as the facilitator of the Word of the Lord. One of the more studious fathers actually organized pre-show briefings for the altar boys. "Now, boys, I would like a tick-tock service today. Let's all work as a team!" But there were others who were definitely performers at heart—insisting on singing as many parts of the mass as possible or shouting during the homily while pointing fingers back at the cross or down to hell. One priest insisted an altar boy hold a handkerchief in case he wept during the homily. If tears were shed, the altar boy would walk out and dab the tears from the priest's face. It was kind of like the dude who brings the cape to James Brown.

I arrived early to mass when I was an altar boy. I liked to prepare myself well in advance. I went to the altar boy room at the back of the church (which I later referred to as the locker room) and picked out a white robe that fit well enough. Bernie showed me how to tie the cool knot in the cord that wrapped around the waist. I'd prepare the stage and the books and the candles. The other altar boys I knew from school or road hockey or from cutting out tongues. My first time as an altar boy, I was a bit nervous.

"You're gonna trip up in that cord and send the father flying down over the incense," an older boy teased.

"He's gonna catch himself on fire and burn to death in front of everyone," another taunted.

"They're just effing with you," Bernie said. He'd been an altar boy for years.

All I did in that first mass was walk in the opening and closing processions. When the time came to sit for the readings, we made our way back to the pew on the side of the altar. The boys before me sat in the pew and spread themselves as wide as possible so that when I got there, there was nowhere for me to sit. I was panicking, pacing back and forth in front of four giggling altar boys. Then, of course, I realized I was being had, a wee hazing of sorts for the first-timer. A rite of passage. One look from the priest and the boys moved over, allowing me to sit with them on the pew, though by this time my face was as red as a beet.

There were more rites of passage to follow. I would come to learn that the national pastime in the Country of Older Altar Boys was to make the younger altar boys laugh out loud during the most solemn parts of the service. I would also add that there is no place on earth in which you can place a ten-year-old boy that will make him want to laugh more than on the altar, dressed in a white robe in front of the whole community and all of his friends. I cannot tell you how many times some friend lifted his leg over mine during the homily and farted on the side of my crotch. I also cannot tell you how many times I did the same to one of them.

The robes we wore were the perfect cloaks for disguising mischief. You could smack, pinch, poke or have a full-on fist fight with the kid sitting next to you, completely out of public view. And we did. Some of the older altar boys got good at dragging their feet on the carpet and electrifying each other during mass. Every once in a while, you'd catch a kid suddenly yelping, which would earn the electrocutee a scowl from the priest, which would cause laughter amongst the others, which would anger the priest even more. It was an endless cycle of forbidden fun.

Despite all the shagging around, I aced my role and eventually could set up the entire mass before the priest arrived. I poured the wine and water. I placed the hosts on the communion plate. I placed the Bible ribbons on the appropriate pages to mark the readings.

For some odd reason, one of my favourite tasks was sliding the cardboard numbers that indicated the hymns into the sign on the wooden wall behind the pulpit. I have no explanation for how much satisfaction I took from this. Perhaps my obsession with getting this sign just right added to my disappointment and annoyance the first time Great Big Sea played in downtown Toronto many years later. We were to play a club on Queen Street. When we arrived for sound check in the afternoon, there was a sign with sliding letters that read:

2NITE FR NFLD

GREAT BIG SEA

It was the coolest thing I'd ever seen in my life. We had most certainly "made it." But when we came back later that night for the show, the wind had blown some letters off the sign, so it read:

2NITE FR NFLD

EAT BIG SEA

Two letters from living the dream—so close to cool.

At church, once I got the sign right, my next task was to check the PA system and microphones. I'd walk with purpose to the altar and say, "Check, one, two" into both mics. I'd seen people on TV doing this and heard my uncle Ronnie do this into his mic many times at band practice and at concerts. I had no idea what this was supposed to accomplish. I just knew that's what you did.

By the time I was a teenager, the thrill of being an altar boy had worn off somewhat, and that's when my latent curiosity took over yet again. It's also when the trouble with the Catholic Church started for me. I was not content to serve the mass without understanding why we conducted it.

One Sunday on the altar during communion, one of the younger altar boys stumbled with the plate of hosts, that is to say the flat little round communion wafers that are given to the parishioners to share in the body of Christ. When the kid tripped, all the other altar boys, including me, giggled. Father Cox's face went red and angry. After mass, Father Cox did not stay by the door to greet the congregation as he normally did. He was so furious at us that he stormed into the locker room and slammed the door behind him.

"How dare you boys laugh at the fallen body of Christ!" he whisper-shouted. "The flesh of Our Lord almost got stepped on," he added while blessing himself with his eyes closed.

No one answered. I eventually spoke up. "But, Father," I said. "Isn't the host just a symbol of Jesus's body?" All the boys nodded in agreement.

"No, my sons! The host is not a symbol of the Body of Christ. It *is* the Body of Christ, transformed in substance by the holy mystery of transubstantiation. And don't forget it, boys. This is not a laughing matter."

He gathered himself by the door, taking a deep breath before leaving. It was the kind of thing an actor would do before walking off stage.

At Sunday supper, while I reached for the gravy, I asked Mom and Dad, "What's transubstantiation?"

"Some kind of railway in Russia, isn't it?" Dad offered.

Mom just shook her head. "Alan, my son, why are you asking such an odd question?"

"Just something the priest said," I replied and let it go.

Later that evening, I went across the dirt road to my grandparents' place. There were usually a lot of people there on Sunday engaging in debate with my ever-spirited grandfather. The chats were often loud enough that you could sneak in and out with the other dozens of grandkids without being noticed. On this day, I needed to get to the back of the living room where my uncle had shelved a complete set of the *Encyclopaedia Britannica* he'd purchased. I loved those books and used them for school projects all the time. In a pre-internet world in a fishing town that was a hell of a drive to a library, encyclopedias were our Google. I found the volume of *T* and leafed through until I came across this entry:

"TRANSUBSTANTIATION, in Christianity, the change by which the substance (though not the appearance) of the bread and wine in the Eucharist becomes Christ's Real Presence— that is, his body and blood. In Roman Catholicism and some other Christian churches the doctrine, which was first called transubstantiation in the 12th century, aims at safeguarding the literal truth of Christ's Presence while emphasizing the fact that there is no change in the empirical appearances of the bread and wine."

I read the entry six or seven times until I figured it out. According to the *Encyclopaedia Britannica*, the father was right. Frig. I went to my devout Catholic aunt and asked my question: "Is the host wafer a symbol of the Body of Christ or is it the real thing?"

"Just a symbol, honey," she said. "And why are you worried about that anyway? Go run up and down the hill."

I asked my uncle Ben the same question. "Just a symbol, b'y. Don't be so stunned. You knows it's not real Jesus meat. He died a million years ago or whatever. Go run up and down the hill."

Over the following week, I asked several other people my question, and the only person who agreed with the encyclopedia was Mr. Kelly, my school principal. He closed his eyes and smiled. "Oh yes, Alan. That is Jesus in the flesh. It is a wonderful miracle that we get to see every Sunday. Bread and wine becomes flesh and blood while still appearing to be bread and wine. Isn't it beautiful?"

He sounded perfectly sure about this. I was not. Moreover, I thought it was kind of gross that we were eating the body of a human being. Wasn't that some kind of cannibalism or something? And if it was, shouldn't the priest make sure everybody at mass knew about this real-flesh thing, because almost nobody did?

All the altar boys went to confession each week, usually at a special student confession session on Wednesdays or Thursdays at the church. When my turn came to confess, I walked into the small room and went through my usual routine. I knew it by rote.

"Bless me, Father, for I have sinned. It has been one week since my last confession. I was disrespectful to my parents again and I lied about my homework again. I punched my brother in the face, but he kind of asked for it. I did not help around the house as much as I should have, according to my sister Kim."

Father Cox went about his usual routine as well. "And, Alan, are you truly sorry for these transgressions and do you hope to do better in the future?"

"Yes, Father."

He laid his hand on my head and said some silent prayer. Then, out loud, he asked God to forgive me. After, he waited for a second or two like he was on hold during a call with the bank. He announced, "Alan, you are forgiven these sins. Go now and say ten Hail Marys and ten Our Fathers and do the Stations of the Cross."

I blessed myself and said, "Thank you, Father," the same as I always did.

But I did not get up as I normally would have and Father Cox must have noticed the pause.

"Is there something else, my son?"

"Father," I ventured. "I looked up that transubstantiation thing in Granda's encyclopedia."

He looked troubled. "Did you? Why did you do that?"

"Because I was not sure what you meant, I s'pose," I said.

"And what did the encyclopedia say?" Father Cox asked.

"It said the host becomes the real flesh of Christ and is not a symbol."

"Yes, Alan. It is a Holy Miracle. Do you doubt it?"

"No, Father, I suppose I don't," I lied, "but I asked some other people this week about this, and I don't think the congregation understands that the host is not a symbol, Father. I don't think many people know they are eating real flesh, and I wonder if we should make that clear to everyone."

"Don't you worry about that, Alan. I'm sure everybody knows enough about this miracle."

I was growing bolder and more insistent now. "No, Father, that's just it. They don't. My principal is the only fella who got it right."

"Well, like I said, Alan, you don't need to worry about that. And we needn't get all the congregation worked up. You should occupy your time with those ten Hail Marys and Our Fathers and make sure you get all your homework done."

"But, Father . . ."

He stood up and ushered me out the door.

I did as I was told. I said my prayers. But as I kneeled, I wondered why Father Cox had not praised me for discovering something that the parish didn't know. The more I thought about it, the more I wondered why he did not seem pleased with me for looking up transubstantiation in the first place. As a matter of fact, not only did he not praise me, he discouraged me from going any further with my research.

As I walked along the Stations of the Cross, I continued to wonder what else I was not encouraged to know. What other questions was I not supposed to ask? I looked up at the image of Jesus falling for the second time and wondered what He would make of this. Would He be pissed to learn that I was looking up transubstantiation in the encyclopedia? Would He be cool with it if He suspected His people were confused? For that matter, were we sure that at the Last Supper He really meant for this wine and bread to actually *become* His flesh and blood? Maybe this was just a way of reminding people that we were supposed to remember His sacrifice for us? Maybe He meant for the host and wine to just be symbols or reminders of His flesh and blood? I was not sure we had this right at all.

I let this go for a while, and then the weirdest thing of all happened. I started to feel guilty about ever thinking about transubstantiation. Why did I feel guilty? Why did I feel like I had done something wrong when I also knew that I hadn't? It was really, really strange.

All through my young, curious Catholic life, I constantly wondered why we were not allowed to ask questions. I remember a conversation in a religion class in Grade 10 between a Sister of Mercy and one of the smarter, nicer girls in my class. The sister told us that birth control and abortion were bad and we should never consider using either method and should actively protest against those who did.

My classmate raised her hand and politely asked, "Sister, I wonder if you and the priest and the Pope feel this way because most likely none of you will ever be faced with being pregnant or getting someone pregnant?"

It was a fair and honest question, I thought, and asked in the most respectful manner. I could not wait to hear the learned and thoughtful answer. But no answer came. The sister grabbed the girl by the collar and dragged her, an A student, to the principal's office. I was gobsmacked. I wanted to march down to the office myself and protest at how badly this girl was being treated. To this day, I am ashamed that I didn't do just that.

I really did not enjoy how religion played out in my high school years. I had read the entire King James Bible, but no teacher ever wanted to discuss it. Bernie and I managed to sneak a copy of *In God's Name*, a book about a papal assassination, into our rooms and read it in hiding, afraid we'd get in trouble for heresy. And when a high school teacher encouraged me to study religion after I graduated, I actually took the advice. There was still an archaic denominational school system in Newfoundland at the time, and she figured a religious studies degree would help me get a job as a teacher. At Memorial University, I took many courses about the history of Christianity. I finally learned very practical stuff that I'd wanted to know for a long time. Dr. Terry Murphy was one of my favourite religious studies professors. He tried his best to satisfy my curiosity, though my lust for answers was so great that he would limit me to five questions per lecture and kept a tally in the upper right-hand corner of the chalkboard. I'm serious.

I learned that the King James Bible was only one of many versions. I learned that the biggest developments in Christianity and especially in Catholicism were made by older white men in strong political positions. These men were not divinely proclaimed at all, and in university, I found teachers who would actually say so. I consumed the teachings of Martin Luther, and was amazed that any organization would kick out a fella as smart and devout as him, which is exactly what the Catholic Church did in 1521. Finally, I learned that my wee little town, the town where I was born and raised, was split in half primarily because of some decision some dude made a few thousand years previous and which now, no one there remembered.

It will be obvious to those of you familiar with the songs I've written how much my fascination with religion has influenced my work. Religion has made its way into my lyrics and reflects at times a most uncertain fella who even today has more questions than answers. "Consequence Free" speaks of Catholic guilt and the desire to be rid of it forever. I make reference to my "Catholic conscience" and how it would be amazing to be rid of it.

The very discussion of it, of course, explains that there still lies in me strong Catholic strains that I am unable or unwilling to shake. Other songs I've written seem downright atheist. Only a person who claims not to believe in heaven and hell could write "Straight to Hell," a tongue-in-cheek look at a musician who's done a deal with the Devil.

But right around the same time as I wrote that, I also wrote one of the most spiritual songs of my life. "Something Beautiful" was meant as a hug of a song for a friend whose husband died of cancer at a very young age. It speaks of hope for a better time and place to come.

I have always insisted that the "Something Beautiful" I'm referring to is life. I wanted my friend to know that her life was not over and that there was so much beauty ahead for her. But I admit that the implications of some kind of afterlife are undeniable.

Can I still call myself a Catholic? I don't go to mass or participate in any of the sacraments, nor do I think the gentleman in the massive cool house in Rome is any more or less than the rest of us. But can you really be un-Catholicized? I don't know. Where I stand right now, I consider myself a religious free agent. I'm more curious than certain about everything.

Reading this, I would not blame you if you thought I was not a Christian. But I'm not sure that would be accurate either. I'm pretty certain there walked among us a great prophet whose life and teachings are worth abiding. I just have not found a single organized Christian religion that seems to honour that legacy sensibly. I've walked through some of the most beautiful and ornate churches and sat through some of the coolest services in the world, and they have never moved me to be more of a believer in any particular faith.

I would think myself agnostic, but in most cases that is defined as someone who is neither a believer nor a non-believer in an all-powerful god or force. I find the whole notion a little too vague to hang my hat on it.

I confess to spending some time in my early thirties trying to convince myself that I was an all-out atheist. I've read many of the books by some of the foremost atheist thinkers and I acknowledge their logic. It's hard to argue that believing in a virgin birth requires delusion, not faith. But the one thing that keeps me from accepting atheism is the fact that I find faith a necessary and positive human quality. Note I say "faith" and not "Faith." I don't mean Faith in a particular god or creed. Rather, I mean the human quality of faith, of believing in things we cannot see or prove, faith in things we are not certain will ever transpire, yet we pursue them, faith in feats and accomplishments that might never happen.

A mountain climber is not certain he'll be able to make it to the top of the mountain safely. But he believes in himself and has faith that he can accomplish it. Without this faith, would he even try? A shipwreck survivor has no idea if she will be rescued, but despite all evidence to the contrary, her faith propels her to survive each day till the ship sails round the corner. Athletes are moved by faith all the time. Sick people look to faith to help them heal. Inventors have faith that inventions which work in theory will work in practice. This small-f faith is such a big part of human achievement, and it almost never gets addressed in the atheist teachings.

I cannot tell you how often faith has gotten me somewhere I would never have come to without it. I have faith that if I am good to the people I am fortunate enough to meet that they will be good to others, and to me. I have faith that if I am a positive person, it will pay off much more than if I'm not. I have faith that if I give myself fully to every performance, the audience, no matter how big or small, will appreciate it and this will lead to more opportunities for me to work again.

This kind of small-f faith helped me get in Great Big Sea and it is one of the biggest reasons Great Big Sea still sails strong to this day. As I type this paragraph, I am at Pearson Airport passing a twelve-hour delay that was completely caused by the error of an airline employee. Many folks would have freaked out at this employee. I chose not to. Instead, I politely opted to tell her I'd make the most of the delay and use the time to write a chapter for my book even though what I really wanted was to get on a plane with my family.

I have faith that this positive use of a seemingly poor bit of luck will pay off in the end. I have decided that atheism is too cold and lonely a pillow on which to lay my head.

So, I restate my place in the world as a religious free agent with more questions than answers.

I'll keep looking.

Me aboard the Dublin ferry, heading to the Mother Country on my first trip off the island of Newfoundland, around 1988.

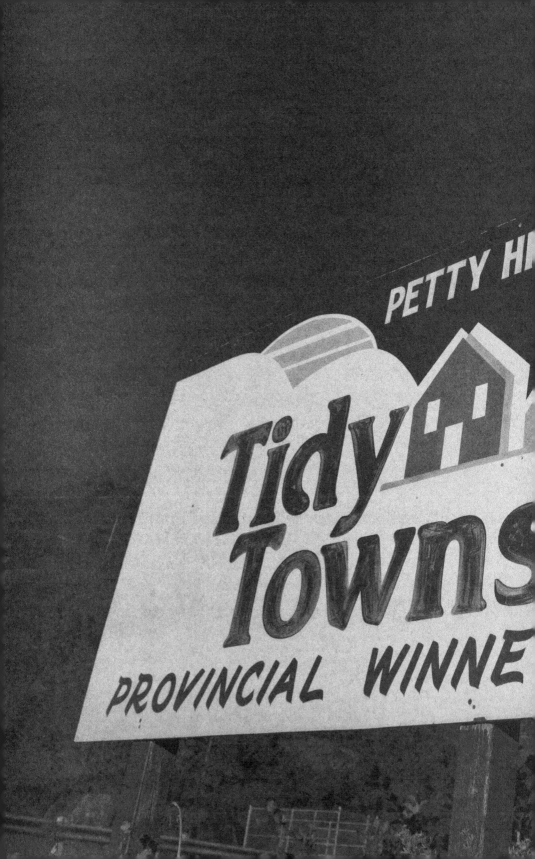

MADDOX COVE

PART 4

2007

CHAPTER 10

The Doyles from Petty Harbour

"You're a Doyle from Petty Harbour. No wonder you can sing and play guitar."

I cannot tell you how often I heard this said to me over the course of my younger life. For generations, the Doyle name in Petty Harbour—all up and down the Southern Shore—has been synonymous with music. The Doyles were a musical crowd, and that was that. If you had the family name and came from Skinner's Hill in Petty Harbour, well, you knew something about songs—for concerts, for masses, for weddings and funerals, and most of all, songs for bands that played in local clubs and at dances.

Many rural Newfoundland towns are rich in musical talent. Newfoundland has been isolated—in many different ways—since the Europeans settled here more than five

Hamming it up at Mom's piano in 1986. In my mind, I can sit at a piano and play sheet music on command. In reality, I cannot.

hundred years ago. Over the centuries, it would have been inevitable that a certain family or group in each community became appreciated for its musical abilities. Perhaps that family, generation after generation, became more musically accomplished. There was probably a favourite musical family or group at the centre of most towns. In Petty Harbour, that family was the Doyles. It still is.

Even as recently as my parents' generation, little radio or television was available anywhere in Newfoundland, so people had to entertain themselves. They memorized and recited stories. They made up skits and plays. They learned to play cheap and simple instruments, like accordions and harmonicas. They wrote and sang their own songs and performed in church halls and kitchens.

You know the tourism myth of the Newfoundland kitchen party and how everyone thinks we Newfoundlanders just sit around a big kitchen, drinking and playing music almost every other night, like it's all a perfect postcard? Well, it was never a postcard for me. It was my reality. It's how I grew up. It's everything I knew.

That's how parties went. That's what my folks did. People came over to our house, we sat around the kitchen or the piano and we sang songs. It wasn't a party unless someone was singing a song. We didn't have a big stereo or many records. Music was homemade.

My mother, my father and just about all my uncles played music probably a hundred days of every year. They got paid a little or a lot for their appearances, depending on where they were playing and for whom, but never once did I hear any Doyle refer to playing music or to rehearsing as "work." Never. Work was work, and music was fun. After all, we were Doyles; we carried music in our blood. Not that this made us professional musicians. To think that way would have been boastful.

When I was starting out with Great Big Sea, my grandmother said it best.

"Alan, honey. Still at the band?"

"Yeah, still at the band, Nan."

"Not working?"

"No. Not working, Nan. Not working."

In our house, there was always at least one guitar, a piano-accordion and, of course, a piano. Mom justified the elaborate expense of almost five hundred dollars on a used

Rick O'Brien

My dad on guitar, my mom on piano-accordion and me on guitar, playing at the wedding of some friends.

piano by charging five dollars per half-hour for lessons to kids from Petty Harbour and the Goulds.

Mom played the organ at masses, weddings and funerals—and at any other social function for the church. To this day, she's an amazing piano-accordion player, and I'm sure it is because of her that I love that instrument so much. Her addition to my dad's and uncles' traditional music collaborations must have made a good thing better. But Mom, of course, did not belong to Petty Harbour. She was from away. And she was considered "the new Doyle" when she married my dad—an honorary and welcome addition to the Doyle family musical tradition.

Like any kid, my ambition when I grew up was to be just like my dad. I wanted to sing like him and play guitar like him. I wanted people to smile when I came in the room the way they did when he announced his arrival with the mock formality of a concert announcer. "Ladies and gentlemen, boys and girls, children of all ages . . . ," he'd say, and then subtly gesture to himself: a man who needed no introduction.

I mimicked the way Dad made foldy bologna sandwiches and I stirred my Tang the way he stirred his tea. And when he would have a drink of rum, I'd sit with him as if in a pub. "Cheers, Alan," he'd say, clinking his rum against my Purity Syrup. Then there was that perfect silence that followed as we'd both enjoy a relaxing sip—it was our moment.

I loved how Dad lit up when his friends came round our house and in no time at all, there'd be rum and whiskey on the table, guitars and accordions in hand and pots of soup on the stove. I would stay awake as long as I could and wonder how he knew so many songs and how one seemed to organically lead to the other.

Dad taught himself to play guitar as a teenager, as did a few of his six brothers. I undoubtedly inherited my love of singing from my father. We also share the unrelenting need to have everyone in a room listening to us and looking at us—preferably at the same time. Neither of us is that fussy on how we accomplish this goal, though doing it

Me and Dad in 2000.

with a song is our preference. Anything from a rousing party tune that gets everyone clapping and singing along, to a mournful ballad that brings a tear to every eye, to a long and exaggerated story that is either tragic or hilarious and may or may not have its basis in fact—if there's a way we can call attention to ourselves, we'll do it. And if it's through music, even better.

My uncles aren't that different. They all sing really well, and when Dad and my uncle Ronnie started their band, they each found their place in it. My uncle Leonard quickly became the instrumentalist of the family, and by the time he was twenty, he could play just about anything with strings on it. He remains one of my favourite guitarists. I've known dozens of more dexterous and technical players, but no one plays a song quite like Leonard. It's kind of like the guitar becomes a different instrument with each song he plays. Sometimes it's a chunky, percussive rhythm instrument, other times more like an Irish harp accompanying a ballad, other times a biting melody instrument that takes the lead solos. My uncle Paul has been writing lyrics for as long as anyone can remember. There are others, my uncles Dennis and Brian, along with their first cousins Gerry, Stan and John Doyle, who grew up next door to us on Skinner's Hill. They all sang or played instruments. A generation before that were two brothers, Joseph and my grandfather, Bernard Doyle, who were well-known singers and storytellers.

In their late teens, my dad and a few of his brothers got on the radio and TV.

On set at the CBC show *All Around the Circle*, my dad's band, the Boys from Petty Harbour. *Back row, left to right*: Uncle Jimmy, Jim Kennedy, Uncle Ronnie, Michael Keiley. *Front row, left to right*: Uncle Leonard, Dad, Jim Keiley, John Doyle (Dad's cousin).

They were asked by the CBC to be recurring guests on *All Around the Circle*, a variety show. They sang Irish drinking songs and ballads, and to Celtic-up the show, they borrowed a banjo. For their first appearance, my uncle Leonard learned to play that banjo on the thirty-minute drive to St. John's. The Boys from Petty Harbour, as this group was known, played together for many years, and still do, in various incarnations.

Just after I was born, in the dying days of the sixties, my uncles Ronnie and Leonard started playing less traditional music and more electric rock 'n' roll and country. My father and Uncle Jimmy were not inclined to be in a rock 'n' roll band, so they did not join Ronnie and Leonard. The band was known first as the Sandelles, then as the Ringdelles, and then as Medicine Jar. There were other names, too. But to me, from the moment I was old enough to know anything, I called them Uncle Ronnie's Band.

Uncle Ronnie's Band often practised across the dirt road from our house in my grandparents' basement. Within earshot of our house, there was always someone learning some new song or tuning a guitar or hauling drums and amps into a station wagon. As an eight-year-old kid, I would watch my uncles loading and unloading equipment before and after gigs. I could often hear them jamming across the dirt road and I'd poke one of Dad's bent screwdrivers between the studs of our unfinished porch to serve as my microphone. From there, I strummed my imaginary guitar and sang along with Uncle Ronnie's Band into the handle of the worn-out screwdriver.

I would listen to rehearsals but also to all the conversation about the gig the night before or the one about to come. About the girls who might be there. About the fights that might happen if the dodgy club owner did not pay them. At three or four in the morning, I'd wake up to the sound of Uncle Leonard getting out of a car and chatting with whoever had dropped him off after a gig. Often, the driver would be some gal he'd cajoled into chauffeuring him all the way down the Southern Shore. I'd kneel up on my bed and peek through the window in hopes of catching Uncle Leonard smooching with some missus.

One Saturday night, after a week of being as good as an eleven-year-old kid trying to stay on Santa's "nice list" can be, Dad let me stay awake long enough for a special treat. He borrowed a car and we drove to the Goulds and parked right under the side window of the Crystal Palace bar, where Uncle Ronnie's Band was about to start the first set. I stood on the hood of the car and watched through the window as the band played about a dozen songs. The dance floor filled the moment they began and my view became obscured by the good times, but I saw what I needed to see and heard what I needed to hear. It was a window to my own Narnia.

Occasionally, like on a Sunday afternoon, my father would go with the band after they had played at the Crystal, or at Darby's in Witless Bay, or at the Station Lounge in St. John's over the weekend. They'd be heading back there to get their gear. I begged to go with them every time and eventually they started letting me tag along.

I remember being just under ten years old, walking into the dim and dingy Crystal Palace on a Sunday afternoon. The place was a mess. It had obviously not been cleaned from the night before. There were beer bottles everywhere, ashes and cigarette butts from wall to wall. A bloodstain smeared the wall near the men's washroom. Uncle Ronnie said there had been "quite a racket" the night before.

On stage, I recognized Uncle Ronnie's silver Ludwig drums, the sticks laid on the snare as if he'd finished playing five minutes earlier. A dozen empty glasses were scattered around the kit. Uncle Leonard's black and white Fender Stratocaster rested against his Fender Super Reverb amp, a burnt-to-the-butt cigarette jammed under the strings at the headstock. A rat's nest of cables twisted and knotted into a ball beside the microphone stand. The place stank of stale beer, cigarette smoke and ashes and sweat.

It was amazing.

The tired, dirty-looking fella that let us in asked Dad and Ronnie if they wanted beer, and of course they did. After all, it was well after 1 p.m. They went straight to the bar, elbows perched on the edge, and they started chatting. I went directly to the stage and sat behind Uncle Ronnie's drums. I picked up the sticks just to feel them in my hands. I was surprised how far I had to reach to get my foot on the bass drum and hi-hat pedals. I pushed my right foot to the floor. The kick-drum beater made a soft and plush sound when it made contact with the bass-drum skin. I pushed my left foot down and yelped a little as my left pinky got caught between the closing hi-hat cymbals. I hit them gently with one of the sticks as I slowly pressed and released my left foot on the pedal. I had always assumed the "sock cymbals," as Uncle Ronnie called them, made only two sounds—the tight *tick tick tick* when they were closed and the *ping* when they were loose and apart. But I discovered I could get a whole variety of sounds in between the two extremes—that *swoosh* sound, like in Eagles songs, that hard clang like in Led Zeppelin. If I hit them while they were closed and opened them right after contact, that was disco. I spent a lot of time discovering those hi-hats while the grown-ups drank beer at the bar.

At one point, I hit the snare drum and nearly scared the crap out of myself, it was that loud. Uncle Ronnie turned my way and smiled. "Give it a good whack, b'y," he said. I did. Wow. It amazed me then and still does to this day how loud a snare drum is. I hit the toms a few times, but they were nothing like the snare. I crashed the crash cymbal and dug it, but nowhere near as much as Ronnie's ride cymbal. His ride cymbal had holes punched in the metal and he had steel rivets bent in from one side to the other. With every touch, each rivet rattled and shimmered like rainfall. I've done dozens of recording sessions with hired professional drummers, and I always ask them to bring a rivet cymbal. They always say yes and then show up with some bathtub plug chain and try to convince me it sounds the same as rivets. (Kris MacFarlane, Great Big Sea's drummer and my drummer of choice for over a decade, had Sabian build me two rivet cymbals so I'd always have one on hand, saving everyone a pile of grief.) But there is no other sound on earth like the sound of Uncle Ronnie's ride cymbal at two in the afternoon at the Crystal Palace. I was imprinted by sound on that day, on that stage, and for better or worse, I've been trying to find the same sound and feeling ever since.

After a good wank at the drum kit, I turned to the next thing I saw on that stage: Uncle Leonard's Strat. I put the strap over my shoulder and it hung so low on me that it almost hit the floor. I flicked on the amp and sat on it. I turned the volume up and played a D chord, as it was the only one I was sure how to play. The guitar must have been in tune, as it sounded pretty good. I turned it up a bit more and it sounded even better. I turned it up the whole way and it rang like rock 'n' roll and started to feedback a tiny bit as it faded away. I wanted that guitar more than anything I'd ever held in my life at that point.

(I kept my eyes on that guitar for years. My uncle sold it to a bandmate, and a few years later, when I was fifteen, I walked up to this fella and said, "I want that guitar."

("You can have it for four hundred, if you've got the cash now."

(I did not have the cash. But a few weeks later, I borrowed enough to buy it. A schoolteacher of mine, who always saw more in me than I did, loaned me the money. I paid her back in a few months. I remain grateful to her for her confidence in me. That guitar has paid for itself a hundred times over. It got me through hundreds of amateur and semi-professional gigs. Out of honour, I insisted that guitar make it onto my first professional recording. There's an electric guitar solo on "Drunken Sailor" on the first GBS album. The guitar you hear is Uncle Leonard's black and white Strat.)

I put the Strat back on its stand and completed my tour of the Crystal Palace stage. I walked up to the lead microphone.

Uncle Leonard's 1972 Fender Strat, easily the coolest instrument in history.

It was way too high for me, so I lowered it a little. I closed my eyes and pressed my lips to the rusty grille. The jagged edges pinched my lips.

It hurt a bit. And I loved it.

I loved the smell of every breath of the night before that still lived on it. It tasted like songs. I opened my eyes and looked over my nose and down the microphone ball to where the silver connector joined the mic to the cable. Past that, I saw the simple dance floor, but I suppose I saw much more than that. I saw a dance floor where dudes might nod to you after the guitar solo. Where girls would shout out loud for you to keep playing or sneak a glance at you over the shoulders of their dance partners. Where a week of working like a dog was erased by the right song at the right time with the right person. A place where a band played and people loved it. A magical place. A band needs a crowd and a crowd needs a band. This is where the two met.

I remember deciding then that I wanted to sing, which I'd kind of always done, but more importantly, I wanted to play guitar. Bernie also remembers me making such a decision. I took to it partly because I saw early signs that I might be able do this one thing better than him. You see, he was quicker, stronger, faster and smarter than me at everything, the way that older brothers often are—a better singer, better at sports, better at fighting, better at getting girls—and he knew more about music by the age of thirteen than I do now. When we both started noodling with the guitar at around ten or eleven years old, I quickly discovered I had an aptitude for it that he did not. Of course, even as

BERRY PICKING TIME

"Berry Picking Time," from our self-titled debut album *Great Big Sea*, remains a popular request at concerts and a bit of a mystery.

While collecting songs for our very first album, I suggested "Berry Picking Time" to Séan, Bob and Darrell. They loved its quaint message but also its authenticity. My grandfather Bern Doyle used to sing it at kitchen parties when I was a kid. It is a courting song that made my grandmother Frances glow and even blush on occasion when Bern sang it and turned her way:

> *We were picking berries at Old Aunt Mary's*
> *When I picked a blushing bride.*
> *As we strolled home together, I just wondered whether*
> *I could win you forever if I tried.*
> *Then at love's suggestion, I popped the question,*
> *And asked you to be mine.*
> *By your kisses I knew, you'd picked me and I'd picked you,*
> *At berry picking time.*

"Berry Picking Time" was known to us for years as a Petty Harbour song. It was a song that lived only in the Doyle family. We could find no other singers outside of Petty Harbour who knew the song. In even the most studious traditional music circles in Newfoundland, I could still find no one who knew its origin. So how did my grandfather, and before him my great-grandfather, come to know this song?

A clue came to me years later when a friend sent me a YouTube link of some country gent from the United States singing the song in the 1950s, but his song was a verse shorter and not the same melody. This confirmed that the song had been passed down from somewhere. I wonder if it was perhaps an old English or Irish song that made its way into American country. Is it possible that my great-grandfather learned it from a Yankee sailor? Or perhaps my grandfather heard it more recently on the radio and decided to try it out himself? No one seems to know the answers, and so, like so many things in Petty Harbour, the mystery remains alongside the tradition.

Before we were Great Big Sea, we were Best Kind. This shot was taken in 1993. Darrell (*left*), me (*middle*), Séan (*right*).

I progressed with the guitar, Bernie was still the one who could sing like a bird.

One afternoon after school when my brother was not home, I snuck Dad's guitar and the big Irish songbook from Mom's piano bench and stole away up to the bathroom. (It had the only door in the house that locked.) By even that young age, I already knew the lyrics to dozens of songs. I learned songs the way a circus kid learns to juggle. I didn't know how I knew them; I just did. It always surprised me at school that not everyone could sing traditional songs like "Rattlin' Bog." I knew that song as well as the other kids knew "Happy Birthday."

In the bathroom with the songbook and the guitar, I opened the book at random and it fell to a page in the middle—"I'll Take You Home Again, Kathleen." I knew how to sing that song, so the guitar chords and melody made sense. I reviewed the chord names and shapes. I knew how to play D and G but not A. That was a tough one, as you had to cover three strings right next to each other in the same fret. Even as a kid, my fingers would not fit. I quickly figured a way to get two strings under one finger. I still play A that way—with two fingers.

Once I was sure about the chord shapes, I strummed the guitar and sang the melody with the chord names inserted into the lyrics. I still do this today to teach people the chords of a song:

> I'll D you G again, Kathleen,
> To A the air is fresh and D . . .

And on it went for a few weeks. I'd sneak away and secretly learn an Irish song or two from that book. I remember learning "When Irish Eyes Are Smiling" and "The Green, Green Grass of Home."

After a month or so, at one of Mom and Dad's kitchen parties, I waited for my chance. It was late, around ten, and Mom was about to send us kids to bed. She'd asked us to go up and get ready, and I knew I could either chicken out now or give it a try.

"Let me play a song first," I said.

"What?" Mom asked. "You can play a song by yourself, can you?" She acted surprised for my benefit, I'm sure, as she would have known full well what I'd been sneaking off to do. Our house was very small, after all.

"Oh sweet Jesus, another one stung with the bug," my aunt Jackie said, mock-rolling her eyes at the thought of yet another Doyle fighting for a concert slot.

Dad had a funny look on his face, but said, "Go on, b'y, have a go." He passed me his guitar and I sat next to him. I made my way through "I'll Take You Home Again, Kathleen."

I'd be lying if I said I blew the place away, because I didn't. I was nowhere near the strongest singer in the room, even amongst the kids. But the fact that I could get through a tune accompanying myself on guitar was good enough.

"Good boy," Mom said. "Now off to bed."

"Oh my lord, Jean. Look at that," one of my aunts said. "Let the boy stay up if he's gonna sing songs."

I did not fully realize it at the time, but I was experiencing something that has fuelled musicians for centuries: Special

Attention. Sing songs for people, and you'll get away with stuff that most others don't. That bedtime extension was the first time I experienced the power of being a musician.

If this was an indication of what playing a song could get a boy, I wanted more of it. Heck, I wanted to be in a band! And of course, being a Doyle and living in Petty Harbour, there was a band really handy.

I knew that I'd have to get a hell of a lot better than I was if I was going to make it into a real band. So I started learning a new chord here and there. I went through just about every song in *The Irish Song Book* and asked for another for my eleventh or twelfth birthday. Dad agreed to take me to town to buy one. We did not own a car, so he borrowed one from my uncle and we drove to O'Brien's Music Store in St. John's.

O'Brien's sits on Water Street. It claims to be the oldest business on the oldest street in North America. I'd seen O'Brien's before when I'd been with my mom shopping for clothes, but I had never gone in there. I was trying to play it cool, but I was pretty excited.

Dad parked my uncle's car and we walked into O'Brien's. The quaint little store had a bell that rang when you entered. It was a long, narrow shop with a display window featuring accordions, whistles, mandolins and various other traditional Celtic instruments. One wall was lined with fiddles and mandolins and guitars—all brand-new instruments with the tags still on them. There were a few brand names I recognized, Yamaha and Fender like I saw on TV. It was an amazing feeling to just be in that shop, where so much cool stuff hung from the walls and so many St. John's musicians must have stood.

Beneath the instruments was a long rack of records and songbooks. Along the other side, the high wall was filled with strings and capos and picks and various other bits and bobs. As soon as I was inside the door and Dad made his way in, the older, well-coiffed gentleman behind the counter said, "Hello, Tom Doyle. How're things in Petty Harbour?"

"Best kind, b'y," Dad replied and after a few more pleasantries said, "This is my little fella, Alan. He plays the guitar now, too."

"Sure you knows he do. He's a Doyle from Petty Harbour," the man said. "And what are you interested in playing, son?"

I told him I wanted a book of rock 'n' roll songs.

"Well, we don't got that sort of book here. We got lots of good Irish and country ones, though."

"He's after learning all the songs in the *Irish Book* I got. He wants something different now, I think."

"Not to worry. You and your father should probably just take a wee stroll down Water Street to Hutton's Music. You'll find what you need there. But before you goes, take a couple of O'Brien's guitar picks with you. God knows I'll see you again."

He was right, too. I've been going to that store for over thirty years. It remains one of my favourite stops on Water Street.

We strolled past the banks and shops, all busy with lines of people. Hutton's was a slightly bigger place with a larger display window and electric guitars in the display case. There was a younger man, probably in his late twenties, behind the counter. I recognized him from music videos on TV. His hair was long and unkempt. He looked like he'd had maybe two hours sleep the night before. This place was way more rock 'n' roll than O'Brien's. I was in awe.

"Hey, man," the guy behind the counter said. "You look like a fella who needs a brand-new electric guitar. I've got the one for you right here," and once he'd started talking, he didn't stop. He went on a mile a minute, until Dad finally cut him off and explained that I wanted a rock 'n' roll songbook.

While my dad wandered the store, the guy picked out a big book called *The Pop Song Book* and explained that it had a few hundred songs in it, most of them with really easy chords. He picked out a few other books as well. Then he looked at me and asked where I was from.

"Petty Harbour," I said.

"Oh! You must be a Doyle. That's your dad, right? Yeah, man, I thought I recognized him from *All Around the Circle*. So Leonard is your uncle?"

"Yeah," I said.

"Well, just stay close to your uncle and you'll learn a lot more from him than you will from any book. But these will get you going. Have fun playing. That's the main thing, man." He winked. Easily the coolest person I'd ever met in my life.

I took *The Pop Song Book* home, and I'm pretty sure I learned every song in it. The Eagles, Rolling Stones, Elvis Presley, Joni Mitchell, John Denver. In the weeks and months to follow, I was given used copies of songbooks by the Beatles,

Cat Stevens and Kris Kristofferson. For almost two years, I learned a song a day. By the time I was thirteen, I could sit at a party with adults and play along with every song they were playing. I'd try to sit close to my uncle Leonard, because he always played the chords differently than they told you to in the books. He could play A and D and E the way Chuck Berry did in "Johnny B. Goode," with the *wuncka chunka wuncka chunka* parts added to the basic chords. The rhythm was awesome.

Watching Uncle Leonard, I learned to play bar chords, where you put one finger across the entire fretboard and use your remaining three to make the chord shapes. I learned that if you make one shape, like an E, with your last three fingers, you could just slide that shape up the neck with a finger bar behind it and play any major chord without changing finger shapes. Same was true for E minor. Also for A and A minor. The progression of E and A major and minor bar chords is one of the most prevalent things you'll notice in just about any rock 'n' roll or country guitar song. Every band, from the Beatles to AC/DC to Chuck Berry to George Jones, uses this guitar-playing shortcut. Most folks have to take lessons for quite a while to get this trick. I was on to it in my living room before I was a teenager.

I played on the odd concert with my brother. Even with me progressing at guitar and a few other instruments, Bernie was the singing star, and I'd support his lead with harmony. We'd sing "The Boxer" or "Kodachrome," with him as Simon and me as Garfunkel. He could flatten a place with his versions of songs by Michael Martin Murphey, John Denver and Stan Rogers. It was great fun to be a part of the community concerts in Petty Harbour. Sometimes I'd accompany the other singers along with my uncle Leonard on guitar or Mom on accordion. Other times, I'd be the lead singer and someone else would be the accompanist. There were usually three community concerts a year—for Christmas, St. Patrick's Day and Petty Harbour Days in the summer, when we'd hold an outdoor fair on the softball field and thousands would come over a weekend. For those events, I'd have to learn at least two new songs really well, so by the time I was around fourteen years old, I'd already sung a dozen or more tunes in front of an audience. Not many people that age have so many stage appearances under their belts. It was a blast, but I needed a musical kick in the pants.

And that's when a lucky break fell into my lap. Call it luck, timing or maybe even being ready for a break when it knocks on the door. It was announced one Sunday while I was serving mass that one of the choir ladies was breaking off from the main group to start a folk choir that would sing for a new Saturday afternoon mass. The choir would not use the organ as accompaniment, but rather the guitar and other folksier instruments. The singers would concentrate on newer hymns that were not necessarily even found in the *Catholic Book of Worship*. Younger people were encouraged to enter the choir.

I can't recall the rest of that mass. I kept thinking about this being my ticket off the altar and my chance to attend Saturday afternoon masses and sleep in on Sundays. Moreover, maybe I'd have a chance to sing and play guitar, and in

The hand program from one of the many community concerts in Petty Harbour.
Count the Doyles on the bill. My uncle Leonard and/or Ronnie would most likely have
accompanied all players as well, though they're not listed on the program.

front of an audience, no less. I even thought I might learn a
thing or two. I told Mom and Dad at Sunday supper that I
wanted in.

"Well, honey, I think folk mass is a grand idea," Mom
said. "Time for you to get off the altar now and let the younger
fellas serve."

"You can use my guitar, but it's got no case," Dad said.
"You'll have to carry it to practice in a garbage bag."

So I was set. I had no idea what a fantastic education I
was about to get. Kathy Hanlon was in charge of folk mass,

and she was an excellent teacher. She had quite a bit of experience with music theory and choir directing and was excited that another guitar player wanted to join. Over the course of the next year or so, I learned some of the most valuable musical lessons I've ever learned.

As a singer, I learned that my natural voice is a little lower in register and most written keys for an average folk or pop song are too high for me to sing without straining. Kathy encouraged me to sing melody for the lower parts, and when the melody got too high for me to sing, she'd let me switch to a lower harmony in my register. In some cases, Kathy sang a higher harmony for the choruses and let me sing a lower one while the rest of the choir sang melody. Without even knowing it, I was learning to map and sing three-part harmony.

Kathy also taught me how to transpose keys to better suit my vocal range. Every now and again, if I was to sing lead on a hymn, we would transpose it down a step or two to suit my voice. A song that was written to be sung in the key of B-flat would be transposed down a step and a half for me to sing in G. Kathy and I would then change the guitar chords as required. B-flat became G, E-flat became C, F became D, G minor became E minor and so on. This made such clear sense to me that after only a few weeks, I could do the transposition without writing it down.

For the non-musicians reading, I cannot stress how important it is to learn your vocal register, especially at such a young age. Likewise, as an accompanist, it is important to be able to quickly transpose your accompanying chords to whatever key best suits the singer. I had almost accidentally learned two of the most important musical lessons by the time I was a young teen.

I have worked on hundreds of songs since then as a writer, singer, player and producer—some with Great Big Sea, some on my own and with other younger and older singers alike. In every case, one of the first considerations is choosing the best key for the vocal range of the singer. If the tune is gentle and simple, should it be sung in the part of the singer's voice that sounds most relaxed and soothing? If it is a rocker of a tune, should it stretch the limits of the singer's upper register to increase intensity? Most people don't learn this lesson until they are well into their adult lives (if ever), and I learned it almost by osmosis as a fourteen-year-old.

I learned other cool tricks from Kathy Hanlon, too. She could play all the regular guitar chords that my father could play, but she also knew the ones that Dad often skipped. She encouraged me to hear the difference between a minor chord and a minor seventh chord—in the key of G, for example, how an A minor 7 led to D so much nicer than a regular A minor; how the D7 anticipated the G far more than a regular D; how the walk up from G to A minor to B minor 7 to C made reaching the D so exciting.

Kathy showed me that Uncle Leonard's bar chord trick worked not only for E and A shapes but for any shape you could manage. All of a sudden, F major 7 could become G major 7 and A and so on, just by moving up the neck of the guitar with your finger bar. She also showed me you did not always need to use a full finger bar. Guitarists: give this a try. Play an A chord with your last two fingers, then start sliding it up the neck, with a finger bar a couple of frets behind. Eventually, you'll get to where your finger bar is on fret 7. That A shape now makes an E chord. Here's the cool trick: take your full bar off and just play the A string in the seventh fret with your index finger. It makes the coolest E chord you've ever heard. I use this trick constantly.

Kathy and I started playing songs at different capo positions, so we were playing the same song in the same key with the same chord sounds, but with completely different chord finger shapes and voicings. For example, in the key of G, I would play with no capo and play the finger shapes of G, C, D, E minor while Kathy would put a capo on the fifth fret and play the finger shapes of D, G, A and B minor. The harmony was amazing.

This alternating capo positioning would become the rhythmic core of many Great Big Sea songs. When Séan and I play guitar in a song, I usually play a lower voicing and shape, while he capos up the neck for a higher voicing. For example, if you listen carefully in "When I'm Up," you'll hear me playing open C, F, G and A minor chords. You'll also hear Séan play in a capo five-position using G, C, D and E minor chords.

While practising for folk mass, I also learned that not everyone sang the same way. Listening to the various singers in the choir, I noticed how some had awesome pitch, while others had a broader range. Some sang louder; others softer. Most of the guys had to sing louder to sing higher, while the girls seemed to sing quieter when they went high.

Here I am, Montreal Canadiens colours ablaze, trying my best to
be the centre of attention at a gathering of high school friends at
a cabin. I'm sure I was thinking, "I bet that girl on the couch to my
left is super impressed by this bar chord."

I played Dad's Marlin guitar for most of the first year or
so that I was in the folk mass. It seemed a very uncool guitar. I walked over Skinner's Hill to folk mass practice with
the Marlin wrapped in a black garbage bag, half the neck
and headstock sticking out. Dad's Marlin was nothing like
the Martin guitar Tommy Hunter played on TV, which, of
course, we couldn't afford. For kicks one night after watching
The Tommy Hunter Show, me and Dad stuck a pencil between
the D and G strings of his guitar and crossed the *l* in "Marlin"
to make it look like a *t*.

Fall came, and it was approaching the time when kids start putting together Christmas lists. I wanted a guitar case for the Marlin so I'd look more like a pro walking up and down the hill. Mom and Dad thought a guitar case was in the price range that Santa could afford—happy news for me. I knew most of the places Santa hid gifts in my house, so I started searching whenever no one was around. Lo and behold, under my parents' bed was a shiny black cardboard guitar case. I was delighted. I was going to look like Bruce Springsteen. Awesome.

When Christmas morning came around, I'd already rehearsed my surprised look of gratitude. I walked downstairs, saw the case under the tree and said, "Thanks, Santa! A guitar case. Just what I wanted."

"Open it," Dad said.

"What?"

"Open the case," Mom echoed.

I walked over to it and unlatched the three brass buckles. I lifted the top and inside lay a brand-new six-string guitar, "Citation" written in clever letters across the tapered headstock.

"Santa figured you should have a guitar of your own," Dad said with a smile. "And God knows I never gets to play mine anymore."

I could not believe it. "It's mine? My own guitar?"

I lifted it out of the case and strummed it, and it was every bit as good as Dad's Marlin, maybe even a bit better. I looked around at my brother and sisters, who all seemed to know that in the world of Christmas gifts, this was a big one. This was way more expensive than any of the other gifts but also the one thing that would be more appreciated than anything else under the tree. My brother and sisters, in their usual way, were so happy for me. They had this look on their faces like they'd just seen a really cool thing: a boy getting his first guitar.

I played that guitar until the brown fingerboard turned white. Grooves formed in the first three or four frets where I beat the wood back. I must have played ten thousand songs on that guitar. It still hangs on the wall of my studio.

My first guitar, a Citation. Check out the wear on
the neck and frets. I played it till my fingers bled.

CHAPTER 11

First Attempt

When I was in Grade 8, I was one of two goalies in the Goulds Minor Hockey League. I had saved up my tongue-cutting money and paid for the registration myself. I knew from day one that I wanted to be the goalie, but Dad was worried that we could never afford the equipment. As luck turned out, the league owned goalie gear, so we did not have to pay that extra expense. At the first skate of the first season, I asked if I could be goalie, and I have never played a single game in any other position.

I wanted to be like Ken Dryden of my beloved Montreal Canadiens. He seemed different from all the other players, even different from all of the other goalies. He was tall, like a basketball player. He was the only English guy who taught himself to speak French. Moreover, he spoke eloquently

The Goulds Minor Hockey Midgets, with me (the largest Midget) in the middle.

about things other than "giving the game 110 percent" and "getting pucks to the net." And when he talked about his team, it was like he was talking about his family. He acknowledged the team's strengths, knew they had a dozen or more superstars, but he was humble enough to concede that the only way they'd ever win was by playing as a team. Then, Dryden did the unthinkable. He quit the NHL to go back to school to finish his law degree. Once finished, he did the unthinkable again. He came back to the NHL and won the Cup a few more times. He was incredible. He was my idol. He still is.

After I started playing goalie, I came to love the position for its unique vantage point of the game. I was in the game, but I could also see it as an outsider, too. To this day, my undiagnosed ADHD runs my life. I am a scatterbrain at the best of times, as easily distracted by squirrels as by bright lights. But when I'm playing goal, I'm totally focused. When a player is approaching and about to shoot, the rest of the world vanishes.

I love hockey now and I loved it in Grade 8 as a goalie for the Goulds team. As luck would have it, hockey led me to one of my earliest and most valued musical friends. He was a goalie, too, a new kid who had just moved to the Goulds from Bell Island. Greg Hawco was his name. He was a strange dude. He would sit next to me on the bench and talk endlessly about the straps of his goalie pads or the laces of his gloves. I did not know it at the time, but I was meeting my first real gear pig.

After a few weeks, I told him I played guitar and was even hoping to get gigs with my uncle Ronnie's band. He looked at me wide-eyed. "I play the drums, you know."

"Really?" I said.

"Yeah. It would be cool if we jammed," said Greg.

From that point on, instead of him talking about the merits of one kind of goalie pad over another, he talked about music, drum gear, guitars and Queen. Yes, Queen, the band. Greg was obsessed with Queen. How Queen was easily the greatest band in the history of music. How they were more orchestral and complex than the Beatles. How they were way more lyrically profound than Bon Jovi or Poison. How Freddie Mercury was the greatest front man and rock singer of all time.

"I like John Denver and Def Leppard," I said. Hawco looked hugely disappointed and paused for a moment. Then he carried on about how Zeppelin and the Doors had a lot more to offer than Ratt.

The next fall, I was going into Grade 9, which meant moving from St. Edward's elementary school in Petty Harbour to St. Kevin's High School in the Goulds. I couldn't have been happier. I was going to school in a town that was not my own, with new people. I knew a few of the fellas in the ninth grade already. Greg Hawco had introduced me to Brian Foley, whose dad was a well-known singer in and around the Goulds. Brian was a great guitar player and, more important, he was willing to play bass. (That's how most bass players are born—by playing guitar first and then turning to bass after.) We three very quickly connected and decided we should start a band. The school band room had a drum set as well as a bass guitar and amp. I borrowed an electric guitar and amp from a guy in Grade 10 who never played it. I could not believe such a thing—to have a piece of equipment like that and not use it.

We asked our music teacher to let us stay after school one day to jam. We had no microphones, but that was not about to stop us. I set the up drums and the amps on opposite sides. I turned them up as loud as they could suffer. After some fussing about, I announced, "I can sing and play 'Summer of '69,' by Bryan Adams."

"Nah," said Brian Foley. "Let's do 'Living After Midnight,' by Judas Priest."

"Queen," Hawco demanded, not even bothering to name a specific song.

"I can't sing their songs," I admitted sheepishly.

"Fine," Hawco said. "Adams it is."

I did not realize the lesson I'd just learned: that in a band, the singer just about always gets what he wants.

We launched in and I gave "Summer of '69" a go. I yelled as loud as I could over the blaring bass and guitar amps. But then the drums kicked in and I was drowned out by Greg's bashing. We jammed that one tune for about two hours—until the school janitor finally kicked us out. When I hitchhiked home that day, my ears were ringing with a high-pitched whistle. But still, I could not wipe the smile off my face.

As cool as that jam was, Brian, Hawco and I knew that if we were going to get serious, we needed a microphone. Brian's dad had a small vocal PA in his garden shed.

"You b'ys clean the junk outta the shed and you're welcome to jam in there," his dad offered.

Brian and I cleaned it out the very next day. Greg was late . . . but that's a drummer for you. Drummers and tardiness go hand in hand. (The stereotype is almost always accurate. Sorry to you most rare punctual drummers out there.)

We cleared a two-by-twelve space, figuring that should do it. The next day, a Friday, we begged Mr. Dave Brown, our music teacher, to let us take the drum kit and bass rig home for the weekend.

"You've got to promise me you'll return it in the same condition. Don't blow my speakers." He could not have been more delighted we wanted to start a band.

"Mr. Brown, when this drum kit comes back, it will be so shiny that you won't recognize it," I assured him. He may or may not have believed me.

That Saturday, we met early at Brian's and set up the drums, amps and one microphone. (When I say "we," I mean me and Brian. See above note about drummers.)

We had no microphone stand, so we jammed a hockey stick into a bucket of rocks and duct-taped the mic to the blade. By the time Greg showed up, we were ready to go. I'd say we jammed for six or eight hours that day and never got through a full song. We did what every young band should. We sucked. It was wonderful. That's how you learn who should play what instruments, what songs to sing and what ones to skip. I always tell young bands, "Don't be afraid to suck in rehearsal." It's the most fun path to discovery.

We fantasized about doing gigs and how one day we'd have a van with all our gear and we'd drive to St. John's to play a club. We switched instruments and argued and fought over who was speeding up and who was playing the wrong part. Just like a real band. It was as cool a day as I've ever had.

After a few of those weekend jams, we set our sights on the St. Kevin's Christmas concert. We figured we could persuade the powers that be to let us play a couple of tunes. Brian was making waves that he should play guitar sometimes and we should get another bass player. Bern was keeping a keen eye on what we were up to, and I asked him if he'd play bass with us at the concert. He agreed but made sure we knew he didn't want to be in the band full-time. That was good enough for us. The gig was booked.

We were to play two songs at the concert—"Summer of '69" and "Johnny B. Goode." I would sing, and Brian and I would play guitar. Greg would drum and Bern would play bass. We rehearsed a few more times in Brian's shed. But winter was coming and it was getting really cold in there. We needed a heat source or we'd be done for the winter.

"Hey, guys. What about this?" I said. I pointed out a coal barbecue in the corner, and beside it, a fresh bag of coals.

The guys looked at the barbecue and then back at me. "Good idea," they said.

For the next few jams, we coughed out songs through thick black barbecue smoke. One day, Brian's dad came home from work early, saw smoke billowing out of the shed and came running over.

"What in the Christ are ye doing?"

We stared blankly. What did he mean?

"Are ye trying to suffocate yourselves?!"

Still nothing but blank stares.

And so, Brian's dad got us a kerosene heater. Admittedly, it burned a whole lot cleaner than the barbecue and kept us warmer, too.

After a few more jams, we were getting the tunes down. Greg started counting us in by clicking his sticks instead of shouting, "One, two, three, four." Our solos were starting and finishing at the right times. We were becoming a band. But we were a band without a name. We argued for a few days over what the band name could be. I think the only band all three of us liked was Van Halen, so we decided our band name should have three syllables and be two words.

"What about 'First Attempt'?" I asked. I figured we may as well let people know that we were new, and if the tunes sucked, maybe they'd cut us some slack.

"Stupid," said Brian.

"Not great," said Hawco.

But no one had a better idea. (This, it turns out, is how almost every single band in history gets named—by default.) So for the Christmas concert gig, Brian and I got a black sheet of cardboard and cut a stylized "F.A." into it, mimicking the famous Van Halen "VH." We stuck the cardboard to the outer drumhead of Greg's bass drum. At least we all agreed on one thing: that drumhead looked incredible.

Later, Brian's parents came in.

"F.A.?" Brian's dad asked. "What's that stand for, F—k Aff?" Brian's mom clipped her husband in the head.

The day of the gig, we went to school early. By "we," I mean Brian and me. We decided that we needed a drum riser that looked more like Alex Van Halen's in Van Halen. From the school cafeteria, we nabbed two long tables with pressboard tops and placed them side by each in the middle of the gym stage. We took the newly adorned F.A. bass drum and placed it up there. We walked to the back of the gym to survey our work.

Unprompted and in perfect unison, we both said, "Deadly."

We took our time setting up our amps on chairs so they looked bigger and higher, like Marshall stacks. We duct-taped our cables and distortion pedals to the stage floor and tried to decide if the mic stands should be straight up and down like Eddie Van Halen's or turned at a sharp right angle like Brian May's from Queen. We jigged and rejigged gear right until it was time to open the doors.

When our time came to do our tunes, we set up behind the curtain and Greg gave a few *thump thumps* on the bass drum. The two tables that hoisted his kit were starting to drift apart. Hmm. Perhaps we should have lashed them together. We asked one of the bigger fellas on the side of the stage to crawl under the tables and hold them together as we played.

"Um . . . sure," the guy said. It surprised me then and thrills me still: it is amazing what the most unlikely folks will do to help out a band.

Dawn, the most awesome MC, took the stage. "And now, ladies and gentlemen," she began, "you are about to hear St. Kevin's answer to the Stones, the Beatles and the Who. Please welcome First Attempt!"

The crowd cheered louder than they had for any other act at the concert, and just as the curtains parted, we launched into "Summer of '69."

I have almost no memory of those next few minutes. I'm pretty sure we played about twenty beats per minute faster than usual. The whole tune went by in a flash. We had rehearsed that song so often, it was like a muscle reflex. I only recall reminding myself that the bridge went to F, an odd but very cool chord progression for a pop song in the key of D major, as it turns out. When we hit the last chord, I finally took a breath and looked up to see everyone in the gym standing and dancing.

I had no idea what to do next. I had not thought of anything to say between songs. I must have had a puzzled look on my face because I looked back at Greg on the kit and he said, "Just go, b'y, go!"

So I started in on the famous opening guitar riff to "Johnny B. Goode." The place got even rowdier. By the time we hit the big guitar solo in the middle, the place was on fire.

Greg kept shouting, "Go, b'y, go!" through the whole song. I still was not sure what he meant.

Then I figured it out. We had used a couple of distortion pedals as links to join three twenty-foot guitar cables together. I ran down the steps and played most of my solo on the gym floor while everyone danced around me. At least that's what it felt like to me. Photos of that moment reveal me playing my solo in the middle of the gym, with one dude dancing close by and everyone else gathered around looking vaguely confused. But that's not the point. The point is it felt like there were hundreds of people dancing with me. And that feeling was awesome.

I made my way back to the stage for the last chorus and the closing riff of *de-na-da, bana-dun, ba-dada-ba-baaaaaa.* The curtains closed. I was sure the entire crowd was on their feet (because there were no chairs), and I was sure they were chanting for more.

Here I am playing with my first band, First Attempt, at St. Kevin's High School. Notice the Eddie Van Halen "Jump" bandana and the Opus penguin shirt. Friggin' Cool.

First Attempt was a hit. The principal said we should learn a few more songs and play a set for the next high school dance. We learned "Bad to the Bone," and "Living After Midnight," and "I Did It for Love" and "Make Me Do Anything You Want." We practised for a few weeks, and the principal let us play a set at the next dance. We set up behind the DJ. He did a great job packing the dance floor before we were up.

When it was our turn, we launched into "Summer of '69" and a blast of feedback came so loud that it almost knocked me down. Our sound setup was so terrible compared to the pre-taped music that people ran from the dance floor. It took two or three songs to get the sound right, and by the time

Another high school concert where First Attempt was rocking out. From left to right, that's Brian Foley on drums, me on Uncle Leonard's Strat (and wearing the same Eddie Van Halen "Jump" bandana), Greg Hawco in the very cool sunglasses and my brother, Bern, with the wicked 'stache.

we played "Make Me Do Anything You Want," some folks got on the floor. We ended with "Johnny B. Goode" and it was finally going well—the dance floor was packed and people were having a good time. When we were done, our fans cheered for more. But we were out of songs. So we did what any band would do. We played the same songs over again.

First Attempt went on to play a few dozen dances at St. Kevin's High School, though I don't recall us ever getting paid. We even got to play for a few dances in St. Paul's church basement, which meant playing for Protestant girls, who I assumed from older die-hard Catholic reports were all scandalous whores who were on the pill and constantly having sex with just about everyone. You can imagine my disappointment when I discovered that these gals were just normal and no more willing to make out with a guy like me than the Catholic gals at my own school.

The band was my first love, but at St. Kevin's I joined whatever other artistic endeavour was on the go. I became entrenched with some of the most creative people I've ever met. We were constantly planning for a concert or a play or something. It would be remiss of me not to mention the artistic melting pot that was St. Kevin's. Here's a quick list of just a few of the people who were part of or hanging with the St. Kevin's gang at that time:

- Perry Chafe, head writer and co-creator of CBC's hit series *Republic of Doyle*
- Allan Hawco, series co-creator and star of *Republic of Doyle*

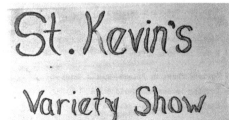

St. Kevin's
Variety Show

may 27, 1986

"Raise A
Ruckus Tonight"

Program from St. Kevin's 1986 variety show. We modelled it after the community concerts in Petty Harbour.

Because I played on almost every song in this show, I must have figured I was a rock star. That's why I autographed the program below for my teacher, Mrs. Chang. Funny that my signature remains laughably similar to what it is today.

PROGRAM

Opening Chorus--Raise A Ruckus Tonight

I Got You Babe--Cindy Smith
              --David Kelly

Believe This, My Friend--Rhonda Whitten

Driving to Mexico--David Stack

Leader of the Pack--Roberta Smith
                  --Rhea Lynn Hale
                  --Donna Williams

I Have A Dream--Mr. Ray O'Brien

Fashion Show--Skit

Overdue Past--Sheila Williams
            --Brian Foley

Johnny B. Goode--First Attempt

INTERMISSION

You May Be Right--David Stack

New York--Peggie Chang

Me & Bobby McGee--Rhonda Whitten
                --Mr. Ray O'Brien

A Word From Our Sponsor

Hello--Cheryl Heffernan

Bad To The Bone--Greg Hawco

Inflation--First Attempt

What She Wants--Alan Doyle

What's Forever For--Bernie Doyle
                  --Roberta Smith

- Greg Hawco, composer, master of percussion and international orchestral conductor
- Jillian Keiley, artistic director of the National Arts Centre
- David Pomeroy, internationally renowned tenor and opera star
- Keith Power, award-winning composer for film and TV
- Robert Chafe, award-winning playwright
- Sheila Williams, principal performer with Spirit of Newfoundland productions

And that's not to mention my little sister, Michelle, who has two music degrees and has starred in a dozen or more musicals, including *Grease* and *Chicago*.

I learned so many lessons with First Attempt. I learned that a fast song gets people on the dance floor, but it needs to be followed by a faster song or the energy will drop. I learned that once the floor is filled, the band's challenge is to keep it that way. And when the energy peaks, it is time for a ballad to give the couples a chance to cuddle. But afterwards, the momentum has to be built up again, often with a fast song that the same couples will want to dance to together. I learned how to use my equipment and that I need heavier strings than most because I play so hard. I came to understand that the technical aspects of concerts were often underappreciated, and that rental and transport of gear was a massive expense.

Of course, there were all sorts of lessons First Attempt failed to learn. Like most young bands, we had no idea what

Brian Foley on drums as I attempt to light St. Kevin's gymnasium ablaze with Uncle Leonard's Strat. The small box blocking my right foot is a jury-rigged strobe light and foot switch. I would click it on and rock out to the high-tech FX during my killer solos. I'm serious.

we were good at and what we were not. We'd play a John Cougar song and do a good job of it. Then we'd follow it with a failed attempt at Zeppelin's very complicated "Stairway to Heaven" or "Subdivisions" by Rush.

As most high school bands do, First Attempt fell by the wayside when we graduated. By this point, I was pretty much a full-time member of Uncle Ronnie's band. But let me backtrack here and tell you how that all started.

I'd been helping Uncle Ronnie and the guys in his band load and set up gear for a few years. He was aware of First Attempt, as he was constantly loaning us gear. All the while, as I helped them set up for parties and concerts, I did my best to not so subtly suggest I knew how to play most of their songs. Underage kids were not allowed to play in clubs, but some exceptions were made if they were accompanied by an adult and left the bar when not on stage. I had a faint hope that one day I might get the nod to sub in.

My high school graduation. I'm grinning because I'm thinking about how all the girls are going to fall for my massively thick and manly moustache.

One Sunday in the spring of 1984, Uncle Ronnie came to our house after mass. He asked Dad to come out on the back step to talk to him. I watched through the door as they spoke for a minute or two. I couldn't hear what was said, but Dad nodded before he came back in, Ronnie right behind him.

"Ned can't make the afternoon matinee gig up at the Squid Jigger," Uncle Ronnie said. "It's only a two-set show, but there's fifty dollars in it for you if you want to play guitar."

A nod from Dad confirmed it. In retrospect, there was no way he was going to say no.

"That would be friggin' awesome," I said.

"Get your gear ready. Pick you up at one."

I spent the next two hours preparing. I restrung Uncle Leonard's Strat and put fresh nine-volt batteries in my pedals. I stood in the mirror with the black and white electric guitar strung around my neck and lowered the strap as low as I could possibly get it and still reach the strings. I packed it up in its case laid it by the back door.

By this time, Bern was home and had heard the news. "First pro gig, Al."

"Yeah. But it's only a small thing."

"Oh no it's not," Bernie said. He was always smart like that.

Ronnie and Aunt Patsy sat in the front seat of the station wagon while me and Uncle Leonard sat in the back as we drove down the Southern Shore. We were cruising past the bar circuit I'd heard so much about, past the Hayloft in the Goulds, and Darby's in Witless Bay, then Hayden's in Cape Broyle and finally to the Squid Jigger in Calvert. It was the coolest drive I'd had in my life.

The Squid Jigger exists to this day and looks pretty much like it did around thirty years ago—a long, narrow building with a bar in one corner and a stage along one short side. When we walked in, there were two couples sat at tables and a few off-duty fishermen leaning against the bar, enjoying what appeared to be nothing like their first drinks of the day. Ronnie said a few hellos and I went to the stage and set up my gear. I plugged in my cable to the Peavey Deuce amp, connected the other end to the output of my Boss OD1 distortion pedal. Then I ran another cable from the input to the output of the Strat. I was ready to go.

Before I could look up and get nervous, Ronnie was on the stage behind the drum kit, and Leonard soon joined with Jerome Hart, the bass player. I must have had a panicked look on my face. They laughed when I asked, "Is there a set list?"

"Don't be so foolish," Uncle Ronnie's booming voice came from behind the kit. He leaned over past the floor tom and gave me a wink of assurance. "'Move It On Over,' in E. Here we go."

Then he swung his mic in place and addressed the crowd. "Welcome to the Squid Jigger, folks. We are the Sandelles!"

Four clicks of the sticks and we were into the downbeat of the Hank Williams tune and I was a professional musician.

After about a dozen songs, we took a quick break and I went outside because I was underage. The club owner followed me out.

"What you doing out here?" she asked.

"I thought I had to wait outside."

She waved me back in the bar and offered me a Pepsi. "No worries, honey. If a Mountie drives down the shore, my buddy in Trepassey will phone me. Sure, what's one more Doyle from Petty Harbour in the bar anyway?"

A while later, we played a quick second set and that was it. I tore down all the gear as Leonard and Ronnie and the grown-ups had a drink or two. By the time they turned around, I had the station wagon loaded and ready to roll.

"Keep this up and you'll be hired on full-time for sure," Ronnie said as he squished two twenties and two fives in my hand, the first money I ever made playing music.

He was right. In no time at all, I became a full-time member of the band. I was barely sixteen years old.

It was an awesome band to apprentice in. Over the next five or six years, I played almost every kind of gig there was to get—weddings, nightclubs, fire-hall dances, concerts. A club date usually consisted of a set of Celtic jigs and reels, followed by a set of older country tunes, then fifties and sixties rock 'n' roll. By the time the last set of more contemporary tunes was done, we'd have covered about five decades of music.

The odd time I would play bass and a keyboard riff, but mostly I played guitar. Uncle Ronnie would play drums and sing. I would sing harmony and play rhythm guitar, with Uncle Leonard playing the solos. He'd give me a nod every now and again to play lead for twelve bars, but I was never very good at lead guitar. I'm still not.

From my time in Uncle Ronnie's band, I learned as much about music as I did about life in general, sometimes the hard way. Like bar fights. You know the kind from the old western movies, where the honky-tonk piano player keeps playing while guys get punched over round-topped tables and go flying through saloon doors and no one really gets hurt. In real bar fights, cops and ambulances are called, and men and women weep and wail. In real bar fights, handfuls of bloody hair are left on the floor, people get jagged glass stuck in their faces and people sometimes even lose an eye. Even the biggest biker dudes squeal in terror when they think they've just lost an eye. Bar fights are no fun.

Not getting paid was no fun either. It happened with sketchy club owners from time to time, but I learned from

The New Sandelles, late 80s. From left to right: me with Uncle Leonard's Strat, Uncle Ronnie, David Stack, Al Hearn. Here, I'm thinking, "Girls are really gonna dig this shirt buttoned right up and how it highlights my Karate Kid guitar strap.

the older gents how to make the most of it. The most fun I had while not getting paid happened in a club halfway down the Southern Shore and it wound up cementing my place in the gang. We'd played Friday and Saturday night and also did a short Sunday matinee. The owner, Dumpy, owed us over a thousand dollars—five hundred each for the two-night gigs, and around $250 for the afternoon one. But the matinee was so poorly attended that Dumpy did not want to pay us for it. Uncle Ronnie was trying to be reasonable.

"Dumpy, b'y, you gotta pay us. We drove down the shore."

"No f—ing way. Ye never even played a full set today. I'm not paying for a full show," Dumpy argued.

"We didn't play because there's no one here to listen to us."

Dumpy was adamant. "Not gonna happen."

As a compromise, he offered to pay eleven hundred and that was it. We could load our stuff and get out and lock the door behind us. He slammed the cash on the bar and walked out the door.

Uncle Ronnie and the gang were not impressed. They were pissed, very much so. But there was also a gleam in their eyes. Club Owner Rule No. 1: Never leave a pissed-off bunch of musicians who you just ripped off alone in your bar.

Without saying a word, Uncle Ronnie went right for the beer cooler and took two two-fours of beer. Another musician, Al, took two forty-ounce bottles of rum and a few bags of chips. We loaded all our gear and our extra stuff into the station wagon.

Once we were done, the two older fellas in the band looked at each other. One said, "We're not full yet."

He and Ronnie walked back into the bar. Ronnie went for the dartboard and scorekeeper, while Al took two dandy bar stools with rounded high backs. By the time we got all our booty in the car, it was just about stuffed, and we were all quite content. But the icing on the cake was to come.

Al turned to me and asked, "You got any quarters?"

"What?"

"I said, you got any quarters?"

I fished into my pocket and gave him four quarters. When he went back into the bar, I followed him. He put two quarters in each of the two pool tables. When the balls came flowing down, he grabbed the eight ball from each table and walked back out the door. Once outside, he stood on the high bank next to the club and threw one of the eight balls as far as he could down into the thick brush. He handed me the second one and paused for my response. I knew what I had to do. I hurled that ball as far as I could into the same bramble. I turned around to see Uncle Ronnie standing there with a proud grin on his face.

"Welcome to the band," he said, and we all piled into our getaway car and raced down the shore.

All in all, I figure I played a couple of hundred gigs with Uncle Ronnie's band, almost all of them before I was twenty. I'll be forever grateful to them for having me along at such a young age and giving me such a head start. I learned how to keep a strong rhythm and play a solid backup, even though it would take a few years of standing in pub corners singing fifty or sixty tunes a night before I could sing lead properly.

And that's exactly where I was headed. During my first year of university at Memorial in St. John's, I joined up with David Stack (another young recruit to Uncle Ronnie's band), and with Greg and Brian from First Attempt. Together, we made a country-rock outfit we called High Tide. We played a few of the old Uncle Ronnie haunts, but that scene was dying right along with the inshore cod fishery.

A few of us moved into a four-bedroom rental house half-way between the university and downtown—7 Suez Street in St. John's. We immediately dubbed it Château de Suez. I lived in that house with a revolving cast of housemates for the next six years. My brother, Bernie, and my oldest friend, Perry, were some of my earliest roommates, and so was Greg Hawco.

He had been playing percussion in a trio with a guitarist and a singer. The singer fella, Jim, had a regular weekend gig in the bar of a dingy hotel in the older part of St. John's. Greg and the guitarist were quitting, and Jim wanted a new partner to do the hotel matinee and a few other gigs.

David Stack, Greg Hawco (on drums), me and Brian Foley, playing a New Year's Eve concert around 1990. Again, I was a chick magnet, what with me playing this far up the guitar neck *and* wearing my cool leather suspenders.

Me and Perry in the kitchen at the Château de Suez. Perry for sure thought his awesome string tie was going to get him girls.

"Why are you guys quitting if Jim is booking you steady gigs?" I asked Greg.

Greg's response was simple. "Because he's crazy."

He was crazy, too, but often in the best kind of way. Jim was a couple of years my senior and had completed a science degree at Memorial University. He was working towards a master's in biochemistry. On Greg's recommendation, I went to see him play one Saturday evening.

It was well known around town that the dingy hotel he played in was really a brothel of sorts, offering half-day and hourly room rates. The bar attached to the hotel had tall booths with curtains that closed. Older gals wearing a little too much makeup sat on bar stools by themselves until old fellas chatted them up and offered them a drink. Then they disappeared for twenty minutes or so. The gal would return to the bar. The old fella would not.

When I visited the establishment, Jim was singing "Taxi," by Harry Chapin. About twenty or so people sat around the bar and at tables. Jim was not a tall fella, but he made up for his diminutive stature with a giant personality. He had his head bent back, eyes closed, wailing at the top of his lungs. I swear he thought he was at Madison Square Garden singing an encore. I could see the veins in his neck bulging, he sang so hard. When he got to the quiet last verse, I thought he was going to cry. Then he launched into "Cat's in the Cradle" and got the crowd clapping to the last chorus. Jim's energy was incredible. He gave 110 percent with every syllable he sang.

Once he was done his set, he left the stage and walked right up to me at the bar.

It turned out Jim knew about me and that I played guitar. He was a very smart and charming fellow, and a great salesman, especially when it came to talking up the number of gigs we could get together.

"Dude, you wail on the guitar and I'll sing the shite out of the songs. I'll get us booked from here to Corner Brook and back. Tons of money. You'll need an extra pocket for the cash and an extra pickle for all the snapper."

I was game for anything and I suggested we get together for a jam and see what came of it. His response should have told me something about him.

"Jam? F—k that. Be here tomorrow at six thirty."

And just like that, I was booked for my first pub-singing gig in St. John's.

The next day, I met Jim in the hotel lobby. There were no hellos or small talk of any kind. There was no discussion of music or pay. His bright, beady eyes curved down the side of his face almost far enough to reach the corners of his massive smile reaching up.

"What a pile of skin here today," he said and disappeared into the bowels of the hotel while I figured out how to set up my gear next to Jim's. About fifteen minutes later, Jim reappeared and said, "Let's get 'er going."

"Is there a set list?" I asked.

"Set lists are for pansies."

With that, Jim picked up his guitar and started strumming a G chord followed by a C and a D in what sounded loosely like the intro to the Eagles' "Take It Easy," but it could have been anything.

"Welcome to the Captain's Quarter Hotel. I'm Jim Benson and this is my long-time sidekick, Alan Doyle. Take it away, Alan!"

Then he stood back from the mic while I awkwardly noodled some lead stuff on guitar. After catching the terrified and puzzled look on my face, he leaned in to me and said, "My throat's as sore as a boil t'day. You sing this one, will ya?"

"Sing what?" I was scared half to death, but he did not answer, just kept strumming and winking at the crowd.

What was I supposed to do? I turned to the mic and started singing the opening lyrics of "Take It Easy." I glanced at Jim, who had a massive grin on his face.

"Oh, good one," he said, and it was only then that I realized he'd had no idea what song he was starting or what I was about to sing.

All I could think was, "Greg was right. This guy is f— king crazy."

And off we went. We played for an hour and a bit. Jim would sing a few and I'd play lead guitar, then we'd switch. He could play guitar quite well and knew hundreds of songs. His singing voice was not always best suited for the tunes he picked, and he often sang tunes in keys that were too low or too high for him. But somehow, he got away with it. Perhaps it was the intensity and the volume of his singing and playing. I thought he would push his right hand through the sound hole, that's how hard he strummed. He barely needed a microphone at all.

We finished the first set and were about to take a short break. Rose, the bartender who I'm not sure you'd call a young woman but who nevertheless wore a tight dress with a plunging neckline and a ton of shiny red lipstick, said, "You wanna come to the back room and get what you came for, Jimmy?"

Jim did not say a word. He just followed her behind the dirty red-velvet drapes. A few people nearby came up to me and said they liked my singing, which was really nice of them. And I think they meant it. Up until that point, I'd never thought of myself as a singer, not like my brother or Uncle Ronnie. They were lead singers. I thought I was going to be Eddie Van Halen, not David Lee Roth.

After a while, Jim came out of the back room with two fifty-dollar bills. He handed one to me and stuffed the other one in his pocket.

Then he shouted back at Rose, "I've got a chem exam tomorrow, Rose. Alan will finish up the last set."

"What!" I said, shocked.

"You've got it covered. Chuck my guitar and stuff in the closet when you're done, will ya? And don't screw any of the young ones. They says they'll do you for free but then some big prick'll come looking for money. See ya."

And he put on his beer league hockey jacket and walked out the door.

What just happened? I wondered. Did I really have to do the last set by myself?

Rose appeared at my side. "Don't worry, honey. You've got a lovely voice. Sing a few of them Eagles songs again. They were nice." I felt her hand slide around my waist. Her arms were almost completely around me when she laid a rum and Coke in front of me and walked back to her stool.

My knees were wobbly. I necked the rum and Coke and walked back up to the stage and picked up my guitar. "Any requests?" I asked the dozen or so people who were left in the room.

"Know any John Denver?" someone asked.

I started singing "Leaving on a Jet Plane" and followed that up with "Country Road." I went on to play for forty-five minutes or so, at which point Rose gave me a wink and made that circle motion with her finger that meant "wrap it up." I played "Take It Easy" one more time, afraid to test the waters with anything more risky.

Once I was done, I packed up my stuff and said good-night to Rose and the rest of the girls, who were really the only ones left.

"Leavin' so early? Have one more drink with us," Rose said.

But the day had gone well and I was too freaked out to stick around and shag it up. That night, I lay awake in bed thinking about what trouble I might have found if I'd stuck around. To this day, in lonely hotel rooms all over the world, I think about that night and continue to wonder what would have become of me had I stayed.

Later that week, Jim phoned the Château. I somehow convinced him that we should rehearse at least once, and he reluctantly agreed. On Thursday evening, he came by the house and we ran through a bunch of tunes that we both knew. It was hardly a real rehearsal, more like a fun "What do you know?" session.

That weekend we played two more gigs at the hotel. I thought they went well, but on Monday Jim phoned and said he wanted us to move out of that dump and go to a different place where we could earn more money. He knew the owners of a bar on Water Street called the Rose and Thistle. They had a Thursday night slot open and Jim figured we could get it.

We set up one more jam at my place, but roommates drinking and frolicking were a problem. Eventually we gave in and stopped jamming serious tunes and joined in the boozing, which led us to discover a mutual talent for writing instant parody songs. Every popular song of the day was easily turned into a tune about sex or fighting or throwing up or whatever we felt like. "Take It Easy" became "Take It, Sleazy." "She Was Only Sixteen," by Dr. Hook, became "She Was Only Fifteen." Bryan Adams's "Heaven" became "Eleven." (Sing the chorus to yourself and switch the word. Then you'll understand the immature shite we'd get up to.)

We decided our parodies would make a great act. This kind of thing had a history in downtown St. John's and Atlantic Canada—Lambert & James were one duo who did blue comedy and music, and MacLean and MacLean had done the same. But we needed a name.

We came up with Stagger and Home. When you said it quickly with almost any Newfoundland accent it sounded like "staggerin' home." Again, no one had a better idea, so Stagger and Home it was. Perfect.

We played our first gig on a Thursday night in the fall of 1990. We sang a bunch of our Eagles and Harry Chapin songs. But it was our parodies that the crowd loved. After closing that night, the bar owner sat us down and offered us every Thursday, seventy-five dollars each, if we'd do a bit more comedy. Without talking it over with Jim, I said, "We'll do it for fifty each to start off if you'll keep Happy Hour prices on all night." (I figured our shtick would only work if people were hammered.)

"Deal," he said.

If we filled the place every Thursday, even for a few hours, we'd ask for more. Plus, if people came for the cheap rum, we'd have a better chance of them having a good time with us and the foolishness we intended to get up to.

Jim was furious that I'd just talked us out of a third of our pay. "You stupid f—ing arsehole," he said. "You play the f—ing guitar, I'll do the deals."

He was probably right. I'm still not good at negotiating fees, but I stood by that decision then to fill the room. I still think it is one of the smartest moves I ever made. Word spread quick that you could get a double rum and Coke at the Rose for five bucks while these two crazy bastards sang delightfully ridiculous tunes about our friends' hot sisters, priests and rum smuggling.

Our rants between songs were almost as awful as the tunes themselves. Jim would say something like, "You think it's hard on the head getting approached by a priest? Well, imagine how depressing it is to be like poor Alan here. He was an altar boy for four years and never got a single feel out of it. Now that's rejection, brothers and sisters. Can I get an amen?"

And the crowd would shout "Amen!" a few times. Then we'd break into our version of "These Are the People in Your Neighborhood." I'll leave the lyrics to your imagination.

The Thursday nights at the Rose became quite a thing. People heard about our gig and wanted to see it for themselves. We'd do most of the comedy stuff in the first set and then cover songs for the rest of the night. But our grand finale was "Thunderstruck," by AC/DC.

I'd put a distortion pedal on my acoustic guitar, and when I played the hammer-on riff—as fast and as loud as I could—it sounded ridiculous. But the real kicker was what Jim did as I played the signature riff. He would prance around like a madman getting everyone in the bar to sing, "A na na na na na na na, THUNDER!" along with him.

When he had the crowd sufficiently engaged, he'd extend his mic stand as high as it could go in the air. Then Jim, a mad hobbit-banshee, would step on a chair and get on my shoulders. From there, he'd continue singing while I played the guitar at the same time—ludicrous but effective. The place went nuts every time.

I'd be lying if I said everyone dug our act, because not everyone did. Some people didn't care for the crass nature of our songs. Some left disgusted. I don't blame them. What we did was not for everyone. But a lot of people loved it. Séan McCann tells the tale of seeing me play for the first time at the Rose and Thistle. He, Bob Hallett and Darrell Power were in a popular traditional band called Rankin Street. They would get big crowds at Nautical Nellies, just across the street from the Rose. Between sets, they'd often leave the building for a break. On one of these breaks, Séan walked across the street for what he thought would be a quiet drink at the Rose. Instead, he was shocked by the sight of a crazy person on the shoulders of another crazy person who was shouting, "THUNDER!!" to a drunken crowd of about thirty other crazy people who were demanding an encore as loudly as a full house at Wembley Stadium. Séan was confused—and not necessarily impressed—but not quite able to look away either. He returned a few more times to see Jim and me as a duo.

In the weeks and months to follow, Jim got busier at school and I ended up doing a lot of the gigs without him. I'd put posters around town that read: "Alan Doyle is Staggerin' Home Alone." The club owners confessed they did not mind having me solo, which again surprised me as I still did not think of myself as a lead singer. Jim was an interesting fella, and I enjoyed my time with him immensely. I learned so much from him about the value of confidence and fearlessness on stage. He was not the best singer in the world, but Jim occupied every song he sang. He taught me how to deliver a performance. It was a great lesson to learn and I'm grateful to him for it.

By the winter, I was doing every Thursday night at the Rose, and doing it solo, and eventually I started playing three or four times a week. I played there so often that I did not even take my gear home. I kept my little PA under the church pew that served as the pub bench. I started getting gigs at other pubs, too—Trapper John's, Bosun's Whistle, Humphrey's, Jungle Jim's. All told, with Happy Hours included, I gigged about seven or eight times a week. Those were long nights, especially for a guy doing four or five shifts a week at the Newfoundland Museum and taking five courses at Memorial University. My day started at about eight thirty. I'd sleep as late as possible and still get to work by 8:55 to open the museum. I'd work until five and go straight to school after. I'd hang at the library and do whatever reading or assignments I had between five and seven. Then I'd head to a night class until 9:45, at which point I'd be bolting to whatever club I was booked in to play from ten to two. I'd get home by two thirty or three in the morning, and the next morning, I'd be up by eight thirty to do it all over again. I didn't get much rest, but I loved the gigs so much that I did not mind the sleeplessness at all.

In 1991 and 1992, I probably played close to six hundred solo pub shows and I learned to be a lead singer. I made some good pocket money doing it, too. I loved it, but at times lamented not being in a band. And I wondered what would be next. Would I graduate from university and become a schoolteacher who had some fun singing in pubs on the weekend? Or was there more to this music thing? I thought about that a lot. I honestly think I would have been happy doing pub gigs on the side. But I decided that if I ever had a chance to take a real shot at the music business, I'd give it a try. I would never forgive myself if I did not.

Every now and again, I'd see Séan or his bandmate Darrell Power lurking in the back at one of my gigs, listening to a song or two. Even then, they were pretty well known, so it was hard for them to hide. Bob tells of how in the dying days of Rankin Street, in 1992, Séan returned to their packed house at Nautical Nellies and whispered to Bob, "I just saw the guy we need for our new band. He's a Doyle from Petty Harbour."

ORDINARY DAY

"Ordinary Day" is perhaps Great Big Sea's most popular song. It has been a high point in concerts for almost two decades and opens or closes many GBS shows. It has been licensed for films, TV shows and commercials and even illegally used in political campaigns. It made its way onto several charts and was the No. 1 video on a couple of music video stations. Many fans have told me that this song has helped them through the most difficult times in their lives. Like most things in my life, it came into being after some struggles, luck and co-operation.

GBS was writing and collecting songs for the follow-up CD to the unbelievable success of our 1995 release, *Up*, which would go on to sell over five hundred thousand copies in Canada alone. We had two albums behind us, but our indie CD was still a very obscure find, so we felt like we were working on the dreaded sophomore release.

I wanted to write a song that could be a single on the radio and prove we were not a flash-in-the-pan success. I wanted a song that embodied the spirit and resilience of Newfoundlanders and Labradorians.

There was an old skipper in Petty Harbour whose attitude was always a source of inspiration to me as a kid. If you asked him how he was feeling, he'd honestly think about it and most often answer, "B'y, I might be perfect."

I once heard someone on the wharf complaining about the weather, and the skipper replied, "It's just an ordinary day, b'ys. No better or worser than any of the rest."

I always thought that line would be a cool to sing. GBS had become well known for incorporating shanties and nautical chants into our tunes, so I came up with the "Way-hey-hey" bit inspired by seafaring songs. The rest of the chorus came pretty easily, as did the first verse about being lucky to live on such a beautiful island as Newfoundland.

A stroke of luck landed me the second verse. I wanted it to be about a specific person, but I did not know who. It had to be someone who had demonstrated that hard times or a bad turn of luck would not so much as break his or her stride. I happened to be flicking through the TV channels when a profile about a young singer gal from Calgary caught my attention. She'd made her way to Vancouver and was so determined to make it in the biz that she busked on the streets to pay her way. One evening, she was mugged and got beaten up pretty bad. Many of us would have packed it all in at that point and headed home, but not this gal. Hours after the mugging, she was right back to work, and after a while she convinced the music industry that it could not go on without her. She would go on to sell millions of albums and become an international star. Her name is Jann Arden.

The single-syllable "Jann" did not fit the rhythm of the melody in "Ordinary Day," so I switched it to "Janey." I got a chance to meet Jann a few times but I never confessed that she was the gal in the song. Finally, I got the courage to fess up and did so live on stage with her at a songwriters' circle event at the Juno Awards in Halifax. She was quite surprised, I think . . . and flattered, I hope. She remains a hero of mine.

All this part of the song had come so easy that I figured

In the cartoon:

20 YEARS AGO, MRS. POWER COULD NOT HAVE IMAGINED HER STUDENTS ALAN, SÉAN, DARRELL, AND BOB WOULD ONE DAY BECOME MEMORIAL'S ALUMNI OF THE YEAR!

IN YOUR MATH TEST YESTERDAY, YOU ALL GOT A GREAT BIG 'C'...

MATH TEST C

THE TELEGRAM '99.

Kevin Tobin

I'd just sum up the tune in the last verse and I'd be done with it. But I could not find any way to wrap up the lyric. I needed a piece of poetry that was beyond me, I suppose. I was on a typically long GBS van ride somewhere in Ontario when Séan noticed my frustration from a seat behind. I explained to him that I was a verse away from finishing what I thought would be a cool song and needed a closing verse that had eluded me for weeks.

I passed him my lyric sheet and about three minutes later he handed it back to me with the perfect concluding lines about double-edged knives and waiting for your ship to come in.

No one in the van knew it at the time, but Séan and I had just written a song that would change our lives.

From our video for "Ordinary Day."

CHAPTER 12

Petty Harbour Dog

One of the luckiest breaks I've ever received fell into my lap in the summer of 1985. A high school teacher of mine, Margaret Chang, called me into her classroom after school. She was impressed by my willingness to stand in front of a crowd of people and sing or act in a play or address an assembly. She had recently left the Newfoundland and Labrador civil service and had many friends and connections in the Historic Resources Division. She asked if I would be interested in being a tour guide for the summer in the Newfoundland Museum or at one of the province's historic sites around St. John's.

This really sounded too good to be true. I told her I was very much interested in any job that got me out of Petty Harbour and the Goulds for the summer and that did not involve night shifts or 4 a.m. rises or direct contact with fish guts, sod rolls or capelin genitalia. She made a few calls, and about a week later I got up at seven thirty in the morning and got Mom to iron a shirt for me. I could tell she was excited that one of her kids was getting dressed up and going to look for a job in St. John's.

"I s'pose you are a bit nervous?" Mom knew I was.

"Nope," I lied.

"Just be yourself, honey, and they'll love you." She thought for a second. "And try not to swear. Not sure they swears in Town like the Petty Harbour crowd."

She made me my favourite ham-and-processed-cheese sandwich on homemade white bread. She put the sandwich and a clean pair of underwear and a T-shirt in a gym bag for me in case I needed them (to this day, I have no idea why).

"Be good," she said.

This has always been my mother's pearl of wisdom, a simple piece of advice she offers just about every time someone walks out the door or every time she ends a phone call. It's one of the most brilliant pieces of advice I've ever heard: Be good. Be good to people. Be a good son to your mom and dad, a good brother to your siblings. Be a good husband to your wife, a good dad to your son. Be a good friend to your friends. Be a good worker to your co-workers, a good band-mate to your bandmates. Be a good celebrity to your fans. Be good.

After her parting words, she sent me walking down Skinner's Hill to thumb a ride to St. John's. I hitched to town with my aunt, who worked at a federal tax office. She dropped me on Water Street around 8:15 and I walked around the early-morning streets of downtown St. John's by myself for the first time in my life, awaiting my nine o'clock job interview. It was the first time I was ever alone in St. John's. I had just turned sixteen a few weeks previous and wondered if that made me a real grown-up. To be there in the big city, walking down the street in an ironed shirt, with a ham sandwich in my gym bag, about to meet someone who might give me a job where I wouldn't have to gut, clean, lift or roll anything felt like I'd come a million miles in one morning.

And I had.

At 9 a.m. on the dot, I walked into the Historic Resources building on Duckworth Street. It had a small reception area and a big office on the main floor. I spoke to a lady at the front desk.

"Hello," I said, but the lady typing did not hear me. "Hello!" I said louder and the poor lady almost jumped out of her skin.

"Jesus, honey. You scared the life right out of me!" I was surprised to hear her swear. I figured I'd left that behind on the wharf, but I was wrong.

"You must be Alan Doyle from Petty Harbour," the lady said, smiling now as I nodded. "My lord, you're cute for a harbour dog. You're here about the interpreter job, right?"

I nodded, though I was very confused by the word "interpreter." Did they think I spoke French?

The kind lady led me upstairs to a back office where two other ladies were talking over a desk. They wore ladies' business clothes like I'd see on *Mary Tyler Moore*. They were beautiful. And not at all related to me. They smiled lovely smiles and put their hands out. I assumed I was supposed to shake them. I wasn't quite sure, as I'd never shaken hands with strangers before. This was one of the things that separated Baymen from Townies. Townies always wanted to shake your hand, and we Baymen felt it was odd. An appropriate greeting for a Bayman when introduced to someone new is to wink and nod and say, "What are you at?" or "Yes, b'y." Still, when in Rome, I figured, and shook the ladies' lovely hands.

"Well, hello. I'm Elizabeth Randall and this is my colleague, Ms. Helena Gibson-Taylor," the taller of the two ladies said. Not sure I'd ever met anyone called Ms. before. Pretty sure I'd never met anyone with two last names either.

"I'm Alan Doyle from Petty Harbour," I said. "My teacher said you were looking for people to work at the museum for the summer."

"Yes," Ms. Gibson-Taylor replied, "we're looking to hire a summer-student interpreter for the Newfoundland Museum in the Murray Premises. Have you ever worked in a museum before, Alan?" she asked, though I'm pretty sure she knew I had not.

"No, Miss, uh, Missus, uh, Mzzz," I said.

"Have you ever done interpreting?" There was that word again. It was beginning to worry me, and I took my time to answer this question. I made a quick decision that I was going to say "oui" when they asked me if I could speak French. In my head, I began stringing together all the French I knew: "Et la première étoile, à choisissez de la *Gazette de Montréal*, le numéro 10, Guy Lafleur!"

All this pondering must have shown on my face, and Elizabeth leaned in and whispered, "Museum interpreter is just a fancy union term for tour guide, dear."

Phew.

"So, have you ever done any tour-guiding?"

"No," I said, "but I've done a lot of talking." They laughed. I had no idea why they thought this was funny, and their laughter made me even more nervous.

"Do you know anything about Newfoundland's history?"

I said I knew a lot about history and am grateful that they believed me, because I was lying. I told them I had a hands-on knowledge of the Newfoundland fishery and could talk at length about it to visitors from other parts of the world. I explained that I could talk about tongue cutting and about Newfoundland's music. I also told them I did not mind singing as a part of a tour, if they saw fit.

"And what would you sing?" they asked, looking both mystified and fascinated.

I told them I knew some traditional songs that might be appropriate, and I sang a verse and a chorus of "Tickle Cove Pond."

When I finished, they clapped, albeit a little awkwardly, and for a second I thought maybe I'd charmed them. This was neither the first nor the last time that having a song ready at the hip wound up being a good thing.

They showed me around the office and introduced me to a few people and then we walked down Duckworth Street to Water Street towards the Newfoundland Museum at the Murray Premises. There I was, Alan Doyle from

Petty Harbour, strutting down Water Street with real live St. John's ladies in business attire. I was doing my best to keep up with the conversation, but what I really wanted was my uncle Eddie to roll by in the Petty Harbour garbage truck and see me. That would have been awesome.

We arrived at the museum, which was closed, and one lady unlocked the small door and the other dashed in to a keypad and typed a code into a security alarm panel. I'd seen those on TV, but never in real life. It was very high tech.

They hit the lights, and the first thing to illuminate was a row of glass display cases that I would later learn contained exhibit highlights. In one was a beautiful model of a wooden ship that served as a teaser for the Maritime History section on the third floor. I had never seen anything quite like it. It had been made by an award-winning shipbuilder, Varrick Cox, and its detail and scale were incredible, right down to the tiny barrels on the aft. Next to that was a long, narrow glass case with a large World War I machine gun in it. There were a few dozen other cases, most notably one housing a stuffed bald eagle.

The two ladies took me on a brief walkthrough of the entire exhibition, and at the end they handed me a binder of information, which I assumed I would have to learn for a final job interview. But what followed was a smile from both ladies and another handshake.

"Tomorrow, we'll introduce you to your co-workers," Ms. Gibson-Taylor said. I was confused. Then Elizabeth went into the staff kitchen and came out with two new white golf shirts that had "Newfoundland Museum" embroidered above the heart.

"What should we put on your name tag?"

I was not ready for this. I had no idea. "Alan Doyle, from Petty Harbour?"

They nodded and smiled and said they thought that was perfect.

And that was it. I had the job.

I could have started the hitchhike home, but I really did not want to. Instead, I walked up and down Water Street and Duckworth Street for the next hour trying to look like everyone else. I was in town. And I loved it.

At the Newfoundland Museum, circa 1992. I'm grinning because I loved that job so much.

I went into the Atlantic Place food court and bought a Pepsi. Over the next hour or so, I watched hundreds of people file in and out. I did not know a single person. It was brilliant. I scanned the different vendors, imagining ordering lunch there in my ironed shirt, glancing at my watch because I was in a hurry. Maybe I'd order chips, dressing and gravy at Skipper's Fish & Chips one day. Perhaps I'd get a Whopper at Burger King the next. At the Chinese Garden, I'd make a point of trying hot and sour soup. I'd never had that before.

I must have sat in that chair for three hours people-watching. I fell in love with the girl at the Tim Hortons counter and consequently finished my first-ever cup of coffee, thus kick-starting a love affair with that beverage that runs strong to this very day. I became aware for the first time that being in an active place is far more soothing to me than sitting in silence. Later, I would come to know that quiet makes me edgy, whereas the sound of people doing something reassures me that the whole world keeps spinning even if I fall asleep.

After a few hours, I decided it was time to hitch home, and I found myself in a car with an older fisherman who was listening to *Open Line* on the radio. We listened intently to the announcer as he described the ever-dwindling cod stocks and said that if things didn't change, the inshore fishery might be halted altogether. The man on the radio worried a shutdown would change life in our fishing villages forever. Without the cod fishery, these vibrant towns would die a slow and painful death, he said, as would the traditions of rural life in Newfoundland. The fisherman laughed out loud as we rounded the corner and Petty Harbour came into full view.

"Towns like Ferryland and Bay Bulls and Petty Harbour will never be the same again," the man on the radio announced. I looked ahead, and there it was: my home. The only home I'd known for the past sixteen years, and for the first time ever, it seemed too small for me. But more than that, this place carved out of rock—rock that had taken a thousand years to trace, this place that had been there for generations, been there forever—suddenly seemed very, very fragile.

I was to be at the Newfoundland Museum at nine the next morning, but it was just before eight when I arrived. I did not want to be late, but I also did not want to be waiting by the door like a lost puppy when the full-timers showed up.

I went for a coffee, fell in love with the Tim Hortons' girl again and returned to the museum at five to nine. It was then that I started worrying that something might be wrong. Surely if work was to start at nine, someone would be there by now? Nine came and went, and at about ten past, the doors opened, revealing a mountain of a man, about six-foot-five and 250 pounds of muscle and gut. His massive forearms sported fading tattoos. His face was leathery and his nose looked like it had been broken a few too many times. Despite his Santa Claus hair and moustache, he looked harder than any fisherman I knew in Petty Harbour.

I stood there with what must have been a silly, scared grin on my face.

"You must be the new summer fella, are ya?" he asked. "Come in, b'y. I'm Ted. What's your name?"

"I'm Alan Doyle from Petty Harbour."

"Oh, a Doyle from Petty Harbour. You must play in a band."

"I do. With my uncle Ronnie."

"Ronnie Doyle is your uncle? Jesus, I've known Ronnie for years. Grand fella. So who's your fadder?"

"Tom," I said.

"Yes, Tom. I know him. He used to work at The Mental, used to sing on *All Around the Circle*. Leonard must be your uncle. Some hand at the guitar."

"Yeah, he is," I said.

Music had given me another in before I'd even started my first day. Ted led me to an office, where we sat at the three-winged desk.

"Well, Petty Harbour Dog, did the ladies walk you through the floors?"

I nodded and said that they had and that I had studied everything in the binders.

"Pile of bull," Ted said. I could not tell if he was kidding or serious. "You mind doing tours?" he asked.

"No, don't mind at all. Can't wait to get started, actually."

"That's great, 'cause I can't stand up in front of people and talk. I gets right worked up and out of breath. I feels like me chest is gonna burst and someone is strangling me." He was getting red in the face just talking about it. His fists were clenched so tight his knuckles were white. "I told the ladies and the bosses I wasn't going at that tour shite and that was that. Glad you don't mind it."

Did I understand this correctly? One of the two full-time tour guides at the Newfoundland Museum did not give tours? It was like a restaurant hiring a chef who refused to cook. So what did this man do?

I later came to learn that before this job, Ted had been a bouncer. He'd most likely managed to get some high-powered folks out back doors when they needed and this landed him a job as a government security guard. When the museum in the Murray Premises was being constructed, he was transferred there in a security function and somehow had become a museum interpreter by default, even while he had no formal education or knowledge about Newfoundland history or even the slightest inclination to learn about it. And he had the above-mentioned aversion to talking to groups of people. Wow. Is this how government jobs worked? I wondered.

"I mostly looks after the security here," Ted said. "Got another six years and then I can retire," he added with a wink.

There was silence and I took the time to turn my attention to the museum binder on the desk.

"How old are you, Alan Doyle from Petty Harbour?" Ted asked.

"Turned sixteen a month or so ago." And that's when the conversation started to turn in a direction I could never have imagined.

The next thing that Ted said to me was: "How many times a day do you pluck your wire? When I was your age I could service meself five or six times a day. Now I can't do it more than once a day, max."

Was he asking what I thought? What was I supposed to say to that?! "As much as anyone, I suppose," was all I could muster.

"Yeah, that's enough to be at it anyway," he said casually, as if we were talking about buying a used car. "Save it for the real turn at the plate, eh, b'y?"

I must have blushed, but somehow I knew that this conversation was a rite of passage.

He continued. "You must be shaggin' all the girls in Petty Harbour, are ye?"

"No, b'y," I said. "All the Petty Harbour girls my age are my first cousins."

"Jesus, that never stopped anyone in Petty Harbour. The closer the kin the better the skin."

I decided to fight fire with fire. "I heard there's a Townie or two going around with an extra toe or finger," I said.

He sniggered. "I'm just effing with you, b'y," he said, impressed that I'd had the gall to rib him back. Turns out he was a great joker, and he loved to make fun of the fact that he was a tour guide who did not do tours.

Some visitors approached the doors and Ted stood and announced, "Welcome to the Newfoundland Museum in the Murray Premises. Come in, come in! This is Alan Doyle from Petty Harbour. He'd love to show you around the floors upstairs." Then he walked into the kitchen and started boiling the kettle.

I spoke to the visitors for a few moments and they were content to head up to the exhibitions on their own.

I returned to the desk and wondered how I might steel myself for further banter when the outside door down the hall slammed and I heard someone approaching. I did not hear footsteps, only loud a cappella singing/screaming: "I AM IRON MAN! DUNNA DUNNA DUNNA DUN DA DUN DUN!"

I expected to see a young punk or some crazy metalhead come around the corner but instead saw a guy in a museum uniform carrying a Walkman and wearing headphones over his thick, curly brown hair. He was shorter than your average man but incredibly stocky and strong, with Popeye-sized forearms. And it wasn't only his head that was covered in curly brown hair; a forest of hair grew out of the V of his golf shirt, running right up his neck and covering his chin and face. It didn't recede until it reached his thick-rimmed eyeglasses.

He repeated the chorus of the Black Sabbath tune one more time before removing his headphones. He grinned a big grin and stuck out a friendly, hairy hand.

"Hey. You must be the summer student. Stan is the name. How the f—k are you?"

"Good," I said, shaking his hand like a Townie. "I'm Alan Doyle from Petty Harbour."

"Well, Alan Doyle from Petty Harbour, welcome aboard. I assume Ted has been giving you a full orientation?"

"Yeah, we've been having a great chat," I said.

"Oh Jesus. Not about jerking off or screwing women?"

"Both."

"Good to know he's going easy on the new fella. You should ask him about the time he got stabbed or about the time he nearly killed a man with his bare hands. But not today. Build yourself up to it."

I swallowed hard.

Turned out Stan was a hard ticket in his own right. He'd been in the armed forces for a period but never finished his career there. He despised authority figures of almost any description, especially as they related to the museum. He set about telling me so in the first five minutes of our acquaintance.

"Gerry McPhearson, the head of Military History up there, wouldn't know a World War II plane if it landed on his head. He was never in the forces. What does he know about hand-to-hand combat? Doctor of history, my arse. Come, I'll show you around upstairs."

Like Ted, Stan was very unsuited to the task of leading people around a museum. He loved debating the conventionally accepted version of military history and often did so with museum patrons or when answering the phones. Both men were doing this job reluctantly and were hence thrilled that I was so eager to do whatever they asked of me. On day one, they sat me down and explained "the rules"—their rules, of course.

"Now the ladies up there don't want me and Stan going to break together and leaving you here by yourself, but you don't mind if we do that, do ye?" Ted inquired.

"Not at all," I said.

Ted asked, "And do you think we should tell them about me and Stan going to have our coffee break together or should we keep that to ourselves?"

It was an easy test. "I figure we can keep that to ourselves."

"Am I right that a young fella like yourself from Petty Harbour wouldn't mind opening and closing the museum and operating the fancy alarm panel?" asked Stan.

"I wouldn't mind that at all," I said. "I'm gonna be here early every day and am in no hurry to get back home, so you guys come and go as you please."

They looked like two fellas who had hit the jackpot.

And so began my days at the Newfoundland Museum. I was so excited to have the job, I was willing to do every tour, open and close every day and go without breaks and eat my lunch at the front desk. It was all such a leap forward from night shift in the fish plant.

I opened and closed the museum just about every day and organized tours for kindergarten classes, for teenagers, tourists and senior citizens. It was a cool way to learn how to tailor a message to an audience, when to be funny and when to keep a presentation moving or when to go into more detail.

Ted would nip off to watch baseball and Stan would spend most of a morning or two a week in the little staff kitchen deep-frying fresh fish. The tables would turn a number of years later when I started playing more and more music and the boys would let me sleep in a bit if I'd

EYE-CATCHING

Interpreter Alan Doyle displays the skull of a minke whale, one of a number of eye-catching exhibits on view at the newly opened natural history exhibit at the Newfoundland Museum at the Murray Premises.

A newspaper clipping from the St. John's *Evening Telegram,* 1993. That's me and a friggin' cool whale head. Great Big Sea was just around the corner.

had a gig the night before. They even let me pip off on a number of occasions while recording the first Great Big Sea album.

"Go on, Petty Harbour Dog," Ted would offer. "I'll close up while you and the b'ys are laying down a few tracks."

"Just don't forget us when you're famous," Stan said and chuckled.

Not much chance of that. Ted and Stan were unforgettable when they were in the best of moods, even more so when they were not. They both had strong opinions and had been working together for so long that they fought like a married couple, or worse.

The most troubling spat happened on my third shift at the museum, when I left Stan and Ted at the desk chatting about baseball, and in the four minutes it took me to go to the Pepsi machine down the hall and come back, they had gotten into an argument that erupted into a full-out brawl. I heard shouting and gagging as I made my way back and then saw Ted had Stan pinned to a wooden post with one hand. He was that strong. He held the other hand back, ready to strike, while Stan's arms and legs flailed and kicked helplessly, unable to reach Ted's face.

I had no idea what to do. I yelled "Hey!" a couple of times but neither of them took any notice of me. I ran downstairs and got Don, one of the maintenance men.

"Stan and Ted are gonna kill each other!"

Don barely lowered the newspaper he was reading. "Ted's got Stan by the throat?"

"Yes!"

"Did you tell them to give it up?"

"They didn't listen!"

"For f—k sakes," he said and slammed his paper down on his desk.

I wanted to run back to the scene of the fight, but Don was just strolling along leisurely, smiling at the museum patrons he passed along the way.

When we got to where Ted and Stan were, Ted's hand was no longer wrapped around Stan's neck, and Stan's feet were back on the floor. But both men were shouting at each other about who had started the fight.

"I never said you were stupid, Ted. I just said you don't know nothing about the Blue Jays pitching rotation!"

As Stan spoke, Ted was making one of those fists where one knuckle sticks out more than the rest. "One more peep from your saucy mouth, Stan, and I'll shove your nose so far back in your head, you'll be sneezing down the back of your neck."

Don shouted, in full earshot of a few flabbergasted tourists: "Shut the eff up, will ye? Ye got the new young fella scared out of his mind!"

And with that, Ted and Stan stopped and both sat at the front desk. Don walked away, shaking his head. Within ten minutes, Ted and Stan were chatting calmly about the Toronto Blue Jays. I was exhausted and went upstairs.

Ted and Stan were not your typical museum employees, but I loved hanging with them. They were hugely entertaining and like no one I'd ever met. I even came to learn a whole bunch from them, whether they knew it or not.

For example, Ted helped me fall in love with St. John's. He embodied the history and spirit of the way the place had been a generation before me—rough and way more clever and complicated than meets the eye. He was an encyclopedia of the recent history of St. John's. You could walk up and down Water Street with him and learn where all the Portuguese sailors used to go to get drunk and shagged. He would point to the old hardware store and tell you what used to be in the renovated buildings on either side of it, and how Sneakers Fagan and his brother Lefty worked there when a fire destroyed the second storey. Stan, a military history buff, taught me more about the history of warfare than anyone, making it simple and palatable. I remember some discussion about prostitutes and venereal disease, and Stan said, "Yeah, just like the Boer War."

"What's the Boer War?" I asked, and the next day Stan brought me four books on the conflict—with pages marked to indicate the most interesting parts.

For most of that summer, I hitchhiked to St. John's every morning and home in the evenings as well. I learned the work schedules of just about every person in Petty Harbour who worked in the city. I knew that if I was up and on the go before seven thirty, I could stand on the bridge and get one of three different rides coming from the Protestant side. If I was a bit later, I would have to walk a little towards Maddox Cove and hitch with some of the Catholic folks who were heading to town. Rain or shine, it did not matter. I always had a gym bag with a raincoat, a can of soup and a pair of spare socks and underwear. Out the door with Mom's "Be good," I was ready for anything.

I worked at the museum for almost a decade, from the summer of 1985 till 1994. It thrilled me that my job was talking to people about the place I loved the most. It was a crash course in all things from Newfoundland. I had no idea how beneficial this would be when researching and learning traditional tunes later in Great Big Sea. I loved meeting people from all over the world and telling them about the history of the country and province of Newfoundland. I loved hearing their stories about where they were from. I loved working with people from all over the island and from Labrador.

Plus, the girls that worked there were not my cousins.

There were many great things that happened to me while working at the museum, but the best thing happened while I was walking up Water Street in October of 1992. Walking towards me was Séan McCann. I remembered him lurking in the back of the Rose and Thistle and I remember secretly hoping he dug what he saw of my performance. By then, his band Rankin Street was pretty much the biggest thing in downtown, and every pub and festival wanted the group as often as possible. Bernie had seen them play a few times and suggested that I check them out.

"You can play the Irish stuff and rock 'n' roll, Al." He was certain. "You'd be a good fit with a band like that."

But I'd heard through the downtown rumour mill that Rankin Street was folding and that some of the members were hoping to form a new band. I decided then and there that I was going to try to make it happen. Right on Water Street. I was about to say hello to Séan, but he beat me to the punch. He had his right hand out before I reached him.

He smiled and I shook his hand. "Hey, man. I'm Séan. You're Alan, right?" he asked with a smile and a twinkle in his eye that made it obvious to me why all the girls wanted to go out with him. His hand gripped mine like he'd never let it go.

"Yeah, Alan Doyle from Petty Harbour. Love your band, man."

But he was not there to be praised and went right back to business. "I saw you play a couple of times at the Rose and Thistle and a few other places."

"Oh, really? That's cool." I tried my best to act like I had not noticed him in the back of the club with a watchful eye and ear.

"Yeah, you're f—king crazy. And you can sing and play guitar really well, man. We're tearing down Rankin Street and building a new band. You want to come jam sometime?"

"Yeah, that would be cool, I suppose."

That friendly chat started what Nan and I could never have imagined. After a generation or two of the Doyles from Skinner's Hill making people dance and sing and smile, the family was about to get its first full-time professional musician. And as he fantasized for nearly two decades, Alan Doyle from Petty Harbour was about to play for a living in a real professional band.

GREAT BIG SEA

On an otherwise ordinary day late in 1992, the trial meeting for the band that would follow the mighty Rankin Street started as an informal jam at Séan's tiny apartment in St. John's. I knew it was a huge opportunity. This was my chance to show Séan and his bandmates that I was the guy they should have in whatever act they formed next. I wanted the day to go well, and the nervous energy had kept me up the night before. I was worried that I wasn't ready. As it turned out, I had no idea how well every experience I'd had up to that point had prepared me for the opportunity of a lifetime.

With my acoustic and electric guitar in tow, along with a small amplifier, I knocked on Séan's door. He greeted me and led me to the living room. He mentioned the next band that he and the boys planned to start was going to be a serious one and a ton of work for not much money at first. I explained about my young life in Petty Harbour and how I'd been working hard and making my own money for over a decade. I told him about cutting out tongues on the wharf and how I had not had a summer off since I was eleven.

He mentioned he planned to take his new band to gigs out of town and even out of province to play clubs in Halifax and Toronto. I could not believe my ears. He warned that life on the road was no bed of roses and there'd be times when we'd have to double up in rooms and share a bathroom. I said I was not too worried about the sleeping arrangements as I'd spent a significant portion of my young life pooping in a beef

bucket. I explained that even at the best of times I was one of five people and a dog sharing a single bathroom, so two in a hotel room was probably not going to be a problem.

He made a point of saying that he'd learned the hard way that not all club owners were honest and that you had to be on your toes when dealing with them. He laughed as I told him how I once stood shoulder to shoulder with a bass player as we flung Dumpy's eight balls into the woods as retribution for not living up to his promises.

We talked about how we'd both learned to sing hymns in church, and he was impressed that I could play a bunch of the folk mass hymns on guitar. Like me, he'd grown up in a very Catholic environment. I told him I'd spent a pile of time on the altar and that I was studying religion at university. Turned out he knew most of the priests I knew, and like me, he had struggled with remaining in the Catholic fold. We even discovered that my high school principal at St. Kevin's in the Goulds, a great woman and prominent Sister of Mercy, was his aunt Patricia.

I told him I'd learned some traditional music from my parents and the Wonderful Grand Band. He was impressed that my dad had been on *All Around the Circle*, a show he'd watched as a kid. He insisted I listen to some other traditional music with him. Séan must have played me thirty albums I'd never heard of—amazing British and Irish bands like Fairport Convention, Steeleye Span and Planxty. I'd never heard traditional music played that way before and I wanted to try it.

I played my electric guitar and did one of the Staggerin' Home tricks of wandering from eighties metal to Irish traditional in one medley. I thought it was hilarious; Séan thought it was no joke at all.

We started jamming and quickly discovered that we could sing in easy harmony with each other because his vocal range practically started where mine stopped. He fed me chili and we sang and played tunes and drank a bottle of rum.

I stumbled out of there late in the evening with a million new songs in my head. The day had been so much fun it certainly did not feel like an audition or interview of any kind. Only as I put on my coat did it even occur to me to worry if I had impressed him enough to get a shot at being involved in whatever project he was doing next.

As it turned out, I need not have worried.

As I walked towards an awaiting orange Gulliver's cab, Séan said, "Deadly, man. Let's book some gigs."

We did not know it yet, but we had just started Great Big Sea.

MUSICAL GUESTS

GREAT BIG SEA

This is our first-ever Great Big Sea poster shot, taken moments after our first opening show for the Irish Descendants, at Memorial University, March 11, 1993. The smiles say it all.

Boy on Bridge

pin the planet like a globe. Does it seem a bit smaller?
Does the Atlantic Ocean appear a little less imposing? Do the Old Country and the New seem just a little
closer? Is that island easier to spot now? Does its shape seem
a bit more familiar?

Look closer and you'll see how Newfoundland reaches
back towards Ireland as it always has, and you'll see the little
bay that leads to that same cove and tiny harbour. The town
around the harbour is almost unchanged. It is still split by
the perfect little river. You'll see the bridge that separates
what people still call the Protestant and Catholic sides of
the town even though religion no longer divides the town
in quite the same way. In a bit more and you'll likely see a
young man on that bridge right where we once saw him as a

boy. I see him there all the time. His foot is still tapping to a song in his head, but it is tapping louder and with growing confidence.

These days, he's always going somewhere, but he's always coming back, too. He's got a few stories to tell from the harbour and beyond, but now in his early twenties, his biggest adventure is just about to start. Those eyes that once followed the valley to the road out of town are about to open wider than he could possibly imagine. He's a pretty big dreamer, but right now on this bridge in time, he could never dream of Great Big Sea.

There was once a boy who lived in a tiny fishing village on an island in the middle of the ocean.

That boy is me. This is my story.

Glossary of Terms
(Mostly for Mainlanders)

Bastarding Doyles: According to shop owner Maureen, the wicked crowd from the other side of Skinner's Hill who left her convenience store door open and wrote nasty songs about local people.

Bayman: a person from the bay or shoreline of Newfoundland, mysteriously with the exception of those from Quidi Vidi and the Battery shorelines of St. John's, who are Townies (see *Townie*), equally mysteriously with the inclusion of people from places like Gander and Whitbourne, which are nowhere near the ocean.

b'y: Newfoundland contraction for "boy"; a term of endearment similar to "pal" or "buddy," often used in reference to a boy or man but just as often used in reference to a girl or woman.

Canadian: A resident of Canada; to my grandfather and others of his generation, a person from the neighbouring country to Newfoundland.

capelin: A schooling fish known in the olden days for its aphrodisiac powers because women wandering in the sea to fetch them had to lift their skirts, revealing the alluring sight of their bare ankles.

cod britches: The roe from a female codfish in the shape of a perfect pair of pink pants.

cutting out tongues: The action of severing the tongue (and the flesh that lies beneath it) of a codfish; a way for young fellas from Petty Harbour to make a small fortune.

fish: Cod. All other fish in Newfoundland are named by species.

gulch: A steep and foreboding crevasse along a rocky shoreline often used for the disposal of adult magazines.

gurry: Fish guts, skin, fins and tails often found in the bottom of a fishing boat or under a splitting table; a grotesque brew that young fellas in Petty Harbour rub on their clothes to gross out their older sisters.

iceberg: A big chunk of ice in the sea that is of interest only to Mainlanders (see *Mainlander*). To most Newfoundlanders, it's about as remarkable as wind.

kitchen party: A gathering in the kitchen to talk, sing, eat and drink. Historically, the kitchen was often the biggest room in a rural Newfoundland home, and it had heat from the wood stove.

Mainlander: A person not from Newfoundland; a Canadian (see *Canadian*).

make-and-break engine: The simplest but most durable engine found in trap skiffs and small fishing boats. Also know as a "putt putt" from its distinctive sound.

making fish: Traditionally means the gutting, splitting, salting and drying of codfish for storage and sale.

Nitzy Pumpkin: A red-haired and freckle-faced person, often of Irish descent.

out-of-oil party: A Doyle-family tradition held in celebration of a lack of heating fuel; an attempt to stay warm in the winter by heating a room with body heat, alcohol and an electric oven with the door taken off its hinges.

pew: Not only a seat found in a church but a single-pronged pitchfork used for lifting fish out of fishing vessels and onto stages (see *stages*).

putt putt: see *make-and-break engine*

Russell knife: A brand of filleting knife used by the best fish cutters in the world; the object of envy of many a young Petty Harbour tongue cutter.

sculpin: The ugliest fish in the world.

sounds: The paper-thin strips of flesh that grow along the spinal column of a codfish; an edible delicacy; proof that some people will eat anything.

stage: A raised platform on a wharf not for live performances but for the making of fish (see *making fish*).

Townie: A person from the town of St. John's; city folk.

What are you at?: A rhetorical question used as a greeting. The most appropriate response is, "What are *you* at?"

Acknowledgements

This book would not exist if not for the patience and professionalism of editor Nita Pronovost. When I needed guidance, she was the perfect teacher. When I needed reassurance, she offered the perfect encouragement. I have learned more from Nita than I can say.

Michael Levine got this whole thing started as he connected me with Scott Sellers, Nita, Kristin Cochrane and many others at Random House Canada, and knew long before I did that I had a story to tell. Thanks also to Zoe Maslow, for shepherding through various changes and corrections to the book and making sure nothing fell through the cracks.

A few select people read advance drafts of this book and their comments were invaluable in its completion. Dawn Chafe, along with husband Karl, Murray Foster, Kerri MacDonald and my brother, Bernie Doyle, all helped tremendously.

Victoria O'Grady did some early leg work for this book, compiling, copying and editing photos and blogs. I am grateful to her for this and so many other things she's done to keep my work and home operating smoothly.

The photos in this book were taken or scanned and reproduced by the amazing Brian Ricks. I am grateful to him and all the folks, especially Margaret Walsh, who so generously made their photos available.

I discovered I knew none of the mechanics of writing dialogue. I explained my problem to my neighbour Ed Riche as we met one morning while putting out the garbage. He set me straight. Helps to have internationally successful writers in the 'hood.

Louis Thomas is my long-suffering manager who never blinks when I come to him with any crazy interest of mine, from music to acting to public speaking to writing. His administration and advice in this project have proved as beneficial as ever.

The cast and crew of Great Big Sea remain at the helm of the Mothership, and I could not have done this without their support.

My mom and dad, sisters and brother gave me not only their stories and permission to use them but also the cheers and praise I needed exactly when I needed it. As always.

My wife, Joanne, and son, Henry, give me every reason to do everything.

Thanks to you all.

I don't know
Where I'm going
But I know
Where I belong

—lyrics from "Where I Belong," Alan Doyle and Russell Crowe,
from Alan Doyle's solo album *Boy on Bridge*, copyright © 2012